Second Psalm & Acts 4:25

WHY DO THE HEATHEN RAGE?

Vol. I

A compilation of newspaper columns which appeared in leading newspapers across the nation from 1962 to 1981.

WHY DO THE HEATHEN RAGE?

FOREWORD

Before publishing this book of articles from the "Why Do The Heathen Rage?" collection, we advertised in the newspapers where we had previously advertised to determine if there was interest enough to warrant this publication.

The response was overwhelming to go forward with the book. The response came from all parts of our country. The comments and location of a few are as follows:

"I really missed it -- I hope the response warrants the publication." *Sabina, Ohio*

"I have missed those Christian messages and have several of them cut out and saved." *Hudson, Florida*

"Yes, I would like a copy of 'Why Do The Heathen Rage?.'" *Tacoma, Washington*

"I did so enjoy reading the Christian message 'Why Do The Heathen Rage?' as it appeared in the Billings Gazette." *Billings, Montana*

"By chance I read your ad in the Rocky Mountain News. Many thousands will not see it. I am sorry." *Littleton, CO*

"The newspaper articles were enjoyed through the years." *Dunwoody, Georgia*

"I not only want a book for myself but would like to put one in every church in America, if possible." *Goldsboro, NC*

"For many years I enjoyed reading the message, 'Why Do The Heathen Rage?' and intended to thank the author." *Austin, Texas*

"I used to read it every Saturday in San Diego Union, and really have missed it very much." *San Diego, California*

"I am sure that much good came from his -- (the author's) life, for his articles were very God-related." *Manchester, CT*

"We will appreciate a copy of the book, as we were admirers of such a dedicated disciple of the Word." *Columbia, South Carolina*

"-- I'm a writer of Christian poetry and got many ideas from the writings of this great author." *Boise, Idaho*

"Sorry he -- (the author) -- died. God bless you for carrying on!" *Carroll, Iowa*

"I could hardly wait for Saturday to come so that I could read 'Why Do the Heathen Rage?'" *Greenville, Florida*

The author, now deceased, expressed his hope that his articles might be published in book form and given free to all who wanted a copy or copies.

We have tried to carry out his desires and have selected the following articles under the appropriate headings. There are many more that are equally as meaningful.

As long as the supply lasts we will be pleased to send additional copies in answer to requests. Please respond to:

"WHY DO THE HEATHEN RAGE?"

Box 765

Scottdale, Georgia 30079

WHY DO THE HEATHEN RAGE?

The Bible - God's Word

Division One

In the 2nd Psalm God asks this question: "Why Do the Heathen Rage?" and then answers it. He tells who the heathen are, why they rage, and His reaction and the consequences of their rage. God also gives instruction, warning, and an invitation. Webster says: "A heathen is one who does not believe in The God of The Bible." This definition fits in with what God says: "People (who) imagine a vain thing -- kings of the earth -- and the rulers -- (who) take counsel against the Lord, and His Annointed, to Break The Bands, cast away The Cords," and restraints The Almighty has thrown across our paths to hold us back from damning ourselves, children and posterity in time and eternity. In other words, their rage is against The Truth of The Bible, God's Moral Law and His Ten Commandments.

In telling of God's reaction to this rage and rebellion, there is a good picture and description of the world today, its present and recent experiences, as God has spoken in His

Wrath, vexing in His sore displeasure, pouring contempt upon kings and rulers, bringing the princes of the earth to do nothing, and making the judges of the earth as vanity. Elijah, the prophet who was taken to heaven without dying, said to King Ahab: "I have not troubled Israel; but thou, and thy father's house, in that ye have forsaken the commandments of God." Said Christ: "If they hear not Moses and the prophets, neither will they be persuaded though one rose from the dead."

Many modern prophets don't believe that Jesus rose from the dead. Probably Herod will have a better chance of heaven than they, for he believed in the resurrection of the dead: He had killed John the Baptist against his own will in order to keep a rash vow -- many of these modern prophets don't hesitate to break a solemn vow they took at ordination -- yet when Christ's fame began to spread abroad, Herod said: *"It is John the Baptist, he is risen from the dead."* Herod believed in the resurrection after a very short period of Christ's fame, yet many of our modern prophets that are "highly esteemed among men" don't believe after nearly two thousand years of His fame of wonder working and power in the lives of men, women, children and nations of every kindred, tribe and tongue! It was just before Christ told of the man in the torments of hell fire that He said: *"That which is highly esteemed in the sight of men is abomination in the sight of God!"* Doesn't that make you tremble? It does this party!

"A heathen is one who does not believe in The God of The Bible." In the April 11th issue of *The Presbyterian Journal* there was a letter from a minister reader in which he quoted another minister as saying to him: "I would not walk across the street to speak to the God of The Old Testament!" Whose minister is this man? Christ identified Himself as being "One" with The God of The Old Testament! *"O God, the heathen are come into Thine inheritance; Thy holy temple have they defiled.* "Psalm 79:1. According to recent published reports in news and church papers, at a recent meeting of The Assembly of one of the great Protestant Denominations, over 350 of the delegates took the position that parts of the Bible were unreliable, and it was not The Infallible Word of God, and only about 70 held to the historical position of the founders and developers of genuine Protestantism, and the great world-wide denominations that have so blessed the world and laid the foundations from which have sprung modern civilization and the wonders of science.

"Genuine Protestantism does not consist only of the doctrines of Justification by Faith and The Supreme Authority of The Scriptures, for it implies, as its name indicates, an energetic protest, formulated in the name of these doctrines, against ecclesiastical abuse of every kind.

"If Modernism was a separate movement in itself, built its own churches, launched its own institutions, projected its own denominations, then we could look at it as just another of the many sects that appear on the surface of history. But Modernism itself builds nothing; it is a parasite that grows on institutions already built. The physician tells us that a given virus can multiply and cause disease only when it is within cells. This is a picture of historical Modernism. It grows on the work, the heritage, the sacrifice of the orthodox. The humble disciples of Christ make the converts, evangelize the fields, build the churches, launch institutions, erect the denominations -- then Modernism destroys the life from within."

Don't know who the author of the above quote is, but he sure "hit the nail on the head" and this is a faithful witness. Probably the Modernists should not be classed as parasites, usurpers, or hypocrites, if they accept membership in the Unitarian-Universalist Church of The Larger Fellowship. But no, doubtless they consider themselves too important personages for that small crowd, too inflated with self, pride and presumption to disappear from the view of mankind in that little bunch, and so as parasites they have wormed themselves way up to some of the top positions, if not in the majority, often of the great Protestant Denominations "While men slept."

Is it not time we genuine Protestants woke up?! If we do not, we are in danger of sleeping the sleep of eternal death, where forever and forever there is no rest day or night! Rev. 14:11. Maybe we can wake up by meditating on the 1st Psalm, and rating ourselves as to whether we in reality belong to The Godly, or ungodly class. Here we have a word picture given us by God of both classes. Consider, and decide from which frame you look out. The picture of the Godly Man has to do with His Walk, His Stand, and His Seat, and these are all determined by that in which *"He* delights." *"His delight is in the law of the Lord; and in His law doth he meditate day and night."* A little while spent while the sun is shining with your Bible, and a little while spent with your Bible after it sets, might fix that up.

This picture further shows the Godly Man to be very fruitful, like a tree planted by the river -- it takes time to grow fruit. The picture of the ungodly man is quickly drawn with just a few words: "He is not so," as the Godly Man, he is chaff driven away by the wind, and he shall not be able to "stand" in the judgment. Which picture "frame" are you looking out of? Rate yourself! We would make a suggestion if you have no delight in The Law of The Lord and are concerned about it, pray and ask God to fulfill His promise and give you a New Heart wherein are written The Commandments of God by the Holy Spirit. If you are sincere, and continue in sincerity in God's good time you will be enabled to rejoice and sing: "I know the Lord has laid His Hands on Me!"

†††

June 30, 1962

About fifty years ago a young man sat in a class at a University and heard an eminent Doctor Professor say regarding the first part of Genesis: "It is a myth." And about the same time another Professor said to his class: "All thinking people have gotten over the idea that the Bible is inspired." Having been raised in the atmosphere and climate of "faith" that "The Scriptures of The Old and New Testaments were the only infallible rule of faith and practice whereby to glorify God," such statements troubled this young man, for he considered that these men had more sense than he did and that they were probably better educated than his former teachers. However, though just a boy as he now looks back, he is thankful for one reaction he immediately had towards the prominent Doctor, for he seemed to "smell a rat," or the odor of hypocrisy and asked himself: "What is he doing in The Church and a prominent officer in his Church and why doesn't he get out?"

Whether the other "bird" was a Church member or not is not definitely known, but think he was. If either of these men had honesty and integrity enough to realize they were breaking solemn vows made to God, in His House, in the presence of His people as witnesses, doubtless their pride and presumption and self-conceit had choked to death at birth any such sentiments, or very soon thereafter! For a time this boy shared some of these men's unbelief, but after "Searching The Scriptures" in order to determine whether to get out or stay in the Church he was fully persuaded to more and more and further and further "get in." He also soon "got the number" of these learned men when he found that "In the wisdom of God, the world by its wisdom knew not God."

For his own profit, and for any he might have opportunity to influence, later on, he made an analysis of these two men. You can make it of yourself or another by knowing or guessing at their age. Make it especially concerning those who attack "The Word of God" -- and today their name is "many legions," even in our churches passing themselves off as Christians and "called of God to preach!" The analysis was suggested by a question God asked of Job when He appeared to him: *"Where were you when I laid the foundations of the world, when the morning stars sang together, and all the sons of God shouted for joy?"* The younger of these two men was probably in his late twenties: so where was he just about 30 years ago? He was in his father's loins -- rather difficult to imagine what he looked like then! 29 years ago he was in his mother's womb. 28 years ago he was a helpless little baby unconscious of being alive, and unable to utter intelligent speech. About 27 years ago he was still a helpless infant but beginning to say, "What's this, what's that, why this, why that, etc?" Marvel of marvels, however, for a little more than a score of years and he is sitting in a Professor's chair in a University passing out the information that The Bible, The Word of God Almighty is not inspired!

The Bible: The Book of Books which has endured through the centuries and has borne the burden and heat of battles with kings, rulers, worldly wise, and men and devils ever since the "Snake in The Garden" lifted up its voice against it! Its enemies have fought it with fire, sword, gibbets, crosses and every sort of torture men and devils could devise! Yet it has come forth victorious over all and still stands to bless or curse mankind: *"The savour of life unto life or of death unto death -- For The Word of God is quick and powerful, sharper than any two-edged sword, piercing even to the dividing asunder of soul and spirit, and of the joints and marrow, and is a discerner of the thoughts and*

12

intents of the heart. "You just ought to read and get familiar with it, and saturate your mind and heart with "every word that proceedeth out of the mouth of God." Don't try to appraise it, but rather search to see how it appraises you yourself! It is your duty if you have taken vows to God in joining some Evangelical Protestant Church. God has given us one day in seven especially for this purpose. "Be sure your sin will find you out!" While this is true concerning every secret sin of the thief, the adulterer and fornicator, the murderer, etc., yet the direct connection in which God speaks these words is to those who made a promise and then failed to perform and fulfill it. Numbers 32:23: "*But if ye will not do so, Behold, ye have sinned against The Lord, and be sure your sin will find you out.*" "But if ye will not do so" has reference to a promise they had made, and a promise which was going to be very costly and self-denying to fulfill. Consider what this passage reveals regarding God's attitude towards our promises to do this, or that, pay our debts, etc., but above all, the promise and vow we made to God in joining His Church! In another place God says that they who make a covenant in His House and fail to keep it "Pollute His Name."

Speaking of "pollution" we do well to remember that God says our very land is "defiled and polluted" by bloodshed in murder, and it can only be cleansed by man shedding the blood of the murderer to make atonement! Is there any rage today against The Lord and His Annointed? Do we not make war on God and fight against Him when we substitute the precepts of man for "The Law of our God?" By the way, God's Word tells us one result of following the precepts of man rather than God's precepts is that *"the wisdom of their wise men will fail"* and *"princes become fools."* Did not our wisdom and the wisdom of our leaders and wise men fail utterly in giving recognition to Russia about thirty years ago? If Stalin made fools of us at Potsdam, Yalta, Teheran,

13

etc., it appears that we are still unwilling to admit it, but go on increasing our folly by rejecting, neglecting and ignoring The Law of Our God for the precepts of man, and are in danger of fulfilling again The Scripture: *"Behold, ye are risen up . . . an increase of sinful men, to augment yet the fierce anger of the Lord . . ."*

"Shall the throne of iniquity have fellowship with Thee, which frameth mischief by a law?" Psalm 94:20.

Doubtless we all share in the responsibility for the serious condition our nation and the world are in, but it especially lays at the door of those of us who have made vows to God and failed to keep them. Our sin is surely finding us out! Is not repentance and restitution in order?

March 26, 1962

†††

Requests for information about the writer of this column have been received a number of times. A recent letter says: "Won't you please tell me who you are that writes the column in each Monday's *Atlanta Journal* 'Why Do The Heathen Rage?" (Understand in some "far away places" this article appears in Monday's *Journal* instead of Saturday.) I have been reading this article for quite some time and look forward each Monday and read the message to our nation, and to each individual as well. So applicable to, and so needed, by our nation today. Daily I cite friends, neighbors and family to this column as a gem from God, hidden in the rough, but to be seized with gratitude, as something to live by."

Truly it has been said that one cannot talk long about "self" without becoming vain. However, the above letter is greatly appreciated, very encouraging, and gives us quite a "lift." It is hard not to make some effort to meet this request. But it is also hard to digress even a little to talk

14

about self when there are so many "gems" from God in His Word: *"The Law of The Lord is perfect, converting the soul . . . more to be desired than gold, yea , than much fine gold: sweeter also than honey and the honeycomb"* -- Psalm 19:7, etc. *"For thou hast magnified thy word above all thy name"* -- Psalm 138:2.

The writer is a layman. Raised in a Christian home that was strict about "Singing the Song of Moses, the servant of The Lord, and The Song of The Lamb of God that taketh away the sin of the world." The burden of Moses' Song is the Moral Law of God, The Ten Commandments that reveal the very character of The Almighty. The message of The Lamb of God is deliverance from the wrath of God to *"Whosoever Will."* The wrath of God is due to our devil perverted nature and acts. The Lamb of God paid our penalty and offers the gift of a new heart wherein are written the Commandments of God by The Spirit of God; and also the gift of Eternal Life in the world to come, which world we enter by "falling asleep safe in the arms of Jesus;" or by being *"caught up to meet the Lord in the air when He cometh to make up His Jewels."* (Hope we are not casting our pearls and gems before swine! We are warned against doing that. If you are a member of a Protestant Christian Church and don't believe these things, in God's Name, why don't you get out? How come you're in there, anyway?)

The writer joined the Church when about twelve years of age. Though greatly blessed with the raising and environment he had, yet when he left school he faced the fact that he was "out of gear" with real Christianity and the vows made on joining the Church. He did not want to, nor did he intend to spend his life striving to fulfill them. "Then get out," he said to himself. "Resign your Church membership, and don't deliberately live the life of the hypocrite." Considering what a serious step it would be to "junk the hope of Eternal Life" offered in the Bible and

15

Protestant Christianity, he purposed before resigning to "Search The Scriptures" himself -- most he knew came second-handed. Since that time, many years ago now, he has read the Bible from cover to cover several times each year. Mostly it was consecutive reading, not stopping unless attention was especially arrested. For quite a while his aim was to read at least thirty minutes a day. Later on he aimed at making 60 minutes out of the 1,440 minutes in every 24 hours, figuring this was not too much time for making preparation for a life that never ends, eternity.

Not so long after beginning this exercise in "Searching The Scriptures" he became definitely aware of "the personality of the devil and spiritual wickedness in high places," and that these fearful enemies were fighting to keep him away from his Creator: fighting him with questionings, doubts, unbelief and even a resentful and rebellious spirit against The Almighty Himself. Through the mercy of God, during all this fearful period he never laid The Bible aside but kept reading it, and kept on outwardly performing his vows by church attendance and striving to obey God's Ten Commandments -- common honesty and integrity required this until he resigned and got out of the Church. The Scriptures say *"In due season you will reap, if you faint not in well doing."* He found it to be true and in due time God's Word became "quick and powerful" in his own life and made of him a man whose greatest desire and ambition was to "Know God and do His Will."

For about twelve years after leaving school the writer was employed as a cotton buyer. After the boll-weevil struck and changed things in that line, he went on a farm and has been there ever since. However, as a result of his experience in "Searching The Scriptures" his main interest has been in Sowing the Seed of The Word of God" in his own heart, and that of others: *"Man shall not live by bread alone, but by every word that proceedeth out of the mouth of God."*

These are the first recorded words spoken by Christ after His Baptism by John the Baptist. Several years ago God opened up the way to begin some "Advertising" of The Word of God. Thank God for all those who have written or by spoken word have said the ads have been helpful and inspiring in their Christian experience. Brethren, pray for me, and pray that "The Word of God might have free course, and be glorified." It is our hope for time, and for Eternity, as individuals, as a nation, and the whole world.

"The Greatest Weapon Ever Forged is "The Word of God!" With it Christ drove off the devil when tempted in the wilderness. Every temptation was met and overcome with The Word of God: *It is written -- it is written -- it is written.*"

"The Next Greatest Weapon is the 'Privilege of Prayer!'" Our Government by law has withdrawn these two great weapons from our schools! We suggest that all the people of God have now a special and important opportunity to use and fight with these great spiritual weapons in the coming election by voting for righteousness: "Righteousness exalteth a nation, but sin is a reproach to any people." It has been suggested, and with good scriptural ground in our judgment, that our Court's action in taking a neutral stand regarding God Almighty and withdrawing The Bible and Prayer from our children, may have resulted in God withdrawing His Presence and Protection from our nation to the place where an enemy was able to cut down the head of the nation. "Not one sparrow falls to the ground without your Heavenly Father" observing and permitting.

In the Book of Ezekiel we find that the "cloud" that hovered over the mercy seat of The Ark of God, signifying the Presence of The Almighty, appeared to become restless: it moved from that place to over one of the doors: later it moved outside of the city, and then later it departed. Not long afterwards Jerusalem and the Temple were destroyed!

17

How would you like to legally vote as many times as you wanted to? Many would spend the day from the opening to the close of the polls voting as fast and as often as they could. Well, you can do that in the Government of The Almighty, the Kingdom of God. You can vote not only on election day, but every day, and Sunday, too, day and night. Regardless of what goes on around you as you sit in church you can keep voting for the right and God's honor, and against evil. God will count every sincere vote. *"In due season we will reap, if we faint not." "And the Lord said, -- But as truly as I live, all the earth shall be filled with the glory of The Lord. For all the earth shall be filled with the knowledge of the glory of The Lord, as the waters cover the sea."* (Numbers 14:20, 21; Isaiah 11:19, and Habakkuk 2:14) The knowledge of the glory of God shall fill the earth as the waters cover the sea -- take heed lest at that time your "ignorance" of the glory of God will have drowned you in perdition, hell's lake of fire!

"An Almighty Justice does verily rule this world. It is good to fight on God's side, and bad to fight on the devil's side!"

"For nothing should the people of God more devoutly pray than that their great men might be good and God-fearing men."

October 24, 1964

†††

Webster says "a heathen is one who does not believe in the God of The Bible." This fits in with what God says in the Second Psalm concerning the heathen. The great Protestant denominations, such as Lutheran, Episcopal, Methodist, Presbyterian, etc. were founded and developed by men who believed in The God of The Bible, that the Scriptures of The

18

Old and New Testaments are the infallible Word of God, the Supreme Authority for Faith and Practice. Or, in other words, *"The Law and the Testimony." "Bind up the Testimony, and seal The Law among my disciples . . . Should not a people seek unto their God? For the living to the dead? To The Law and The Testimony: if they speak not according to this word, it is because there is no light in them."* Isaiah 8:16, 19, 20.

The Law and The Testimony were the great Foundation Stones of The Reformation of the 16th Century begun by Luther, and established by Calvin, Knox and other mighty men inspired by God. The same great Foundation Stones, The Law and the Testimony, were also the basis of the 17th Century Revival and Reformation, sometimes called the Puritan Reformation. The Law and The Testimony were words frequently on the lips of John Wesley, and were the great Foundation Stones of the 18th Century Revival led by Wesley, and which Revival saved England from experiences similar to those of France at the time of her Revolution when the streets of Paris ran with blood, and which Revolution was greatly contributed to by Voltaire and his cohorts as they mocked, despised, and rejected The Law and The Testimony!

Not only did the Wesleyan Revival greatly bless England, but its fire leaped across The Atlantic Ocean and kindled itself in North America by the hands of such men as Whitfield, Asbury, Coke, Jonathan Edwards, and others, and spread rapidly over our country, producing such men in political and civil life as George Washington, Patrick Henry, etc. Patrick Henry "cried aloud, spared not, lifted up his voice like a trumpet: 'Give me liberty, or give me death!'" As an individual, I have often thought of and thanked God for what Patrick's zeal and efforts, along with kindred spirits, has meant to me personally, and our nation, but have often thought that he "stopped short," and should have gone further and said, "Give me righteousness, or give me death," for without the "righteousness of God imputed to us by faith" we go to death in time, and in eternity!

Liberty without righteousness usually produces "license," which in turn produces and provokes the "wrath of God" upon men and nations! Through the blessings of God which have come from our rich and godly heritage, we have freedom and liberty, which we have turned into "license!" If not so, from whence comes all this *"bleating of the sheep in mine ears, and the lowing of the oxen which I hear?"* If this quote means nothing to you, then read the 15th chapter of 1st Samuel, especially verses 10-23. By the way, why don't you get familiar with your Bible if you have taken the vows to join a Protestant Christian Church -- or if you have not joined -- get familiar with all of it? If your auto has some of its numerous parts missing, you are in for trouble sooner or later. Read all of it, make a life effort that occupies part of every day, even if you now have to begin at the eleventh hour. Ask the Author and Finisher of Faith to give you a believing heart: *"Faith comes by hearing, and hearing by The Word of God."* If you read it and decide you don't want to or can't trust The God therein revealed then resign and get out of The Church and relieve it of some "dead wood and excess baggage," and "paddle your own canoe" on into eternity, in the boat formed by your own wisdom and skillful hands!

A great English Historian standing on the high ground of his vast knowledge of the English people, and looking at their varied experiences across the centuries said: "The lapse of church discipline was a certain symptom of social and political anarchy!" If you can help cleanse the Church by getting out of it, do so! Many members by their neglect of their vows are in reality already out but won't ask that their names be removed from the rolls, and it appears the church is so sick and weak she can't lift her foot high enough with force enough to kick 'em out! Many of you old timers can remember when you could not live just any way and remain in the church membership; they just treated them like most of the civic, fraternal and other organizations do today.

In the Book of Malachi God says to try offering to your Governor what you offer me, and I am a Great King! Did not Christ say, *"I would that you were either hot or cold, but because you are lukewarm I will spue you out of My mouth!"* Many are there today who are fulfilling the Scripture written in Psalm 78:36: *"Nevertheless, they did flatter Him with their mouths, and lied unto Him with their tongues! The sheep are bleating, and the oxen are lowing,"* but many of us are like King Saul, insisting we are serving and obeying God!

The great and inspired men of God mentioned above were all in one accord and in one respect: "They believed in The God of The Bible." Not only that "it contained The Word of God," but that it "was The Word of God." They accepted at face value the first recorded words spoken by Christ after His baptism by John, and The Holy Spirit visibly descending upon Him from Heaven in the form of a dove: *"Man shall not live by bread alone, but by Every Word that proceedeth out of the mouth of God."* Matthew and Luke 4:4.

As a result of the Puritan Revival and the Wesleyan Revival in the American colonies, and later the states, many of God's laws were written on our statute books and are still there, though scorned and mocked at by many today as "blue laws," outmoded and out of date, etc. These laws were put there without serious objection by a population that was about 75 percent or more non-professing Christians. Today the picture is just about reversed, with about 75 percent, or a little less, professing to be Christian, we see the laws of God being taken off our statute books, or

21

compromised, or watered down to where they mean almost nothing to the morality of our times! What makes the difference? The answer lies in the fact that "The Word of God is quick and powerful" when really believed, practiced, and enforced! But it is weak and ineffective when meddled and trifled with by unbelief of a generation that "are lovers of pleasure, more than lovers of God," and run after the world, the flesh, and the devil, which is certainly characteristic of our day and generation! Is it any wonder that the "hell bombs" hang heavy, heavy over our heads, and we are in danger of God again *"cutting off the righteous with the wicked."*Ezekiel 21:4.

"The Law of The Lord is perfect, converting the soul, The Testimony of The Lord is sure, making wise the simple . . . Who can understand His errors?" Psalm 19: 7, 12. It appears that we have waxed so wise today as to understand the "errors" of The Almighty, and are going about to correct them! If the Almighty has foreknowledge, how is it that He did not foresee that our present Supreme Court would, in 1954 A.D., disapprove of His making some white, some black, and some other colors, and have to declare a law, an edict, or what have you, to correct this error of The Almighty? "There is a great day a coming!" We can look forward to the time when no one will have cause to call some "poor white trash" and others "nigger," but we will all be dear brothers "in the bonds of mongrelization." Mongrelization was advancing entirely too fast before the Supreme Court, the powers of Government, Army, Air Force, etc., joined in the procession. Don't you imagine the Almighty is highly pleased that his wise creatures have taken in hand to "understand and correct His errors!"

February 23, 1963

†††

22

"The Bible is the Word of God," said John Wesley.

"I beg leave to propose a short, clear and strong argument to prove divine inspiration of the Holy Scriptures. The Bible must be the invention of good men or angels, bad men or devils, or of God.

1. It could not be the invention of good men or angels, for they neither would nor could make a book and tell lies all the time they were writing it, saying *'Thus saith the Lord,'* when it was their own invention.

2. It could not be the invention of bad men or devils, for they could not make a book which commends all duty, forbids all sins, and condemns their own souls to "hell" for all 'eternity!'

3. Therefore, draw the conclusion that the Bible must be given by divine inspiration!"

This is mighty strong reasoning and logic. Over 1700 times in the Old Testament appear the words *"Thus saith the Lord,"* or similar phrases that state or indicate God Himself is speaking; and in the New Testament there are 850, or more, quotations from or references to passages in The Old Testament, and also Christ's words of approval such as *"Man shall not live by bread alone but by every word that proceedeth out of the mouth of God -- Search the Scriptures, for they testify of Me -- The Scriptures cannot be broken."*

This count was sparked by the statement to the writer of two young men who were studying for the Protestant Christian ministry in one of Atlanta's prominent Theological Schools to the effect that one of the Professors told his class that the Prophet Ezekiel was "neurotic," or in other words a "nut," more or less "cracked." The New Testament says he

23

was *"a holy man of God, moved by The Holy Spirit."* The above count was never checked, so if you find we are in error, please advise in order that we might check and correct.

Consider the ages of history and behold The Bible standing *"The Rock of Ages,"* the great "Anvil" on which the hammers have worn themselves out, the "Mighty Fortress" towering over the wrecks of nations, generations of men, evil angels and devils, as they have battered themselves to pieces and passed into oblivion after raging against this Rock which God has given for a refuge for the sons of men that *"Fear God and keep His Commandments, which is the whole duty of man!"* Over 400 years ago Martin Luther wrote: "Infinite potentates have raged against this Book, and sought to destroy and uproot it -- King Alexander the Great, the princes of Egypt and Babylon, the monarchs of Persia, Greece, and of Rome, the emperors Julius and Augustus -- but then nothing prevailed; they were all gone and vanished, while The Book remains, and will remain forever and ever, perfect and entire, as it was declared at first. Who has helped it, -- who thus protected it against such mighty forces? No one, surely but God Himself, who is Master of all things."

Consider another quote from Luther: "I admonish every pious Christian that he take not offense at the plain unvarnished manner of speech of the Bible. Let him reflect that what may seem trivial and vulgar to him, emanates from The High Majesty, Power, and Wisdom of God. The Bible is the Book that makes fools of the wise of this world; it is only understood by the plain and simple hearted. Esteem this Book as the precious fountain that can never be exhausted. In it thou findest the swaddling-clothes and the manger whither the angels directed the poor, simple shepherds; they seem poor and mean, but dear and precious is the treasure that lies within."

One night about 200 years after the time of Luther, John Wesley listened as one read some comments of Luther on The Bible, from the Book of Romans, and his heart became "strangely warmed" and he went forth to be a mighty instrument in the hands of God to greatly bless mankind and the world, and was especially used to save England from such experiences as France had at the time of her revolution when the streets of Paris ran with blood, which revolution was greatly aided and abetted by mobs whose hearts had been "violently warmed and heated" by Voltaire and his cohorts as they attacked The Bible, and The God of the Bible. John Bunyan was another man whom God greatly used to bless mankind whose heart also was "strangely warmed" by reading the writings of Luther. Elisha the Prophet who was present when Elijah was taken to heaven without death, in a chariot of fire, and horses of fire, and who at the time received a double portion of God's Spirit, the account of his death and burial is in 2nd Kings, Chapter 13. Later, another man was being buried near his grave when a band of the invading enemy appeared. They threw the body in Elisha's grave and ran. On coming in contact with Elisha's bones, the dead man came to life! It is interesting, instructive, and inspiring to consider the large numbers of men of God who greatly blessed mankind whom it appears came to life by coming in contact with the "spiritual bones" of Luther -- Bunyan and Wesley were two of them !

Why not set yourself to get in the way to let God "touch your heart" by getting familiar with every word of God. If you think you are too old to start, I would ask do you not hope to live throughout all eternity? Do you think it too big a job? Did you ever hear the story of the clock that at the close of the year figured out how many "ticks" it would have to make in the new year, and on facing the enormous sum said, "It is too much. I can't make it." But on further thought said: "It is only one 'tick' at a time," so got on the job and ticked the year off without strain. Thirty minutes a day out of the 1440 in every 24 hours -- 60 minutes would not be too much time to spend with God -- given to reading The Bible consecutively would in a few years cause you to know ' *'what God hath said,'* '' and if you purpose to *"do his will"* -- without which purpose no one can enter Heaven -- He will give you what understanding is necessary as you may have need to make application of it in your life and testimony.

Adam failed. Christ, the Second Adam, came down and kept God's Word perfectly, and imputes that perfect righteousness to all who believe in their hearts. Those men who have best known and obeyed God's Word have been the greatest benefactors in the salvation of their fellow men, and in blessing the world.

November 16, 1967

Applied Christianity

Division Two

On a certain day two sermons had been preached, one by Martin Luther and the other by a friend and his co-laborer we will call Doctor B. Luther said to his friend: "You preached a good sermon, but I liked mine better than yours." "Well, Doctor, I will acknowledge your superiority." "No," replied Luther, "that is not it. The reason I liked mine better than yours is that every child and illiterate servant present could understand mine and knew what I was talking about, but much of yours was only understood by the learned and the scholars."

Some years ago there was a prominent politician in this State who had some oratorical ability along with a "flowery gift of gab." After one of his speeches two farmers met and one asked the other if he had heard the speech, and on learning that he had not he said, "Man, you don't know what you missed. Believe that was the finest speech I ever heard. He sure went to town!" "What did he talk about," asked his friend. After hesitating a little: "I don't know, he never did say what he was talking about!"

On a number of occasions letters have come asking the objective of this column, which probably is another way of asking "what are you talking about?" Our first article appeared on the first Saturday of March, 1962, and with the exception of the following week there has been one in every Saturday paper, and in the first one and in all the following ones, directly or indirectly, we have talked about the fact that generally speaking, the Church is corrupt and has junked discipline, and the results of "corrupting God's way in the earth" will mean in the end, and the end might be near, the visitation of the wrath and curse of God upon us as individuals, our nation, and the world, calling attention to the fact that this was the cause of the destruction of the world in the days of Noah, the cause of the visitation of the wrath and curse of God upon the Jewish people down through the centuries, the cause of the disappearance from the face of the earth of great cities and nations and kingdoms of antiquity, and the cause of all the disasters, troubles, etc. of mankind, including the calamities we read about in every day's newspaper!

The "heathen rage" to get rid of God's Moral Law, Ten Commandments, and The Almighty holds them in derision, laughs and vexes them with all adversity. We have also in these articles continually talked about the fact that God sent His Son to the earth to keep His Commandments perfectly, and that He will impute that perfect righteousness to every soul that sincerely accepts and believes on Jesus Christ, and will write His Commandments in their hearts, or in other words, fix them up where they will want to "obey God, and keep His Commandments, which is the whole duty of man."

"It is singular how long the rotten will hold together, provided you do not handle it roughly." Picture a rotten apple hanging on a tree or elsewhere. It holds together a long time unless it falls or is handled a little roughly, and then you have "rotten apple sauce." One meaning of "corruption" is "rottenness." The earth became corrupt, or rotten in the days of Noah. God handled it rather roughly. It went to pieces and there was none left except for the man who found grace in God's sight, the man who feared God, and obeyed Him!

Some have estimated there might have been 480 billions of people in the earth when the flood came! The Jewish nation as a whole became corrupt, rotten. God has handled them roughly through the centuries and behold their history, suffering, and how they have been scattered. There is much rottenness and corruption in the home and family life of our nation; there is much rottenness and corruption in the political life of our nation; the main cause of the corruption and rottenness in the family and governmental life of our nation can be traced to corruption and rottenness in our Protestant Christian Church life, and every one of us who have taken such vows are especially responsible!

Did not God handle us roughly when He permitted our President to be assassinated? No doubt in our mind but that this "permissive providence" of The Almighty is a rebuke to the entire nation! Generally speaking, The Church refuses to "get rough" with its own rottenness of unbelief, apostacy, rejection of God's Laws and Word, and so the corruption holds together and increases; the civil powers of government refuse to "get rough" with murder, robbery, vile immorality -- I have heard it said time and again that the City of Washington, the seat of the great power of this nation, is the worst "sink of sin and cesspool of iniquity" of such crimes in all this great land, and therefore, corruption and rottenness "hold together."

What can one man do? He can do the "one thing needful," read what it is in Luke 10:41, 42: *"And Jesus*

28

answered and said unto her, Martha, Martha, thou art careful and troubled about many things: But 'one thing is needful'; and Mary hath chosen 'that good part,' which shall not be taken away from her.''The good part Mary chose was to "sit at the feet of Jesus and Hear His Word." Go and do likewise, get rid of the corruption and rottenness, become "good fruit by the power of God!"

December 7, 1963

†††

In the First Psalm, God says the man that delights himself in "The Law of the Lord" shall be like a tree planted by the riverside, his "leaf shall not wither and whatsoever he doeth shall prosper."

"But the wicked are like the troubled sea, when it cannot rest, whose waters cast up mire and dirt. There is no peace, saith My God to the wicked." Isaiah 57:20, 21. We cry peace, peace, but make little effort, if any, to cut out our personal wickedness and indifference, or to rise up and put away the lawlessness all about and around. In Amos 5:23-24, God says: "Take thou away from me the noise of thy songs, for I will not hear the melody of thy viols. But let judgement run down as waters, and righteousness as a mighty stream." In plain everyday language God is here saying: I am sick of your songs and music, take it away. What I want is judgment and righteousness established in the land like mighty rivers and streams that bless the earth and her inhabitants. That God's Kingdom might come and His will be done on earth as in Heaven!

"The lapse of Church discipline was a certain symptom of political and social anarchy," said the English Historian, Terry, as he looked across centuries of experiences of the English people. Church anarchy in doctrine and conduct produces political and social anarchy. Neglect and unbelief of God's Book, The Bible, produces Church anarchy! If you are a Church member you can do something to correct this situation by being faithful to your vows to serve God. *"When thou vowest a vow unto God, defer not to pay it, for He hath no pleasure in fools; Pay that which thou hast vowed.* Eccles. 5:4

All that has been said in the above concerning God's message in the Second Psalm, might be summed up in just one short verse of The New Testament, Romans 6:23: *"For the wages of sin is death; but the gift of God is eternal life through Jesus Christ our Lord." "Sin is any want of conformity unto, or, transgression of the law of God."* It is the duty of every true and faithful witness of Jesus Christ to "cry aloud and spare not" to denounce every transgression of the law of God, and the rejection and departure from "one jot or tittle" of God's Ten Commandments which reveal the very character of the Omnipotent Creator. Such witnesses are not your enemies, but friends in that they seek to turn you away from the wrath of God. The wages of sin is death, and these faithful witnesses are seeking to "smite death's threatening wave before you."

This quote is from the old and beloved Christian Hymn: "God be with you till we meet again, smite death's threatening wave before you, keep love's banner floating over you, --"

The Almighty has engaged Himself by means of the New Covenant, and the work and ministry of The Lord Jesus Christ and The Holy Spirit, to write these Laws upon the hearts and in the minds of true and faithful believers. "We are workers together with God," don't rage against Him!

"The wages of sin is death; but the Gift of God is eternal life through Jesus Christ Our Lord." Death does a mighty big business every day! Probably all over the world

at this moment there are between 150,000 and 200,000 dead bodies waiting to be buried. And tomorrow there will be an additional like number, with you and me included in one of those tomorrows! If just one day's "crop of death" was gathered in one place, what a territory would be covered! Great nations, great institutions, companies, unions, and concerns of all kinds also die, perish off the earth. John Bunyan said, give a little thought every day to your own funeral in order that you might be prepared! "O Death --!" The Lord Jesus Christ is the Mighty Conqueror of Death! He raised the dead! He raised Himself from the dead! Don't neglect and reject Him and His "Wonderful Words of Life." Surrender! Submit! -- We deliberately use the word "Submit" rather than "Commit", as it appears to us there is quite a difference. In Mark 1:15, Jesus said, *"--The time is fulfilled, and the Kingdom of God is at hand; repent ye and believe the Gospel"*

"God be with you -- smite death's threatening wave before you!"

May 31, 1975

†††

"Heathen" are those who do not "believe in the God of the Bible." The second Psalm identifies them as people "who imagine a vain thing" and support kings and rulers who set themselves to break the Bands and cast away the Cords of restraints of the Laws of the Commandments of God Almighty and His Anointed, Jesus Christ!

Consider the broken Bands and cast away Cords of restraint regarding God's Commandments for His people to *"Remember the Sattath Day to keep it holy."* "The great Desideratum in the Council Chamber of the infernal king has always been how man's innate religious feeling should be

31

satisfied, and yet God be not served. How could the heart be kept from God and the clamors of conscience be silenced, and yet the demands of an instinctive religious feeling be answered? The arch enemy of man's immortal hopes solved the problem. The solution appears in the cunning devices he has sought out by which to beguile unwary souls. He has varied his plans to suit times and circumstances, the condition of man, the progress of society, the character of human governments, and the condition of the human mind!''

For our generation and such a time as this, doubtless one of his biggest devices to accomplish his design is to encourage ''church going'' for a little while on Sunday in order that one might feel free to spend the rest of God's Day in pursuit of ''the lusts of the flesh,'' instead of using it to find and feed the soul with ''The Bread of Life.'' Jesus Christ said, ''*I am the bread of life. He that eateth of this bread shall live forever, never die!*'' It is mighty costly to break the Bands and cut the Cords that bind the soul to God and His Commandments.

Also, consider the broken Bands and cast away Cords of the 5th Commandment: ''*Honor thy father and mother that thy days may be long upon the land which the Lord thy God giveth thee.*'' Note, ''That thy days may be long.'' You who today are clamoring for and desiring ''long life'' for murderers, rapists, traitors, and the rebellious against decency and God ordained authority, and wretches who for other reasons the Creator commands that their life be cut short (See Ecclesiastes 7:17) to stop the contagious spread of ''devil diseases and plagues'' to others -- ''a little leaven leavens the whole lump'' -- you would promote longevity much better if you spend your concern and energies and ''cruel pity'' in practicing and teaching God's 5th Commandment, instead of trying to ''cut its cords,'' for it carries the promise of long life to the obedient who honor

32

father and mother. Kings and rulers are named especially as "ragers" against God's Laws. Is not our Government and those in authority over us seeking to relieve children of their duty and privilege to honor and take care of their parents and elders! And we, the people, "imagine a vain thing," and love it that way!

Those who reject the Word of God and Jesus Christ ought to have the name Christian stripped off them if they have not the honesty and integrity to resign and get out of His Church! The Apostle Peter had just had a revelation from the Heavenly Father as to who Christ was, had been blessed for his faithful and true testimony and told by Christ that Truth would stand forever. But shortly after this, Peter rebuked Christ for saying He must die at Jerusalem for the sins of mankind. Did Christ enter into a dialogue with Peter to straighten him out? No, indeed! He quickly cut the conversation off by turning upon Peter and saying, *"Get thee behind me, Satan. Thou art an offense unto me; for thou savorest not the things that be of God, but those of Men!"* Matthew 16:23 and Mark 8:33. In Matthew 15:3-9, and in Mark 7:6-13, Christ gave His approval of the death penalty for breach of the 5th Commandment, and later took that death penalty upon Himself in order that those guilty might not die eternally!

We have another suggestion for those to spend their concern and energies in a more profitable way than in the effort to save the temporal life of criminals, and that is to testify against and fight birth control. We give a reason or two. That's God Almighty's business, and not fallible men! Thank God such folks did not have control of John Wesley's parents -- John was about the 17th child! Multitudes of other men and women who have been a blessing to mankind have had many sisters or brothers older than themselves. In the 38th Chapter of Genesis we have the account of God slaying two men who deliberately wasted "the seed of human life."

33

One of these men might have been named among those from whom Christ came after the flesh.

This chapter also reveals that a woman, Tamar, received that honor because of her desire for the "fruit of the womb," a child. Her rights to marriage according to the customs of the time had been neglected by her father-in-law, Judah, who said of the affair: *"She hath been more righteous than I; because that I gave her not to Shelah my son!"* Tamar's name is on the first page of the New Testament! What will be the record in "God's Book of Life" concerning those so presumptuous as to decide that some "seed of human life" should not come to fruition!

JULY 14, 1973

††

The Voice of Retribution: *"For I the Lord thy God am a jealous God, visiting the iniquity of the fathers upon the children unto the third and fourth generation of them that hate me; and showing mercy unto thousands of them that love me and keep my commandments."* -- Part of the Second Commandment, Exodus 20:5-6. If you are one of those who belong to a Protestant Christian Church, and yet rail at God here revealed, may we suggest that you make haste and delay not to have your name rubbed off the rolls -- if it may be a lengthening of your tranquility!

History makes some singular developments in respect to the retributive justice of God. Nations, communities, families, individuals, furnish fearful illustrations that "the wicked is snared in the work of his own hand," and that "the way of the transgressor is hard!" Wrong doing, oppression, crime, are, by no means reserved only for a future retribution. They draw after them an almost certain retribution in this world. "There is no peace to the wicked,

34

saith my God!'' He may seem to prosper -- riches may increase -- he may revel in pleasures, and shine in honors, and seem to have all that heart can wish; yet there is a canker-worm somewhere gnawing at the very vitals of happiness -- a blight somewhere upon all that he possesses. History bears at least an incidental yet decisive testimony on this point.

Perilous it is indeed to a man's well being in this life -- to his peace, his reputation, his best interest -- to do wrong. Possibly the wrong doer may not suffer himself, yet most certainly his children, and his children's children will pay the penalty of his misdeeds. Man is undoubtedly so constituted, whether regard be had to his physical, social, intellectual, and moral nature, as to make him a happy being. The right, the unperverted use of all his powers and susceptibilities would not fail to secure to him a high and continual state of earthly happiness and prosperity. And not only is the human machine itself so fitted up as to accomplish such an end, but the whole external world, the theatre in which man has to live, act, and enjoy, is fitted up in beautiful harmony with the same benevolent end. Every jar of human happiness, every arrest or curtailment or extinction of it, is the fruit of transgression or perversion. The violation of a natural law is as sure to be followed by retribution as the violation of a Divine Law. The history of individuals, families, communities, nations, is full of such retributions!

"Be sure your sin will find you out" -- Numbers 32:23.

"It shall not be well with the wicked." Ecclesiastes 8:13.

"As I have done, so God hath requited me." Judges 1:7.

"Oh, that they would consider their latter end." Deuteronomy 32:29.

"The domestic peace and prosperity of the good old

35

patriarch Jacob was sadly marred. He is compelled to become at an early age, an exile from his father's house -- to flee before the aroused wrath of his brother -- to suffer a long oppression and wrong in the family of Laban, his kinsman; and no sooner is he relieved from these domestic afflictions, than suddenly he is bereaved of his favorite wife -- Joseph is violently torn from his embrace by his own sons -- and at length Benjamin, the only object on which the affections of the aged father seemed to repose, must be yielded up to an uncertain destiny, and his cry is heard: "All these things are against me!"

Pharaoh defied the God of heaven and raised his hand to oppress the chosen people, and he perished miserably amid the ruins of his own kingdom. Egypt never recovered from the sock of Pharaoh's sin, but since has been the "basest of kingdoms."

David was a good man, yet he sinned a great sin. And his sin was of a domestic character. And how grievously was he afterward afflicted in his domestic relations, his subsequent history remains the sad memorial: The Voice of God announced, *"The sword shall never depart from your house!"* His son Amnon raped his half-sister Tamar. Absalom, her brother, killed Ammon! Later on Absalom usurped his father's throne and drove him out, etc., etc. Yet David was a "man after God's heart" -- a man after God's heart in the way he repented and accepted the severe judgment of God, reminding one of the words of Job: "Yea, though He slay me, yet will I trust Him!"

Adonibezek, who had conquered 70 kings, and having cut off their thumbs and big toes, made them eat under his table, is at length conquered by the invading Israelites, who in turn cut off his thumbs and big toes. He acknowledged the retributive justice of the act when he said, *"As I have done, so God hath requited me."*

36

Examples crowd upon us from every quarter; every neighborhood furnishes them! Haman was hung on the gallows he built for Mordecai. Dogs ate the carcass of Queen Jezebel, and licked up the blood of her husband, King Ahab. The Herods furnish fearful examples. But consider Pontius Pilate: many of us quote his name every Sunday in public worship: "Suffered under Pontius Pilate!"

"Pilate, vacillating between the monitions of conscience and a miserable time serving policy, delivered up Jesus to be crucified. He believed him to be innocent; yet that his own loyalty to Caesar might not be suspected, he did violence to his conscience and condemned the innocent. He must secure his friendship of Caesar, though it be at the expense of the most appalling crime. But how miserably he failed; and there was in the retribution which followed a striking fitness of the punishment to the crime. He hesitated at nothing to please his imperial master at Rome. Yet but two years afterward he was banished by this same emperor into a distant province, where, in disgrace and abandonment, and with a burden on his conscience which was as the burning steel, he put an end to an existence which was too wretched to be borne!" *"Be sure your sin will find you out!"* "He that confesseth and forsaketh his sin shall find mercy."

October 30, 1965

Morality: Social Issues & Sin

Division Three

In Jeremiah 6:16 we read: *"Thus saith the Lord, stand in the ways and see, and ask for the old paths, where is the good way, and walk therein, and ye shall find rest for your souls. But they said, 'We will not walk therein!'"* Is not that the answer the "run-of-the-mill" church members and so-called Christians give the Lord today? The following article first appeared in the column on Nov. 24, 1962, Thanksgiving Season. We believe it can be helpful to you to

37

"Remember all the way the Lord our God hath led our nation," and to be obedient to the above commands: "Stand in the ways, and see, and ask fo the old paths, where is the good way, and walk therein," to the end and we might find rest for our souls.

"Democratic Institutions exist by reason of their virtue. If ever they perish it will be when you have forgotten the past, become indifferent to the present, and utterly reckless as to the future." This quotation was copied from the Monument of Thos. E. Watson on the Capitol grounds in Atlanta. Are our Democratic Institutions now headed for wreck and ruin on the rocks of socialism and communism? "Lord God of hosts, be with us yet, lest we forget, lest we forget!"

(NOTE: Most of the following facts of history, etc., are taken from the Book *"The Hand of God in History,"* written about one hundred years ago by Rev. Hollis Read, A.M.)

"The Mohammedans," says M. Oelsner, "would have discovered America even centuries before Columbus, had not their fleet been wrecked in a tempest, after clearing the straits of Gibraltar." Is not this something for us to still remember, and for which to thank God?

The great navigator Columbus is said to have been a diligent and devout student of prophecy, and he was actuated in no small degree in his venture westward, "by the hope he cherished of extending the Kingdom of Christ." And in the mind of his royal patroness (Isabella of Aragon), the conversion of the heathen to Christianity was an object "paramount to all the rest."

The first discoverers of this continent were Roman Catholics, and America was taken possession of and made subject to Catholic governments. Nothing seemed more probable at one time than that France would be the owner of New England -- and these hills and valleys would have languished under the crucifix and the mitered priests, and groaned beneath the heavy rod of The Roman Pontiff -- even as has Mexico, Central and South America for hundreds of years! (It appears today as if we might be on our way back to superstitious and spiritual slavery!) "Eternal vigilance is the price of liberty!" New England was early an object of desire of the French. As early as the year 1606, De Mont explored and claimed for France, the rivers, the coasts, and the bays of New England. The hostile savages first prevented their settlement. They did not yield their purpose. Three times in the following year the attempt was renewed. Twice they were driven back by adverse winds, and the third time wrecked at sea. Again did Pourtrincourt attempt the same enterprise, but was, in like manner, compelled to abandon the project. At a still later period, a French armament of forty ships of war, under the Duke D'Anville, was destined for destruction in New England. It sailed from Chebucto, in Nova Scotia, for the purpose.

In the meantime, the pious people, apprised of their danger, had appointed a day of fasting and prayer, to be observed in all the churches. While Mr. Prince was officiating in Old South Church, Boston, on this fast day, and praying most fervently that the dread calamity might be averted, a sudden gust of wind arose so violently as to cause the clattering of the windows (till then, the day had been perfectly clear) The Reverend gentleman paused in his prayer, and looking around on his congregation with a countenance of hope, he again commenced, and with great devotional ardor, supplicated the Almighty to cause that wind to frustrate the object of their enemies. A great tempest ensued, in which the greater part of the French fleet was wrecked. The Duke and his principal general committed suicide, thousands were drowned, and many died of disease, and a small amount returned to France, without health and spiritless, and the enterprise was abandoned forever!

"The first colony in North America, save Mexico, was a

Protestant colony, planted by Caspar de Coligni, as a City of Refuge for Protestants. It was destroyed expressly as Protestant! Thus was North America baptized by Jesuit priests with Protestant blood; yet despite all the machinations of Rome, God has confirmed the covenant and made this land the asylum and home of the Protestants." Bancroft.

There were many varieties and sects of the Protestants, but it was the Puritans that were chosen by God as the materials with which to rear the superstructure of religion and government in the New World. Before the arrival of the Pilgrims, a grant had been given and a colony had been established in New England, called Plymouth. But this did not prosper. A new and modified patent was then granted to Lord Lenox and The Marquis of Buckingham. But no permanent settlement was made. It was reserved to the Puritans! Here should be nurtured, in the cradle of hardships, and perils from the savages, and from the wilderness, and sufferings manifold and grievous, a spirit which should nerve the moral muscle of the soul, and rear a soldiery of The Cross made up of steadier stuff, and animated by a purer spirit than the world had before known. The Pilgrims were the best men, selected from the best portion of the best nation on the fact of the earth.

"The institutions of this country, both civil and religious, were cast in the mold of Puritanism. Had any other of the colonies been allowed to stand in this relation to the whole, how different would have been the cast of American liberty and religion! As it was, men of the most unbending integrity and untiring industry; men humble and unobtrusive, yet courageous and immovable at the post of duty; yielding when wrong, yet inflexible when right; plain and frugal, yet intelligent and liberal; men who had been nurtured in the school of persecution, and suffered the loss of all things, that they might breathe the uncontaminated air of freedom; men who hated oppression, abhorred ignorance and vice -- who were in their very souls, republicans and Christians -- these were the men, chosen out by sovereign Wisdom, to control the destinies of the New World. And they have done it.

The enterprise and intelligence, the undying love of liberty, the religious spirit -- I may say, the population of our Puritan colonies, have spread themselves over the whole continent. And what is worthy of special remark, these only prosper in our country. You look in vain over the wide expanse of our territory to find thrift and prosperity, temporal and spiritual, except under the auspices of our Puritan influence. Who people our wide western domains, and plant there the institutions of learning and religion? Who found our colleges and seminaries, publish our books, teach our youths, sustain our benevolent enterprises, and go on pagan lands to make wretchedness smile, and ignorance to speak wisdom? By whose skill and industry rolls the railroad cars over the length and breadth of our great land, and whiten the ocean with canvass? Who, if not the sons of the Pilgrims, nerved with the spirit of the Pilgrims? Tell me in what proposition, in any section of our country, the people are leavened with the leaven imported in the Mayflower, and I can tell you in what proportion they are enterprising, prosperous, moral and religious people.

"Compare Massachusetts and Mexico. Mexico was colonized just one hundred years before Massachusetts. Her first settlers were the noblest spirits of Spain in her Augustan Age; the epoch of Cervantes, Cortes, Pizzaro, Columbus, Gonzalvo de Cordova, Cardina Ximines, and the great and good Isabella. Massachusetts was settled by the poor Pilgrims of Plymouth, who carried with them nothing but their own hardy virtues and indomitable energy. Mexico, with a rich soil, and adapted to the production of everything which grows out of the earth, and possessing every metal used by man -- Massachusetts with a sterile soil and uncongenial climate, and no single article of transportation but ice and rock! How have these blessings, profusely given by Providence, been improved on the one hand, and obstacles overcome on the other? What is now the respective condition of the two countries? In productive industry, widespread diffusion of knowledge, public institutions of every kind, general happiness and continually increasing prosperity; in letters, arts, morals, religion -- in everything which makes a people great, there is not in the world, and there was never in the world, such a commonwealth as Massachusetts. And Mexico -- what is she?

The object of the brother who wrote the above about a hundred years ago was not to disparage our neighbors to the South, but rather to remind North America "Lest we forget," as well as to bear witness to all men that it is "The fear of the Lord, and obedience to His Commandments" that makes individuals and nations strong, virile, and blessed of The Almighty. *"And thou shalt remember all the way which the Lord thy God led thee --"* Deut. 8:2. *"Lord God of hosts, be with us yet, lest we forget, lest we forget!"* Lord God of hosts, we have forgotten, have mercy upon us, that we may repent and bring forth fruit meet for repentance! *"He that hath eyes to see, let him see."*

July 15, 1968

†††

The late great Evangelist "Billy Sunday" said, "Put a pole cat in the parlor: which changes first? Parlor or pole cat?" He did not give the answer to this problem, probably thinking all would have sense enough to figure it out! Surely there has been tremendous change in Churches since his day! Could it be caused due to Spiritual Pole Cats getting in the Church! The 10th chapter of Leviticus tells of *"the fire of God"* *flashing up and burning to death* two of The High Priest Aaron's sons because of their offering "Strange Fire" in a worship service!

In the 5th chapter of Amos God tells His people He *"hates"* and *"despises"* their offerings of worship and will not accept them. There is nothing to their worship -- except offense -- unless they rise up and put away evil, crime, lawlessness, etc. with which their land is filled, and with which their land is defiled. Verses 12-24: *"I hate, I despise your feast days, . . . Though you offer Me burnt offerings and your meat offerings I will not accept them; neither will I regard the peace offerings . . . Take thou away from Me the noise of thy songs; for I will not hear the melody of thy viols. But let judgement run down as waters, and righteousness as a mighty stream!"*

The article in this column two weeks ago told about the writer's effort to obey this command of God to *"Let judgement run down as waters, and righteousness as a mighty stream"* in his contact and experience with a hold-up man. Quote: I told Mr. Hold-up if I had the responsibility and power of the law in my hands, his body would probably now be in his grave, and his evil spirit -- unless he truly repented, and it don't take long to repent -- would be in hell with his "daddy, the devil!" For with two witnesses, or definite proof of his guilt he would have been shot at sunrise or sunset, whichever was nearer! Genuine Christianity doesn't tolerate evil! One branch of Christianity is charged by God Almighty to take vengeance for Him and do away with evil against law and order. Read the 13th chapter of Romans. The Bible not only says *"Resist the Devil,"* but it also says *"Give no place to the Devil!"*

What do you think? If men knew this was the law in Atlanta, and knew and believed it would be promptly and faithfully enforced, would it not do away with hold-up pests? If it was known that this was the law regarding murder, rape, homosexuality (crimes for which God Almighty's Law demands the death penalty), and men believed and knew it would be promptly and faithfully enforced, would it not cleanse the city of murder, rape, homosexuality, etc., etc.! Would you like to live in a city, a state, a nation where these abominations have been stamped out? I would! I expect to in due time.

Abraham, The Friend of God, The Father of The Faithful, *"looked for a city which hath foundations whose builder and maker is God."* At least three times God promises that *"the earth shall be full of his knowledge and glory of The Lord as the waters cover the sea."* Where will you be then in view of your present attitude, and actions, and witnessing concerning the abominations that fill the earth, almost as the waters do the seas? Your present attitude, and actions, and witnessing concerning the Abomination of *"Taking the Name of The Lord thy God in vain"* by claiming to be a Christian and remaining a member of His Church; concerning Sabbath Desecration, dishonoring of parents, and the abominations of murder, rape, homosexuality, stealing, covetousness, etc.?

May another question be asked for your consideration? Can one be a Christian that rejects Capital Punishment? Was not Christ's Crucifixion on the Cross Capital Punishment? Though innocent He offered Himself to die for the guilty! *"God so loved the world that He gave His only begotten son"* -- gave Him for Capital Punishment that God's righteous and holy Law might be carried out: *"the soul that sinneth shall die"* -- *"that whosoever believeth in Him might not perish but have everlasting life."* "Believeth in Him," that He substituted His Sinless Self and took Capital Punishment that my Sinful Self might live eternally a redeemed soul!

44

"I thought on my ways, and turned my feet unto Thy testimonies. I made haste, and delayed not to keep Thy commandments." Psalm 119: 59-60.

"Ye that love the Lord, hate evil." Psalm 97:10.

"For this is the love of God, that we keep His commandments; and His commandments are not grievous." 1st John 5:3.

December 30, 1972

††††

"Man, when left to himself, is half fiend and half brute!" Bishop Hall.

"Man, when left to himself, is a motley mixture of the beast and the devil!" William Law.

The dread foes of man are not belligerent circumstances, but the riotous passions - the leopard of incontinence, the lion of violence, the wolf of avarice. Incontinence means "lack of restraint, especially undue indulgence of sexual passions; licentiousness, etc." Great nations and empires of history as a result of this sin have rotted from within, decayed, perished. Is not our great land in danger of the same curse? "Chastity is driven away as an enemy by all men, like a snake!" Is not the "lion of violence" and the "wolf of avarice" back of and the cause of riots, strikes, etc.? It is said that a wolf is hungrier after food than before!

"A man may foretell as plainly as can be what will become of us, if we grow indifferent and lukewarm in repressing evil. Make it a shame to see men bold in profaneness, and God will bless you. Be confident that our liberty and prosperity depend upon reformation -- if not, what difference is there between a man and a beast?

45

"Beware of making laws in the face of God -- telling The Almighty you will meet all His Dispensations, and stay things, whether He will, or no.

"God will curse me, if I put personal interests above duty!" -- Oliver Cromwell. (Consider this last statement, remembering Pontius Pilate: "Suffered under Pontius Pilate" because of conflict of interest!).

Devoutly thankful ought we to be for the gift of great and good men. They are God's noblest work -- For nothing should the people of God more devoutly pray than that their great men may be good men. (If we had been doing that during the past few decades, do you reckon we would today have a Supreme Court such as is; one that has taken away from our schools and children, God's Book, The Bible, and The Lord's Prayer? I think not. Or, we would have such men in authority over us that let them get by with it? I think not.) One honest statesman -- one great, sanctified, devout, Christian man in the Senate or Cabinet of a nation, or at its head -- is worth more to a nation than all the riches of El Dorado, and is a surer defense than all her armies and navies!

Every young man should strive by the best possible improvement of his talents and opportunities, to make himself a great and a good man. This is a true and noble ambition. A great and a good man is the noblest work of God . . . strive then, my young friend, to fit yourself for the times in which you live.

God give us preachers, teachers, and students that put "the study of their own hearts" -- above the study of their books. "Search the Scriptures" for it is the mirror by which God reveals to us our hearts: *For the Lord seeth not as man seeth; for man looketh on the outward appearance, but the Lord looketh on the heart,"* 1st Samuel 16:7.

"For all flesh is as grass, and all the glory of man as the

46

flower of the grass. The grass withereth, and the flower thereof falleth away; but the Word of the Lord endureth forever. And this is the Word which by the Gospel is preached unto you." 1st Peter 1:24-25.

"For all that is in the world, the lust of the flesh, and the lust of the eyes, and the pride of life, is not of the Father, but is of the world, and the world passeth away. And the lust thereof: But he that doeth the will of God abideth forever." 1st John 2:16-17.

November 20, 1971

†††

The subject of this article is suggested by the 1st verse of the 40th chapter of Isaiah: *"Comfort ye, comfort ye my people, saith your God."* In our judgment, "all God's children" are conservatives unless perhaps they are "babes," or "lambs," lost, strayed, or stolen by leftists or devils!

In the Presidential campaign last year Senator Goldwater asked one of his opponents to put down in writing what the word conservative, extremist, or ultra-right meant to him. For our own benefit and profit we undertook to do this and came up with the following: "Ultra-right means Perfection, Holiness. Extremist is the pursuit of Perfection and Holiness is God-likeness!" The Bible says: *"Follow peace with all men, and Holiness, without which no man shall see The Lord,"* Hebrews 12:14. "Without which no man shall see The Lord!" We sure do want to "see the Lord" and behold His Glory when we are through this life and enter Eternity!

I have seen too much of the devil already down here below, too much of him in our own experience and life as we have sought to obey the commands: "Resist the devil, give

47

no place to the devil!'' In The Sermon on The Mountain Christ called on His followers to be "ultra-extremists," or so we interpret His Command: *"Be ye therefore perfect, even as your Father which is in Heaven is perfect!"* Matthew 5:48. However, if ever we try to appraise our own accomplishments along this line we think of the words of Job in 9:20: *"If I justify myself, mine own mouth shall condemn me; if I say, I am perfect, it shall also prove me perverse."*

When the children of Israel left the bondage of Egypt there went up with them a "mixed multitude." Later this "mixed multitude" fell a lusting and caused much trouble -- their "lust" appeared to be very contagious! In our judgment the Church today is badly afflicted with "a mixed multitude which have fallen a lusting!" Instead of using "discipline" and getting rid of them, it appears we are trying to keep them contented by "feeding their lust!" Christ ordered "discipline" in His Church and gave grounds for excommunication. Christ exercised "discipline" when He made a whip of cords and drove some wretches out of His Father's House! -- "The lapse of Church discipline was a certain sympton of social and political anarchy," said an English Historian as he looked across the centuries of the experiences of that people.

"Judgment must begin at the House of God!" Last week we called attention to the visitation of God's wrath on account of corruption in the city of Jerusalem. It was indeed terrible; no mercy or pity shown to old or young, maids, little children, and women! It is so terrible we prefer to just quote from God's Word in the 9th chapter of Ezekiel: *"And the Lord said unto him, go through the midst of the city, through the midst of Jerusalem, and set a mark upon the foreheads of the men that sigh and cry for all the abominations that be done in the midst thereof. And of the others [those with destroying weapons] He said in mine hearing, go ye after him through the city, and smite; Let not your eye spare,*

48

*neither have pity; slay utterly old and young, both maids and
little children, and women; But come not near any upon
whom is the mark; And begin at My Sanctuary. Then they
began at the ancient men which were before the House!"*
Remember The Word of The Lord in Isaiah 55: 8-9: *"For My
thoughts are not your thoughts, neither are your ways My
ways, saith The Lord. For as the heavens are higher than the
earth, so are My ways higher than your ways, and My
thoughts than your thoughts."* Doubtless, among the
conservatives there are many of the "lusting mixed
multitude." In spite of this we think there is good cause for
comfort and encouragement in the conservative and rightists
camps. There is still great cause for "sighing and crying"
and getting God's Mark on you in view of the abominations
that be done in the midst of our cities, land, and world,
beginning at the House of God, yet there is cause for
gladness and comfort when you consider the great number
of organizations that have arisen in recent time whose object
appears to be to obey The Word of God found in Jeremiah
6:16: *"Thus saith The Lord, stand in the ways, and see, and
ask for the old paths, where is the good way. And walk
therein, and ye shall find rest for your souls. But they said,
we will not walk therein."*

Generally speaking we take the position the Conservatives
are those who believe the Old Paths of The Bible and our
forefathers are The Good Ways, and the good things this
Country is enjoying today are the fruits of their faith in
God's ways, and obedience. On the other hand, the liberals
and leftists are those who say: "We will not walk therein."
Hence the crime, troubles and vexations promised to the
heathen *"Who rage against God, His King, Laws and
Reign."* Psalm 2:4-5. The fact that over twenty-six million
responded to Senator Goldwater's call last year to return to
the "Old Paths" is cause for Comfort, Rejoicing, and
Encouragement. We believe that number has, and is

49

increasing in spite of "The Raging of the Heathen" -- if not mistaken, some of them have admitted it. If correct, it is due to the blessings of God in the hearts of His people, and there is cause for thanksgiving. Comfort ye the Conservatives!

Judgment began at The House of God with all except those who had God's Mark on their forehead! Have you noticed in recent days accounts of mobs issuing out from Churches, Houses dedicated for the worship and promulgation of the Gospel of the Cross, and marching forth to defy legally constituted city, county and state authority, when they well know it will foment discord, strife and ill will. The Bible says to the Christian, why do you not rather suffer yourself to be wronged or defrauded, rather than promote discord? Do you think such folks, regardless of what they profess, have God's Mark on them? Our witness is that they do not, for the Christian is called upon to suffer, suffer, bear the Cross, and to endure suffering and wrong treatment even as Christ did when crucified!

In God's Name, let us suggest that colored and white better be more concerned about whether you are going to spend Eternity in the blessing of Heaven, or in the fires of Hell, than about the questionable right to vote! We say a "questionable right" because of the conviction that there are myriads of white and colored who are not qualified to vote on account of lack of character, integrity, decency, and no telling what else! In nearly every election the writer questions his own qualifications to vote on some of the matters on account of ignorance. Usually he skips such things and doesn't vote on them unless he feels he can obtain advice from parties who have the good of the community at heart, and not some political or other kind of self interest. "It is appointed unto man once to die, but after this the judgment!" Every man must give account of himself unto God!

March 20, 1968

Government /Rulers

In the 2nd Psalm God tells us the Heathen are *"people who imagine a vain thing, kings and rulers who set themselves to break The Bands and cast away The Cords"* of restraint of God's Laws and Commandments. In Acts 4:25 the disciples of Jesus Christ, God in the flesh, lifted up their voices in prayer to God, acknowledging the fulfillment of the prophecy of the 2nd Psalm in their own observation and experience as they had witnessed the death of Christ at the hands of the religious and secular leaders and rulers who were now threatening them.

Persecutions among the heathen were supported under the pretense that Christians brought in new gods. The persecutions under the Roman Catholics were under the pretext of the Protestants introducing heresies into the Church.

However, does any know of an instance, among mankind, of rulers persecuting "religion itself"? Well, we submit that the "powers that be" in this great land are doing that very thing today! The ruling and edicts of our Supreme Court is openly and avowedly against: "Prayer," the greatest key to every blessing -- that is, in so far as our children and young people in the public schools! Surely the Almighty did not speak in vain when He said a number of times in His Word of supposedly His people: "Worse than the heathen!"

We certainly should not put all the blame on the Supreme Court! Look to yourselves, as well as the President, the Senators, the Congressmen, the Judges, etc., great numbers of whom either support the High Court, or are more or less indifferent to the whole matter! Is not the great power of the Army, Air Force, Navy, F.B.I., etc., standing by, if needed, to fight to enforce the decrees to prevent prayer in our public schools : "Prayer, the greatest key to every blessing!" Are not the high and mighty offices and pulpits of the clergy, the great doctors and scholars of the great seats of learning, largely filled with such as are in accord with the persecution of religion itself: "Prayer itself," the greatest key to every blessing!

When I read the title of the first chapter of Mr. John Stormer's book, "None Dare Call It Treason"; "Have we gone crazy," the answer that came immediately to my mind way: "No doubt of it!"

The heathen had a reason for persecuting. The Catholics had a reason for their persecutions. We asked if any knew of an instance, among mankind, of rulers persecuting religion itself: "Prayer," the greatest key to every blessing! Maybe we also have a "first" -- or a "scoop" as I think they say -- in another matter: Does any know of any civilized or enlightened people of history that allowed her citizens to go about in public in near nakedness? Has not that always been reserved for the pagans, savages, and benighted people who sexually live more or less and dogs and the beasts that perish?

But let us talk of a remedy. The Scriptures in Luke 8:27, etc., tells us: *"When Jesus went forth to land, there met Him out of the city a certain man, which had devils long time, and wore no clothes . . . !"* Read on and you will find that after Jesus treated him and the folks of the city came out to see what was done: *"They found the man, out of whom the devils were departed, sitting at the feet of Jesus, 'clothed,' and in his right mind; and they were afraid."* However, the change was not without cost, somebody lost some hogs in getting rid of the devils, and they did not want to pay the cost. They preferred to have a man walking about naked and full of devils than suffer the loss of some hogs.

They asked Jesus to leave! Ruskin said the trouble with most of us is: "We cannot see in a plain way!"

A certain historian says that after the fall of the western part of the Roman Empire, for generation after generation there was murder, rape, pillage, fire, etc., and one thing, and only one thing, kept Europe from returning to the days of the savage and hyena; and that was the humble followers of Jesus Christ. The proud, the presumptous, the lecherous, the coveteous, the hypocrites, the heretics, the apostates and their kinsfolk have got our nation and generation on the toboggan slide headed towards the dogs and hyenas.

It is time for the humble followers of Jesus Christ to get busy and bring our "naked" day and generation to Him who is able to cast out legions of devils and cause her to get in her right mind, put on "clothes" and sit at His feet. An approximate quote of Martin Luther: "Prayer is the only omnipotent empress of human affairs; by her we can change all things and overcome all evils; mend that which might be repaired and reclaimed, and take away that which is too evil and bad to mend." It has been said that John Knox prayed Mary, Queen of Scots, off the Throne of Scotland, and maybe to her death at the hands of Queen Elizabeth!"

It may be, for the benefit of some of our modern college students, and maybe doctors and professors, too, it should be pointed out that this was not the present reigning Queen Elizabeth, no indeed, but the great queen who reigned several hundred years ago. Am prompted to make this explanation in view of the meager intelligence some of them manifest in view of their conduct in many schools and universities all over the nation. Also, judging from several letters I have had from some of these "brilliants," the way they handled the subject matter under discussion, it is surprising they are not still "walking on all-fours."

April 23, 1966

53

In the Gospel of Luke, chapter 16, verse 15, we read these words of Christ: *"For that which is highly esteemed of man is abomination in the sight of God!"* The dictionary defines "abominable" as meaning "hateful; odious; offensive; unclean." This is a terrific statement, a terrible one, if one lets its significance sink down in their minds and hearts. Its terrific force, its terribleness is greatly magnified when one considers who made the statement -- none other than God in the flesh, The Lord Jesus Christ, man's Creator; man's Redeemer; man's Preserver, of whom the Scriptures testify: *"By Him and for Him, were all things created and made."*

The context of this 15th verse tells us what prompted, or provoked, Christ to make such a statement: It was the conduct of men who "justified themselves in the eyes of men," while God was looking upon them and knew their hearts to be *"deceitful above all things and desperately wicked: who can know it? I, The Lord, search the heart, I try the reins, even to give every man according to his ways, and according to the fruit of his doings. As the partridge sitteth on eggs, and hatcheth them not; so he that getteth riches and not by right, shall leave them in the midst of his days, and at the end shall be a fool."* Jeremiah 17:9-11.

"And at his end shall be a fool!" Consider the word picture of a man to whom God said: "Thou fool!" "The ground of a certain rich man brought forth plentifully; and he thought within himself, saying, what shall I do, because I have no room to bestow my fruits? And he said, *'This will I do; I will pull down my barns and build greater; and there will I bestow all my fruits and my goods, and I will say to my soul, soul, thou hast much goods laid up for many years; take thine ease, eat, drink, and be merry.'* But God said unto him: *'Thou Fool, this night thy soul shall be required of thee,'* then whose shall those things be, which thou hast provided? So is he that layeth up treasure for himself, and is not rich towards God!"* Luke 12:16-21. God grant these three words may sink down into our minds and hearts: "So is he; so is he; so is he." that means me, that means you, that means every man that spends his life laying up treasure here below, and fails to become rich towards God!

Also, there are others of whom God says, *"Thou fool!"* In Psalms 14:1 and 53:1 God calls the man "fool" who says there is no God. If I listened too much, and paid too much attention to such folks as this, I fear it might indicate I was in the same category.

"This night thy soul shall be required of thee!" In Luke 16: 19-31, Christ gives us a word picture of a certain man whose soul had just been *"required of him."* *"He died and was buried; and in hell he lifted up his eyes, being in torments - - - Father Abraham, have mercy on me, and send Lazarus, that he may dip the tip of his finger in water and cool my tongue; for I am tormented in this flame. But Abraham said, Son, remember that thou in thy lifetime receivest the good things - - - between us and you there is a great gulf fixed - - - Then said he, I pray thee therefore, father, that thou wouldest send him to my father's house; for I have five brethren; that he may testify unto them, lest they also come into this place of torment - - - They have Moses and the prophets; let them hear them - - - If they hear not Moses and the prophets, neither will they be persuaded, though one rose from the dead."* Such a passage as this causes me to be thankful that over and over again the following passage of Scripture has been presented in these articles:

"And further, by these, my son, be admonished; of making many books there is no end; and much study is a

weariness of the flesh. Let us hear the conclusion of the whole matter: 'Fear God and keep His Commandments, for this is the whole duty of man.' For God shall bring every work into Judgement, with every secret thing, whether it be good, or whether it be evil.'' Eccles. 12: 12-14. It appears to us that many who claim to believe and make much of the resurrection of Christ from the dead, attempt to use this belief to "cast away the Law of the Lord of Hosts," and this sort of testimony largely accounts for the lawlessness, crime, anarchy, etc., sweeping over our nation and the world, and in spite of the fact "there is no end to our churches, righteousness appears to be as scarce as 'hen teeth.''

"For that which is highly esteemed of men is abomination in the sight of God!'' This article was begun with the purpose of commenting on the subject of "voting," and qualifications. If we mistake not one thing highly esteemed of men these days is the slogan "Vote as you please, but please vote." Would like to give several reasons why this slogan is highly esteemed of men, in our judgment falls in the category of things abominable to God Almighty. If it pleases a man to vote for evil, regardless of whether your pleasure is due to ignorance, or coveteousness, or immorality, lust, dishonesty, lack of integrity, or any other evil, the result in the long run will be a curse to you, your family, your state, nation and the world: For you are responsible to God Almighty for your motives, acts, words, thoughts, and He will bring you into Judgement to "require your soul of you!" In the passage quoted above from the 17th chapter of Jeremiah God hath spoken: *"I the Lord search the heart . . . even to give to every man according to his ways, and according to the fruit of his doings,''* "Say ye to the righteous, It shall be well with him. Woe unto the wicked.''

The right to vote has been won at exceeding great cost and

56

sacrifice down through the centuries. The price paid is far above the value of gold and silver, jewels and precious stones. To hand this treasure over to the ignorant, the immoral and dishonest, lacking in character and integrity, might be likened to *"giving that which is holy to the dogs and casting your pearls before swine!"* In the Sermon on The Mount, Matthew 7:6, Christ said: *"Give not that which is holy to the dogs, neither cast ye your pearls before swine, lest they trample them under their feet, and turn again and rend you."* It appears that this Scripture has been largely fulfilled in our great nation in recent years by removing just about all good qualifications to protect the ballot and turning it over to the ignorant and immoral in many instances, and even to children in some states. And there are many records of some of these turning against the government to rend it apart. Did you ever hear of the experiences of some of the citizens of Atlanta: we refer to one whose place of business, a cafe, was "miserably messed up," and another being deprived of his business which had taken many years for him to build up? And these abominations were permitted, if not encouraged, or winked at, or "passed by on the other side" by many of our "highly esteemed authorities in the political, educational and ecclesiastical, and editorial world - - highly esteemed Priests, Levites, Reverends (?), and Doctor Divines (?). The Bible says, *"Whatsoever things are true, pure, of good report . . . Think on these things."* We trust and pray that some of these guilty "highly esteemed" will think on these things, turn, repent, and make what restitution possible, lest they be found abominable in the sight of God *"When He cometh to make up His Jewels, and require of them their souls! Is it well with your soul?"*

"To them that have shall be given, but from them that have not shall be taken away that which they have," said Christ. If we fail to use and protect the blessing of the right to vote, it will be taken away from us! Has it not already

been taken away from many of the peoples of the world? They vote, but with instructions who to vote for!

Did you know that one of the Presidents of the United States, the 12th, Zachary Taylor, "never bothered to vote?" We do not mention this in order to suggest that you do likewise, but rather to point out that it is not the right to vote that really exalts a man, but rather character, integrity, ability, etc. Or, to put it in Scriptural language:

"Righteousness exalteth a nation; but sin is a reproach to any people." Proverbs 14:34. And this truly applies to the individual.

May 21, 1966

†††

The information herein concerning President Zachary Taylor is from the National Geographic magazine of January, 1965. He became President in 1849, but died after being in office only about a year and a half. He was the first Professional Soldier to occupy the White House. He lacked political experience, and never voted -- probably a wise thing to do when you do not know what you are doing. Here is a man that never voted, and yet his fellow citizens voted him the highest office the country could give. He was so honored because of his ability, character, integrity, and devotion to duty in the defense and protection of his country. U.S. Grant, who served under him, said years later: "No soldier could face either danger or responsibility more calmly than he. These are qualities more rarely found than genius or physical courage."

Taylor treated bullets as trifles and never lost a battle. In the battle of Buena Vista, February 1847, General Taylor

58

with 4,700 inexperienced invaders defeated the Mexican Army of 15,000 troops, and became a national hero. In February 1850, President Taylor held a stormy conference with several southern leaders who threatened secession. Taylor told the southerners that to enforce the laws he would lead the army in person, and if they were taken "in rebellion against the Union," he would hang them with less reluctance than he had hanged deserters and spies in Mexico. It is believed that this unwavering stand delayed the Civil War 11 years. Ironically, his only son, Richard, served as a general in the Confederate Army.

"Never bothered to vote": We do not mention this to suggest that you do likewise, unless you do not know what you are doing, but rather to point out that it is not the right to vote that exalts a man, but rather character, integrity, ability and performance. Or, to put it in Scriptural language: *"Righteousness exalteth a nation: but sin is a reproach to any people."* Proverbs 14:34. And surely this applies to the individual.

It has been said, and doubtless very true, that mobs are seldom or never guilty of atrocities till they are deluded and misled. Do we not need intelligent and principled votes? Are we not striving to produce them? Can it be done by removing prayer and Bible reading from our public schools? And teaching that God is dead? *"Whatsoever a man soweth, that shall he reap!"* We have seen time and again of the communists announced plans to delude and mislead some of the most ignorant and immoral of our citizens in mobocracy in order to rend our government apart, and it appears they won the support of many of our "highly esteemed" in the government and colleges, churches, etc.

"For that which is highly esteemed among men is abomination in the sight of God!" We submit that the highly esteemed slogan: "Vote as you please, but please vote,"

59

falls in the category of things abominable to God; for if it pleases a man to vote for that which is evil, regardless of whether his pleasure is due to ignorance, coveteousness, immorality, lust, dishonesty, lack of integrity, or any other evil, the result in the long run will be a curse to the man, his family, state and nation: For he is responsible to God Almighty for his motives, acts, words, thoughts, and He will bring you into judgment to "require your soul of you!" In the 17th chapter of Jeremiah God hath spoken: *"I the Lord search the heart . . . even to give every man according to his ways, and according to the fruit of his doings."*

The right to vote has been won at exceeding great cost and sacrifice down through the centuries. The price paid is far above gold, silver, precious stones, etc. To hand this treasure over to the ignorant, immoral, dishonest, lacking character and integrity, might be likened to "giving that which is holy to the dogs and casting pearls before swine!" In the Sermon on the Mount, Christ said: *"Give not that which is holy to the dogs, neither cast ye your pearls before swine, lest they trample them under their feet, and turn again and rend you."* It appears that the Scripture has been largely fulfilled in our great nation by removing just about all good qualifications to protect the ballot and turning it over to the ignorant and immoral in many instances, and even to children in some states. And there are many records of some of them turning against the government to rend it apart.

Did you ever hear of the experiences of some of Atlanta's citizens: we refer to one whose place of business, a cafe, was "miserably messed up" and another being deprived of his business which had taken many years to build up? And these abominations were permitted, if not encouraged, or winked at, or "passed by on the other side" by many of our "highly esteemed" authorities in the political, educational, ecclesiastical and editorial world -- highly esteemed Priests,

Levites, Reverends (?), and Doctor Divines (?). The Bible says: *"Whatsoever things are pure, true, of good report . . . Think on these things."* God grant that some of these guilty "highly esteemed" may think on these things, turn, repent, and make what restitution possible, lest they be found abominable in the sight of God. *"When He cometh to make up His Jewels,"* and requires of men their souls! Is it well with your soul?

"To them that have shall be given," said Christ, *"But from them that hath not shall be taken away that which they have!"* If we fail to use and protect the right to vote, it will be taken away from us! Has it not already been taken away from many of the people of the world? They vote, but with instructions who to vote for!

May 28, 1966

†††

In the second Psalm God asks a question, and then answers it. He tells who the heathen are, why they rage. God also gives us instruction, warning, and an invitation to blessings.

Webster says a heathen is one who "does not believe in the God of The Bible." This definition fits in with what God says in this Psalm: "The Kings of the earth -- and the rulers, and the people (who) imagine a vain thing, and support them as they take council together, against The Lord, and His Annointed."

Does a Supreme Court "believe in the God of The Bible" if they reject this Book for our public schools and children? Surely, the right answer is, No! Does a Supreme Court believe in "The Lord's Annointed, The Lord Jesus Christ," when they reject the Prayer He taught His disciples, for our schools and children? Surely, the right answer is No! Does a

61

President, a Senator, a Congressman, a Governor, a Judge, etc. "believe in The God of The Bible, and His Anointed Jesus Christ" if they support decisions taking The Bible and The Lord's Prayer away from our school children and young people? Does not reason and common sense dictate the answer, No!

This is no light matter for the believer of The Bible! The ages of Eternity are at stake! Not only the well being of our nation, government, our people, and our prosperity are at stake for time, but also their well being and salvation for all eternity is at stake! Being persuaded, and conscious, and convicted of these truths, millions of people before our day have chosen to perish from the earth by fire, anguish, and cruel torment, rather than reject "The God of The Bible, and His Anointed, Jesus Christ!"

We should be careful about "passing the buck" of all responsibility to those in authority over us! Thus saith the Lord: *"For promotion cometh neither from the east, nor from the west, nor from the south. But God is the judge; He putteth down one, and setteth up another."* Psalm 75: 6-7. Generally, the Scriptures reveal that the kind of rulers God puts over men are symbolic of the overall national character and integrity, or the lack of such. In other words, God usually puts over us authorities representing a cross-section of the national conscience. Like with the individual, this may become "seared as with a hot iron." An indication of the condition of the national conscience is revealed by our attitude towards lawlessness, crime, immorality, etc.   Do we tolerate and excuse it, or are we intolerable and fight it to the death?

God Almighty's appraisal of the natural human heart is: *"The heart is deceitful above all things, and desperately wicked; who can know it?"* Jer. 17:9. This condition of the natural heart accounts for God's revelation to the great world ruler, Nebuchadnezzar, that His judgment upon him was *"To the intent that the living may know that the Most High ruleth in the kingdom of men, and giveth it to whomsoever He will, and setteth up over it the basest of men."* Daniel 4:17. Thank God for the exceptions, instances where nations or men learn "to fear God and keep His Commandments, the whole duty of man," and God sets up as rulers good men!

"The lapse of church discipline was a certain symptom of Political and Social anarchy," said the English Historian, Terry, as he viewed the centuries of their experiences. Protestant Christianity produced this great nation, and her good assets of every kind. Protestant Christians have no one to thank but themselves for the sad conditions we now find ourselves in! We are Jonahs! *"What meanest thou, O sleeper? arise, call upon thy God, if so be that God will think upon us, that we perish not!"* Jonah 1: 6. The following Scriptures are quoted with the hope and prayer these Words of God will quicken and wake up many of us. *"This people draweth nigh unto Me with their mouth, and honoreth Me with their lips; but their heart is far from Me. But in vain they do worship Me, teaching for doctrines the commandments of men."* Matthew 15: 8-9.

Consider the results of "vain worship:" *"Not every one that saith unto Me, Lord, Lord, shall enter the kingdom of heaven; but he that doeth the will of My Father which is in heaven. Many will say unto Me in that day, Lord, Lord, have we not prophesied in Thy Name? and in Thy Name cast out devils? and in Thy Name done many wonderful works? And then will I profess unto them, I never knew you; Depart from me, ye that work iniquity."* This quote is from The Sermon on The Mount -- Matthew 7: 21-23. In the remaining verses of this chapter Christ says those that reject His sayings are like a fool which built his house on the sand. The house could not stand the winds, the rains, the storms that beat upon it, it fell, and great was the fall thereof. Surely, it will be "A Great Fall" if America goes down.

"*Why even of yourselves judge ye not what is right?*" Luke 12:57. Did not our founding fathers, the early Pilgrims and Puritans build on "*the firm foundation, laid for the saints of The Lord In His Excellent Word: The Rock of Ages, The Word of God, and His Anointed, The Lord Jesus Christ?*" Believe it or not, these foundations account for the greatness, the power, the liberty, the prosperity of this great nation! Believe it or not, these benefits at the present are slipping away! The reason: our foundations are slowly but surely shifting to treacherous, shifting quick-sand!

"*What meanest thou, O sleeper? arise, call upon thy God, if so be that God will think upon us, that we perish not!*" Jonah "came out" all right, but it was not until he denounced "*lying vanities*" and said: "*I will pay that that I have vowed. Salvation is of The Lord!*"

March 7, 1964

God and History

Division Five

Queen Mary, known in history as "Bloody Mary," sat upon the Throne of England from 1553 to 1558. She was a violent persecutor of Protestants. After having brought multitudes in England and Scotland and Wales to the "block" and had their heads cut off, and others to the "stake" to be burned alive, she stretched forth her hand to strike them of Ireland. In 1558 she signed a Commission authorizing the persecution and annihilation of all Irish heretics. The Commission for execution was committed to Dr. Cole, a zealous son of Rome.

For a little sample of Queen Mary's work, we quote from an English History: "Among the first victims were John Rogers, the Bible Translator, and Hooper the Bishop of Glouster-Coverdale was saved by the interposition of the king of Denmark; but Ridley and Latimer sealed their faith at Oxford, Oct. 16, 1555 . Latimer was now in his 77th year, hale and hearty and merry to the last. 'Play the man, Mister Ridley,' he shouted to his fellow, as the executioners were fastening them to the stake, 'We shall this day light such a candle in England, as I trust by God's grace shall never be put out!' ''

"Of all Mary's victims none perhaps merited her vengeance more than Cranmer. She would not be a woman to forget the part which he had taken in fastening the stain upon her birth. Cranmer's courage which had never been of the stoutest failed him. He shrank from the torture of the heretic's death, and in hope of gaining his life recanted. His enemies, however, had no idea of allowing their victim to escape and he was condemned not-withstanding. As the end drew near, he recovered his spirit and boldly facing death, withdrew his unhappy denial of The Protestant Faith, thrusting his right hand into the flame first, "that unworthy right hand," as he sadly exclaimed, with which he had signed the recantation! The persecutors thought the "smell and sight of death" would frighten them into speedy acquiescence. But these were different men whose faith was now put to the test; nor could their firmness be shaken by the sight of flames. Spectators who came to scoff and jest, went away thoughtful and reverent.

"Genuine Protestantism does not consist only of the doctrines of justification by faith and the supreme authority of the Scriptures, for it implies, as its name indicates, an energetic protest, formulated in the name of these doctrines, against Ecclesiastical abuse of every kind." These, and many other men and women, died cruel deaths, some even rejoicing in their sufferings in order to be faithful witnesses to Genuine Protestantism!

Protestantism lived on in England and Scotland and Wales to bless those people and the world. Hear now, how

God Almighty protected and preserved the Protestants of Ireland at that time from the designs of Queen Mary and her supporters: Doctor Cole, on receiving the Queen's Commission, immediately goes to Ireland to execute the bloody mandate. At Chester, where he is to embark, he communicates to the mayor the nature of his errand to Ireland, at the same time pointing to a box, which, to use his language, contained "that which will lash the heretics of Ireland." The good woman in the house where they were, (Elizabeth Edmonds), a friend of the Protestants, who had a brother in Dublin, hearing these words, was not a little troubled. Therefore, watching her opportunity, she opens the box, takes out the Commission, and places in its stead a piece of paper in which she had carefully wrapped a pack of cards, with the knave of clubs uppermost. Suspecting nothing, The Doctor, the weather favoring, the next day set sail for Dublin. He immediately appears before the Lord Deputy and the Privy Council, makes his speech, declaring the nature of his Commission, and presents the box to the Lord Deputy; which, on opening, nothing appears but a pack of cards, the knave of clubs staring his Lordship in the face! The Lord Deputy and Council were amazed, and the Doctor was confounded; yet insisted that he started with a Commission such as he had declared. The Deputy answered: "Let us have another Commission, and we will shuffle the cards in the meantime."

The Doctor, chagrined, returned to England, appears at the Court, obtains another Commission, but is now detained by unfavorable winds, and while waiting, Queen Mary died, being called to her dread account! And thus God preserved the Protestants of Ireland! (MSS of Sir James Ware, copied from the papers of Richard, Earl of Cork, and found quoted by Mosheim, Vol. 2, p. 42. Also, Universal History, Vol. 4, p. 278.

"He that sitteth in the Heavens shall laugh: The Lord shall have them in derision!" So, says the 4th verse of the

2nd Psalm concerning heathen, kings, rulers, and people who imagine a vain thing and rage against The Commandments, The Acts, The Ordinances and Providences of "Him that sitteth in the Heavens."

Psalm 138, verse 2: *"For thou has magnified Thy Word above all Thy Name."* Herein can be found genuine Protestantism.

"Democratic Institutions exist by reason of their virtue. If ever they perish, it will be when we have forgotten the past, become indifferent to the present, and utterly reckless as to the future." Quoted from the Monument to Thos. Watson on the Capitol Grounds in Atlanta.

It appears to us that Our Supreme Court, the supporting Powers that be, including most of the High Ecclesiastical Powers, in their treatment of The Bible, God's Word, which He has magnified above all His Name, are seeking to destroy Genuine Protestantism just as surely as was Queen Mary. They will never do it, thank God: "He that sitteth in the Heaven shall laugh!" In the meantime, let all "genuine protestants" stir themselves up to improve their conduct in "honoring all God's Commandments," and improve their "prayer life," especially remembering that prayer the Government forbids the schools: "Deliver us from evil!" "God moves in a mysterious way His wonders to perform." It has been well said that sometimes God's doors swing open or shut on strange and peculiar "hinges!"

January 19, 1974

†††

We quote from a letter received giving a reader's reaction to a past Saturday's article about King Charles The First of England, and Oliver Cromwell:

"While I have admired some of your editorials, I cannot

67

agree with your surmise of Oliver Cromwell as detailed in a past issue of The Atlanta Journal. You suggest that in Oliver Cromwell, God 'Found his man to stand in the gap' whereas history shows him to be a cold-blooded murderer of women and children.

"Herewith I list some of the slaughterers of mankind. 1. Pharaoh of Egypt at the time of the birth of Moses (He was a heathen). 2. Herod about the time of the birth of Christ (He was a stooge of Roman Empire). 3. Attila, the Hun, Scourge of God (He was a heathen). 4. Genghis Kahn (Mongol heathen). 5. Tamarlane (Oriental heathen). 6. Catherine de Medici, Regent of Charles IX, King of France (She engineered the Massacre of St. Bartholomew). 7. Oliver Cromwell, Commander of The Praying Puritans, he invaded Ireland to put down a rebellion, and had his 'Roundheads' slaughter Men, Women and Children at Cork and Wexford. How can a man of God violate the 6th Commandment and permit the useless slaughter of innocent children, thereby earning the worst malediction one Irishman can hurl at another Irishman, 'The Curse of Cromwell Be Upon You . . .'

"There can be no question as to the stabilizing influence Cromwell had on the British Government during his term of office, but the stain of blood of innocent children of Cork and Wexford can never be erased. I suggest you remember this when you are tempted to extol the virtues of Oliver Cromwell. I am not an Irishman. Yours very truly."

We wish to thank the writer of this letter for sending it, for his desire, and for his effort to "straighten me out." However, will have to admit he has failed, for we are not "straight," according to his "measuring stick." However, we are giving him the opportunity to "straighten out" any of our readers if they feel the need of it.

I consider our disagreement is due to the difference in the character of "The God" they profess to worship and serve.

68

No doubt he will say that "his God" created all these "Slaughterers of Mankind" such as Pharaoh, Attila, Genghis Kahn, Tamerlane, Cromwell, etc. But I can't go along with this letter writing friend, not especially with "his God," for it appears to me that "his God" after creating all these "big boys" lost rule and control of them to the extent where they did a slight devilment and dirty work. Such a god ought to be ashamed of himself -- started to say somebody ought to "kick him in his pants," but that might be too rude -- recall in one of my articles, I told how I thought God rebuked me a couple of times for mistreating snakes!

I certainly do believe, testify and bear witness to the fact that the God I believe in created every one of these great "slaughterers of mankind" and many others, but He never lost control over any one of them for even a fraction of a second, and on the contrary, everything and anything they did was with His Permission and the result of His exercising righteous Judgments and "Paying the Wages of Sin: Death!" They were his Judgments and Curse being visited upon Sin, Rebellion, Anarchy and Rage against "God who is a spirit, infinite, eternal and unchangeable in His being wisdom, power, justice, holiness, goodness and truth."

He is the God who on two different occasions turned the devil aloose on Job: first on his family, and then on his person. But in each instance, He kept the Devil under control and said, *"Go so far, but no further!"* If you have genuine and true faith and "Fear of the Lord" in your heart, should you worry unduly about those who die and are slaughtered? Has He not said "Not one sparrow falls to the ground without your Heavenly Father!" The Almighty created my Grandfather Adam out of the ground, and in introducing Himself to His New Creature He said: *Obey or die!* In Luke 13:3, Christ says to us: *"Repent, or Perish!"* May I ask: What is your experience in this subject of Repentance?

"For the eyes of the Lord run to and fro throughout the

*whole earth to show Himself strong in the behalf of them
whose heart is perfect towards Him!"* 2nd Chronicles 16:9.

*"And I sought for a man among them, that should make
up the hedge, and stand in the gap before Me for the land,
that I should not destroy it But I found none!"* Ezekiel
22:30.

Again this writer suggests that "God found His man to
make up the hedge, and stand in the gap," in Oliver
Cromwell with the result that England, Scotland and Ireland
were not destroyed, but saved and greatly blessed. Be
careful you know what you are doing and "Don't bear false
witness against your neighbor," Oliver Cromwell.

Unless there is a change of mind the writer intends next
week to give account of Cromwell at Cork and Wexford
according to his understanding.

July 27, 1974

†††

We trust it will be an encouragement to all the true and
sincere people of God to be reminded of several long periods
of time in the earth when men dwelt without fear for their
families, loved ones, and property, due to kings, rulers, and
governing authorities who would not countenance or put up
with lawlessness. May I ask any or all in whatever category
you may belong who claim to believe that the "death
penalty" does not prevent crime: Did you ever see a dead
man commit murder? Did you ever see a dead man rape a
woman or girl? Do you reckon there was any rape, adultery,
homosexuality, or other crimes in Sodom on that morning
shortly after Lot went out of the City and God rained fire and
brimstone from heaven upon it?

The following statement is made not for the purpose of
offending any man, but rather for the purpose of the writer
not offending God Almighty: From my knowledge of The

70

Bible, if I take the position the "death penalty" does not restrain and prevent, I make God out to be a liar many times in His Word, and in fact reject the entire economy of The Almighty revealed in John 3:16 : *"For God so loved the world that He gave His only begotten Son, that whosoever believeth in Him should not perish but have everlasting life."* Maybe we need to meditate on these words of The Lord Jesus Christ: *"Ye do err, not knowing The Scriptures, nor The Power of God!"* Meditate on them, and repent!

Regardless of what others do, or profess, you continue to "Fear God and keep His Commandments: for this is the whole duty of man." "Be not weary in well-doing, for in due season we will reap, if we faint not." *"Thy Kingdom come, Thy will be done, in earth, as it is in Heaven. Deliver us from evil."* Remember that a number of times God has told us in His Word: *"The earth shall be full of the knowledge of the glory of the Lord, as the waters cover the sea."* For nothing should the people of God more devoutly pray than that "their great men might be good and God-fearing men!"

"Democratic Institutions exist by reason of their virtue. If ever they perish it will be when you have forgotten the past, become indifferent to the present, and utterly reckless as to the future." "When you have forgotten the past!" The following is a reminder of a few incidents of the past:

Not forgetting the past: let's turn to Oliver Cromwell about the 1650's A.D., and remember that God used him in England, Scotland and Ireland to put down evil, rebellion and disorder.

Not forgetting the past: in the year 617 A.D. Edwin was crowned King of Northumbria, one of the seven divisions of England in the period of The Heptarchy. It was from this King that Edinburgh got her name. It was said first of him that in his days "a woman with her babe might walk scathless from sea to sea." The people tilled their fields and gathered their harvests in quiet and safety. Men no longer feared the thief and robber; stakes were driven by the roadside spring, where the traveler found a brass cup hanging for his use, and no thief durst carry it off . . . "Thus the church as the great civilizer, had already begun its work in Teutonic Britain."

Again, not forgetting the past; in the year 1066 A.D. the grandson of a Norse pirate was recognized as King of England. His ways were masterful and his measures severe, but the results were beneficial. He was a hard drillmaster; but England needed a drillmaster, and the English were the first to recognize it. Life and property were protected as they had never been done and protected under native English kings. Even the Chronicle is forced to recognize "the good peace he made in the land, so that a man might go over the realm alone with his bosom full of gold unhurt. Nor durst any man slay another, how great so ever the evil he had done." "The good peace he made in the land!"

Don't forget again that the conqueror's son, Henry I, demanded respect and obedience to his laws, and won the title -- "Lion of Justice." "And no man durst misdo against another."

Not forgetting the past: around 1200 to 1230 A.D., Genghis Khan came out of the Gobi desert and conquered the cities of civilization. No other man except Alexander the Great, long before the time of Genghis Khan ever made such a change in the world during one lifetime. Southern China was conquered, he swept over Russian princes, and over the brave Poles and Hungarians. His general, Subotai, got as far as Vienna, where his forces turned back from Europe of their own accord -- doubtless because France and Germany went to their knees in prayer to God Almighty! Genghis Khan demanded obedience to his Law: Mongol accounts say cart loads of gold and silver stood nearby without any guards to watch over them, so utterly was the Law of Genghis Khan, which forbade stealing, obeyed!

72

Somewhere, somehow, this Magnificent Barbarian had gotten ahold of God Almighty's Commandment: *"Thou shalt not steal."* He believed it! He enforced it! (Would God we would do the same!) Because of that Law peace prevailed for thousands of miles around him. At a "Council of his Conquerors," he said, "I have gained the mastery by carrying out our Law. Only severity keeps men obedient . . . An action is only good if you carry it out to the end." His commandments were obeyed even after his death. It was as if he sat on the raised throne of the council of the Mongol Khan. Everything written down in his Law was carried out by the generations that followed him. When his grandson, Batu Khan, ruled there was a saying in Russia that "a dog cannot bark without permission of Batu Khan." And it was also said that a young girl alone could carry a sack of gold safely from the River Don to the City of The Khans. What is wrong with such power when it is used to stop stealing, and protect women?

Above records of five rulers testify to the ability of men to keep law and order. Suggest we think on our ways.

What is the trouble? The answer is as plain as the nose on your face: We have forsaken the Commandments of our God!

March 8, 1975

†††

In the year 1625 Charles the First ascended the throne of England. The political creed of Charles was a short one; he believed in "the divine right of kings," and also the "divine right of his bishop." There was no place for a Parliament in his system, except as a cumbersome and annoying method of securing money for the purpose of government.

From the first, Charles was at war with his Parliament,

and soon there was an era of arbitrary government --
1639-1640. It has been estimated that at the outbreak of the
American Revolution seventy-five percent of the people of
English blood of the northern colonies were descendants of
men and women who had been driven out of England by the
tyranny of Charles and his little arch-bishop -- by the way,
these are the two responsible for the "Declaration of
Sports" promulgated in those days that made it legal for the
profanation of the Sabbath -- both of these boys ended up by
losing their heads on the chop block, however, to their
worldly credit it might be said they were not "chicken"
about doing as they pleased on God's Day!

During this period of arbitrary government "The Star
Chamber Court" made history by passing out judgements
and sentences for "flogging, for one or more ears to be cut
off, or slitting noses, or for face branding." In spite of these
severe judgements, and censoring of the press, many hardy
souls fought on "underground," some enduring more than
once the atrocities of the court! With such conditions, is it
any wonder that Civil War broke out in 1641, and all the
nation was in uproar? Scotland was hostile. One of the worst
massacres of history occurred in Ireland in 1641 and all that
nation was in uproar. The great mass of the English people
were disloyal and ready to take advantage of the first sign of
weakness on the part of the government.

Civil War! Take a glance at the opposing forces: The
king's forces and supporters were thorough courtiers, many
of them soldiers of fortune, princes of royal and noble blood
such as two nephews of the King, Prince Rupert and Prince
Maurice, gay worldlings who hated Puritanism and despised
Puritans -- doubtless there are multitudes of their
descendants in our land today. On the other side supporting
Parliament were the great mass of "God Fearing"
yeomanry, tradesmen of the towns, etc.

74

For ten years the Great Civil War desolated England. The economic life of the nation suffered terribly. Thousands of individuals had been ruined, and public works abandoned and, in cases, destroyed altogether. Thousands of acres had been thrown out of cultivation. Little respect was shown for civil law, crime and violence had increased steadily; murder, arson and highway robbery were common events of daily life -- sounds about like our day, is it not so? These were only symptoms of a deeper malady, the general decay of civilization.

God, in His mercy, gave Parliament the victory, 24 years after Charles was crowned, on the 30th of January, 1649, after á trial by the High Court of Justice, King Charles was condemned to die. Three days before the Court had given its decision, declaring Charles Stewart to be "a tyrant, traitor, murderer, and public enemy to the good people of this nation," and fixed the death penalty. On the 30th he was led out to Whitehall to die: "And when the tragedy was over, and the masked executioner held up the gory trophy of his art, he shouted to the horror-stricken crowd 'Behold the head of a traitor!' "

A few years after the king's death, England, Ireland and Scotland were at peace and prospering. When Charles ascended the throne, England's government and power were looked down upon, if no scorned, by other nations. At the time of the death of The Protector, Cromwell, England was respected and feared both as a land and sea power -- someone said of the Prime Minister of France: "He was more afraid of Cromwell than the devil!"

"Watch God work!" Consider the change God wrought in England, Ireland, and Scotland between 1641 and 1659: from chaos and confusion to order, peace, and prosperity. Consider the human instruments with which He worked. We quote Ezekiel 22:29-30: *"The people of the land have used oppression, and exercised robbery, and have vexed the poor and needy; yea, they have oppressed the stranger wrongfully. And I sought for a man among them, that should make up the hedge, and stand in the gap before me for the land, that I should not destroy it: But I found none!"*

We suggest that in Oliver Cromwell God "found His man to stand in the gap." During the first few years of the Great Civil War, Prince Rupert's horsemen and Cavaliers swept the cavalry of Parliament off the field of battle. However, the sturdy Puritan infantry and foot soldiers of Parliament forces victoriously withstood the king's infantry. There was a country squire by the name of Oliver Cromwell. He had a cousin among the nobility by the name of Hampden by whose influence he might have obtained military preference. However, he asked no special favors for himself but appeared to be content with the office of captain in the cavalry. When Prince Rupert's Cavaliers played havoc with Parliament's horsemen, Cromwell managed to keep his men together and from being routed and scattered. Cromwell analyzed the success of Prince Rupert's Cavaliers, and said to his cousin, Hampden: "Your troops are most of them decayed serving men and tapsters, and such kind of fellows, and their troops are gentlemen's sons and persons of quality. Do you think that the spirits of such base and mean fellows will ever be able to encounter gentlemen that have honor, courage, and resolution in them?" Cromwell then went to work to raise a cavalry regiment of a very different mettle. As he himself expressed it, he proposed to match "men of religion" against the "king's gentlemen of honor." The result was the organization of the famous "Ironsides," a body of men who possessed the loftiest religious enthusiasm, tempered and hardened by the severest discipline.

Cromwell's Ironsides were men that had the true "fear of God" in their hearts; and gradually lost all other fear:

76

"Truly they were never beaten at all," he says. They swept Prince Rupert and his Cavaliers off the face of the earth. The Prince then took a job of Admiral in the king's navy, but it was only a question of time until Cromwell's Ironside Navy swept Prince Rupert and his ships off the ocean, or to its bottom -- have forgotten just what did happen to the great Prince in the end, but the last I recall he was wandering about.

Do not forget the "past." The above recalls to remembrance some very significant history of our past. It is the first step in the downfall of our "democratic institutions": forgetting. The second downward step is indifference, and the third utter recklessness." Are not our "democratic institutions" now failing in favor of institutions of socialism and communism? Lord God of Hosts, be with us yet, lest we forget! Lest we forget!

November 2, 1967

Hell and Judgment

Division Six

"I will also forget thy children!" Is there not something wrong with the young people today? Maybe some light can be thrown on the situation by considering this quotation, for it is God Himself speaking.

"My people are destroyed for lack of knowledge: because thou hast rejected knowledge, I will also reject thee, that thou shalt be no priest to me: seeing thou has forgotten The Law of Thy God, I will also forget thy children!" Hosea 4:6.

Weigh these words! It is a terrible message of judgement! Destroyed on account of "lack of knowledge" or ignorance. Rejection and ignorance of "The Law of Our God!" The results: they shall be no priest to God, and God will forget their children, seeing they have forgotten "The Law of Thy God!" -- Protestantism gives us the true teaching of God's Word that every sincere believer is a priest unto his God. Have we not forgotten "The Law of Our God!" We "breach the Sabbath," and destroy "The Goods of God!" We mock and scorn His Laws regarding the home, marriage and sex relations. Our land is lousy with murderers, and yet quite a number of our states have decided that The Almighty did not know what He was talking about when He said:

"Whoso killeth any person, the murderer shall be put to death -- Moreover ye shall take no satisfaction for the life of a murderer, which is guilty of death: but he shall be surely put to death -- So ye shall not pollute the land wherein ye are: for blood it defileth the land: and the land cannot be cleansed of the blood that is shed therein, but by the blood of him that shed it. Defile not therefore the land which ye shall inhabit, wherein I dwell: for I The Lord dwell among the children of Israel." Numbers 35: 30-34.

Our land is also filled with stealing, lying and coveteousness. If this writer's appraisal is correct even many of the laws of our nation and states encourage its people to covet that which in God's sight belongs to another instead of teaching and urging them to take heed to one of the very first laws of God to fallen man to live by "the sweat of his own brow." We are trying to run over Almighty God Himself! And in order to make peace with men who deny and blaspheme The God we claim to serve, we turn and make war on God Himself! Shall we have peace with man by making war on God Almighty? Was it not Bill Shakespeare who said: "What fools these mortals be!"

"My people are destroyed for lack of knowledge!" What is your vocation, doctor, lawyer, teacher, etc.? Say you are a lawyer: If you had spent that same amount of time on your law books, court cases, decisions, etc. as you have on

78

studying the Law of God and His Judgements, what kind of a lawyer would you be? If a doctor, what sort of doctor would you be if you had spent no more time studying the necessary subjects than you have spent learning of The Creator of the body -- "we are fearfully and wonderfully made" -- and taking heed to the injunction and invitation of The Great Physician to "Learn of Me?" Whatever one's vocation may be, their success or failure doubtless depends on their knowledge of the subject and their ability to make application of same. But fail or succeed, it is only temporal. But the knowledge of God, or lack of it, has to do with our Eternal Life, or eternal death! God says: "Cursed be the man that trusteth in man," and "He that trusteth in his own heart is a fool!"

"Search the Scriptures, they testify of Me," said Jesus Christ. "The Scriptures cannot be broken." Search and you will find the Almighty pleading with you:

"And the Lord said unto me, -- O that there were such an heart in them, that they would fear me, and keep all my commandments always, that it might be well with them, and with their children forever!" Deut. 5: 28-29.

"Oh, that my people had hearkened unto me, and Israel had walked in my ways! I should have soon subdued their enemies, and turned My Hand against their adversaries. The haters of The Lord should have submitted themselves unto Him: but their time should have endured forever. He should have fed them with the finest of the wheat: and with honey out of the rock should I have satisfied thee." Psalm 81: 13-16.

"Thus saith the Lord, thy Redeemer -- O that thou hadst hearkened to my commandments! Then had thy peace been as a river, and thy righteousness as the waves of the sea: thy seed had been as the sand." Isaiah 48: 17-17.

79

For the sake of the children we should not forget the "Law of Our God!"

May 19, 1962

†††

"Who is on The Lord's side?" This quotation is from Exodus 32: 26. Moses asked the question of the children of Israel and called on all those who were on The Lord's side to come to him, and all the sons of Levi gathered themselves together unto him. Moses himself belonged to this tribe of Levi which God had set aside for His special service. These men were ordered to do a terrible thing, witness: "Thus saith the Lord God of Israel, Put every man his sword by his side, and go in and out from gate to gate throughout the camp, and slay every man his brother and every man his companion, and every man his neighbor. And the children of Levi did according to the word of Moses: and there fell of the people that day about three thousand men!" Was not this a terrible thing to do, and a terrible thing to have to take part in? About this time, or just a little later, there were numbered of the nation 603,000 men 20 years of age and over that were able to be soldiers and go to war, and this indicated there were probably over three million men, women, and children total population. The killing of the three thousand is not so terrible when you consider that they perished instead of the three million, for God had told Moses: *"Now therefore let Me alone, that My wrath may wax hot against them, and that I may consume them and I will make of thee a great nation"* -- God's anger bursting into flame and burning them up!

The object of this article is to present the facts, the setting, the context, concerning the question *"Who is on The Lord's side?"* which appears nowhere else in The Bible, we think, in just these words. We carelessly and

80

glibly sing the song "Who is on The Lord's Side" and doubtless feel that means us because we have joined the Church and have not been put in jail, maybe because we did not get caught, not yet. About six weeks before Moses asked this question he stood with the others at the foot of Mt. Sinai: Picture in your own mind what they saw as recorded in Exodus 19:17, etc.: *"And Moses brought forth the people out of the camp 'To meet with God' . . . and Mt. Sinai was altogether on a smoke, because the Lord descended upon it in a fire: and the smoke thereof ascended up as the smoke of a furnace, and the whole mount quaked greatly. And when the voice of the trumpet sounded long, and waxed louder and louder, Moses spake, and God answered him by a voice."*

Out of this fearful and terrible scenery they heard the voice of God speak the Ten Commandments. *"And all the people saw the thunderings, and the lightning, and the noise of the trumpet, and the mountain smoking; and when the people saw it, they removed and stood afar off. And they said unto Moses, Speak thou with us, and we will hear, but let not God speak wth us, lest we die."* *"And so terrible was the sight, that Moses said, I exceedingly fear and quake."* -- Hebrews 12:21. After God finished speaking the Commandments to the people, He called Moses up into the Mount. There he spent forty days with God, receiving detailed laws concerning the peoples relations with one another, and to their God; and also instructions for building a tabernacle for God to come and abide with them; and then God gave him "The Ten Words" written on two tables of stone. *"The stones were the work of God, and the writing was the writing of God, written with the finger of God."*

Beginning with the 32nd chapter it appears that Moses conference with God was interrupted, and He told Moses to go down and see about his people for they had quickly forgotten their experiences and promises at Sinai, had made a golden calf an idol and were worshipping it! It was then that the wrath and anger of God would have burst into flame and consumed all the three millions of them had not Moses stood in the breach and interceded for them, and as a result of Moses' mediation, they escaped with only three thousand being slain, instead of the three millions! When Moses stood in the gate of the camp, and said, Who is on the Lord's side? Let him come unto me! These were called upon to execute the vengeance of God!

If we consider ourselves as "being on The Lord's side" we would do well to consider our attitude towards the terribleness of sin and rebellion against God's Commandments: "The wages of sin is death, eternal death, but the gift of God is eternal life through Jesus our Lord." When Moses saw the idolatry of the people, and how in their perverted worship they "sat down to eat and drink and rose up to play" -- this makes one think of things going on in many of our churches these days -- he became angry and threw down the two tables of stone on which the Commandments were written, and broke them. Later, God told him to cut out two stones and present them to God for a rewriting of The Commandments *"with the finger of God."* God now calls on you and me to present the tables of our heart to Him in order that The Spirit of God might write His Commandments upon them. Beware, take heed, if you are one who thinks and claims "Christ is in you" and yet there is not the desire to be obedient to every Commandment of God: *"Blessed are they that do His Commandments, that they may have a right to the tree of life, and may enter in through the gates into the city."* Rev. 22:14. *"Who is on The Lord's side?"*

January 4, 1964

†††

"Blessed are they that do His commandments, that they may have a right to the tree of life, and may enter in through the gates into the City."

Note the place and position the above verse occupies in The Bible -- it is the eighth from the end. Just seven more verses and God's written Revelation to man closes. These seven last verses contain one of the most wonderful and glorious invitations of God to men. Also, one of the most terrible and awful threats of God Almighty's judgments:

The Invitation: *"And the Spirit and the bride say, Come, And let him that heareth say, Come. And let him that is athirst, Come. And whosoever will, let him take the water of life freely."*

The Warning Threat: *"If any man shall add unto these things, God shall add unto him the plagues that are written in this book; and if any man shall take away from the words of this prophecy, God shall take away his part out of the book of life, and out of the holy city, and from the things which are written in this book."*

The blessing and the curse are set before men, over against one another, from one end of The Bible to the other: In the garden of Eden, by Moses in The Laws of God, by example after example in the experiences of the nations and their kings and rulers and peoples; in the Psalms, and in the prophets, and in the gospels and in the epistles, and here in the last few words of Revelation.

Surely we are without excuse if the curse becomes our potion! The invitation is Come, Come, Come! And we are on our way to our spiritual "space flight" to other worlds and eternity! The late Sam Jones said: "The heart in your bosom is a 'muffled drum' beating a march for you to the

83

cemetery." How old are you? Is your "drum-beat march" near its end? A few days ago there were sixty or more notices -- funeral -- in just one paper of men and women and maybe children who had just left on their trip to outer-space to keep The Appointment God made for them: *"It is appointed unto men once to die, but after this the judgment."* Hebrews 9:27.

Enoch and Elijah's trip to "outer-space" is exceedingly interesting! Also, in the 16th chapter of Luke, Jesus Christ draws back the veil and gives us a little view of the "Space-flights" of the souls of two men to other worlds: one carried by the angels to Abraham's bosom, the other died and was buried, and in hell he lifted up his eyes, being in torments -- not much about the details of the trips but very definite about the destinations and the conditions found at the end of the journey. Let any mock and scorn who will, but as for me let me stir up myself to "Fear The Lord and depart from evil."

"Why do the heathen rage?" A heathen is one who does not believe in "The God of The Bible." The ones who rebel and rail against the righteous Laws of The Holy God, and pull down His wrath, curse, scorn and contempt upon the human race in judgments. While the Second Psalm gives us a picture and the cause of present world conditions and tells us the way out, yet turn back to the First Psalm and look at a different scene, a beautiful and fruitful tree planted by the side of a river: It is the blessed man *"That walketh not in the counsel of the ungodly, nor standeth in the way of sinners, nor sitteth in the seat of the scornful. But his delight is in the law of the Lord, and in His Law doth he meditate day and night."*

"In His Law doth he meditate day and night." Concerning the warning above of taking from, or adding to God's Word, doubtless many of us who would not dare think of such a

thing, have actually taken it all out of circulation so far as our own reading and meditations are concerned, and have added and substituted the devil's library! If so, is it not time for a change?

"I thought on my ways, and turned my feet unto thy testimonies. I made haste, and delayed not to keep thy commandments." Psalm 119: 59-60.

March 31, 1962

†††

"Forget Hell!" Recently we saw this sign on the front end of an automobile -- beware of this man's "front end service," -- such a "front-end loader!" "The heart in your bosom is a 'muffled drum' beating a march for you to the cemetery," and God Almighty's Judgment: *"As it is appointed unto men once to die, but after this the judgement"* --Hebrews 9:27.

However, the above-car owner's "front end service" seems to be the kind of service we have been getting from most of the pulpits and clergy for many years -- adopting an attitude as if "that which is not talked about does not exist!" About 25 years ago the writer heard a sermon on the subject of "hell" preached by a man reputed to be orthodox and "sound in the faith." He announced it was his first sermon on the subject of hell after a ministry of 18 years. The reaction of this hearer was that to a large extent the Scriptural Truth was fulfilled that says: *"To him that hath shall be given, but from him that hath not shall be taken away that which he seemeth to have."* Or, in other words, he did not now accept and believe the Scriptures he had neglected so long!

Many years ago the writer had the privilege a number of times to hear the late Bishop Candler -- it is my

85

understanding that the Emory Candler School of Theology was named in his honor. Many interesting and striking incidents were told of his experiences. We undertake to tell one of them -- it could be that we might get two of them mixed into one story, yet we think we are careful to stress points that are faithful to the Bishop's teaching and testimony.

One Sunday morning The Bishop was standing in the front of a hotel in a city where he was to preach, waiting for his carriage or conveyance. He noticed a man in some activity that in those days was considered Sabbath Profanation --in our day it would probably be all right as it appears we have developed such a religion and faith that puts no difference between the "sacred and profane," "the holy and unholy." The Bishop stepped over to the man and said: "Friend, you ought not to be doing that on The Lord's Day, The Holy Sabbath! Aren't you afraid the devil will get you?" "Naw," replied the man, and then looking closely at The Bishop he said: "Where in the hell have I seen you before?" "Well, now," said the Bishop, "just what part of hell are you from?"

It is said that Dante told this story on himself: One day as he walked down the streets of Florence he noticed two women in a doorway looking hard at him, and overheard this remark: "There is the man that goes back and forth to hell every day!"

There was a cause, and good grounds for Dante, as well as all men who sincerely believe in "The God of The Bible" and accept His Word as Supreme Authority, to meditate upon and seek to visualize the horrors of hell. Just about all that we have in The Scriptures of the awful subject fell from the mouth of The Lord Jesus Christ, and from His Beloved Apostle John, found in the Revelation of Jesus Christ given unto John by God's angels. Dante in his vision of the Inferno

86

sees hell divided into nine or ten "pits" or "circles." It appears there is segregation in each pit: for example, the sexual, sensual, lustful sinners are together in one pit -- but they are not enjoying one another's company. The gluttons occupy a pit of their own and so on.

Remember the preacher's question to the Sabbath desecrator: "Well, now, what part of hell are you from?" Let us look and behold what Dante saw "in that part of hell" he called the fourth "pit" or "enclosure!" There he sees the Demon Plutus, with hoarse voice and inflated lips, symbolizing "Pride of Health!" These occupy the same pit where the misers and prodigals are made to herd together. Their mutual hatred makes them form into opposing bands, which attack one another without ceasing, reminding one another at each encounter of the degrading vices that have brought them down. Amongst them are clerics and cardinals and popes! "Now, my son, thou canst discern the shortlived vanity of those possessions that are committed to fortune, for which the human race is ever wrangling. For all the gold that is under the moon, or that ever existed, would not give rest to these weary souls!" This fortune that makes people so contentious, is hidden like a snake in the grass. It enters, however, into the plan of Providence, and it is through its influence that peoples are great or weak, that one nation rules and another languishes."

Is the Bishop's question relevant for you, for me? "What part of hell are you from?"

The late Dr. Leen G. Broughton, who for many years was Pastor of the Baptist Tabernacle on Lucky St. in Atlanta, and under whose ministry the present building was erected, told of this experience in a revival meeting: He had preached the sermon, and in giving the invitation for the people to forsake their sins and come forward and publicly accept Christ, he asked the Christian people who were willing to go about the

87

congregation and give people a personal invitation, and offer to come forward with them if desired. There was a well known and brilliant lawyer on the back seat. The Doctor noticed a young man, known to be about half-wit, get up and go straight to the lawyer and speak to him. After a word or two the lawyer's face flushed, he got up and went out. The Doctor was afraid he had ruined things in so far as that prospect was concerned.

It was near the end of the week before he learned what had happened. The lawyer came to see him and told this story: The young man came to him and abruptly said: "Do you want to go to Heaven?" It offended and angered him so much that he said, "Naw!" "Well, go the hell then," the boy replied. However, regardless of the provocation, he had been unable to shake off the fact that he had said he did not want to "go to Heaven," and he had faith enough to believe the alternative was as the boy said: ' 'Then go to hell!'' The man was unable to find peace of soul until he acknowledged his lost condition, and called on The Saviour to Save. It appears that it took quite a shock to wake him up to his spiritual condition, and God used this poor boy to produce the shock needed!

"Is it well with your soul?" Beware -- Don't forget Hell -- remember Him who came to save.

April 13, 1974

†††

Dante, the great Christian poet, in his immortal work, *The Divine Comedy,* says he saw Cleopatra and Helen of Troy in Hell! Others also he saw there, and called names. Some were emperors, kings, great generals, popes, cardinals, priests, and others of the great or small of the earth!

Dante was born in 1265 and died in 1321 A.D. The

literature on his life and work is enormous. The first complete American translation of *The Comedy* was that of Longfellow in 1867, in three volumes. Here are a few quotations from some familiar with his life and works:

"As a Christian poet, his name occupies a foremost place in the line of genius. His immortal work, *The Divina Commedia,* expresses such views of religion and the Church that he is numbered among the forerunners of the Reformation. To use his own words, 'The subject of the whole work, taken literally, is the state of the souls after death regarded as a matter of fact; taken allegorically, its subject is man, in so far as, by merit or demerit in the exercise of freewill, he is exposed to the rewards of punishment or justice.'"

"The Inferno represents the summing up, by perhaps the keenest observer the world has ever seen, of The Papal system judged by its results." Dante was a Catholic, as were most all men at that time who called themselves Christian; and no doubt from his knowledge of God, his love of righteousness, and his experiences in life, he knew what he was talking about.

Another says: "Dante had the art to make men tremble six centuries after recital of his words!" Ruskin said: "The more I think of it, I find this conclusion impressed upon me . . . the greatest thing a human soul ever does is to 'see something,' and to tell what he sees in a plain way. Hundreds of people can talk to one who can think; but thousands can think for one who can 'see.' To see clearly is poetry, prophecy, and religion -- all in one." The Apostle Paul could "see," and what great things he accomplished: *"Whereupon, O King Agrippa, I was not disobedient to the 'heavenly vision.'"* Acts 26:19. God opened the eyes of others and enabled them to "see" and tell in a plain way what they "saw." Luther, Calvin, Knox, Bunyan, Wesley, and many other mighty men of God, and what great things they have done in blessing mankind in time and eternity!

From our meager knowledge there are three things that stand out in the life of this great man: His fear of The Lord; his faith in "every word that proceedeth out of the mouth of God;" and his love of righteousness -- *"Ye that love The Lord, hate evil."* He could "see," and he told in a plain way the things he "saw." Over the portal of hell was this alarming inscription: "Through me is the way to the city of woe!" Through me is the way to eternal sorrow! Through me is the way to lost people! Justice moved my High Creator! The Divine Power, Supreme Wisdom, and Primal Love, made me! "Before me were no created things, but eternal, and I eternally endure! Give up all hope you who enter!"

In some eight or nine separate "pits," "Circles," or "enclosures," Dante sees and tells of the punishment of souls, according to their particular kinds of sin, evil and rebellion against God. He pictures the above and punishment of the "lukewarm" -- remember Christ said to the lukewarm: *"I will spue you out of My mouth, unless you repent"* -- who were mingled now with a band of lukewarm angels who, when Lucifer rebelled, were neither rebels nor faithful to God. Heaven drove them out! Here, also, were men who did not act a manly part in life, who did not know how to make up their mind and take a decisive step, but preferred to await events and reserve to themselves freedom to join the successful side. Justice and mercy hold them in equal contempt! Shall you, shall I, be there? In other "pits" are pictured the condition and punishment of Gluttons, Misers, Prodigals, those inflated by Pride of Wealth; the spirits of the Wrathful, Sullen, Slothful; and in another enclosure the Heretics with the followers of all kinds of Sects -- So great was Dante's hatred of heresy he describes the stench at this point of his journey as something awful -- He saw where and how were punished those guilty of Violence, Fraud, Grafting, Stealing, Murder, Flattery, and Simony -- simony means trying to buy the gifts of God with money or rewards; also he saw in hell the place reserved for the punishment of Diviners, Soothsayers, False Prophets, Witches, Sorcerers, and the like!

But let us note more in detail the place where he saw Cleopatra and Helen of Troy! In this pit were punished the Carnal, The Sensuous, The Incontinent, etc. (Carnal means "pertaining to the body, its passions and its appetites; Sensual: gratification of the senses; Incontinence: "lack of restraint, especially undue indulgence of sexual passions." Are not such as these especially applicable to our day and generation?) Dante sees these souls standing on the precipitous edge of a cliff down which they are hurled. As he approached the cries of despair were already audible, as they shriek, and wail, and blaspheme The Divine Power. In their new abode they are caught up in a whirlwind, or tornado, that blows and bears them up increasingly, whirling and buffeting them, so as to cause endless sufferings. They not only have no hope of any rest, but not even the slightest alleviation of their pain. Like cranes that form themselves into a long line in the air and go chanting their lays, so these souls, borne along by the winds, come uttering lamentations. The whirlwind that blows them around is symbolic of the tumult of their passions!

Do you admire and envy Cleopatra, Helen of Troy, or present-day movie stars who, through carnality, sensuality and incontinence, cast aside the laws of God and a decent civilization regarding the marriage state, and the God ordained and declared proper relations of the man and the woman? "That which is highly esteemed among men is abomination in the sight of God!"

Does Carnality, Sensuality, and Incontinence dominate

91

and prevail over The Spiritual in your life? *"He that hath not the Spirit of Christ is none of His!"* If you "see" the imperative need of the Spiritual over the Carnal, then give attention to "Searching the Scriptures," The Prayer Closet, "Keeping the Sabbath Day Holy," and Your Church vows: *"Whatsoever your hand findeth to do, do it with your might, and as unto The Lord."*

"He that endureth to the end shall be saved," said Jesus Christ, in at least three different places!

July 6, 1963

†††

The object of this article is to give somewhat a review of the contents of several of our recent columns, together with the suggestions of a personal applicaton of these Biblical Truths. Then, a prediction of some of the results to be expected by those who do make faithful application.

Three Bible Stories were presented. Recognition was duly given to those to whom "Bible Stories" are considered as Fables, Jewish History and Traditions. Our witness and testimony is that all such are people in whose hearts The Holy Spirit of God has not done His work with "The Sword of The Spirit, which is The Word of God." Certainly, you are at liberty to take that position, but if you know the meaning of the word "integrity" and a partaker of its Virtue, you surely have no right to be in a Church and partake of its Holy Sacraments if you fail to believe and accept The Scriptures of The Old and New Testaments as The Infallible Word of God, the only rule to direct man how to obey and glorify God. If you are such a one, this scribe would like to tell you that if he had the authority and was in a position to do so, you would be put out of the Church and refused as a partaker of The Lord's Supper; not for the purpose of offending you but for

92

fear of offending God Almighty and the fear of "your blood being on my hands!"

With God's permission, the Devil swept away Job's earthly substance, and his family with the exception of his wife. Then, in a second blow, the devil swept away Job's health and left him sitting in an ash heap covered with boils from the top of his head to the bottom of his feet! Mrs. Job said: "Do you still retain your "integrity? Curse God and die!" (Mrs. Job knew her husband had integrity! Does your wife know you have integrity and zealously hold on to it? Does the world of your acquaintances know you have integrity? Recall the time you stood up in the House of God, and in the presence of His people and took vows to serve and obey God, and then check your integrity in the light of your performance of faithfulness to such vows.)

But to those *"whose hearts God has touched"* -- see 1st Samuel 10:26 -- "Bible Stories" are Revelations of God Almighty Himself and His Truths. Have you ever asked Him to touch your heart? Do you give Him the opportunity to "Touch your heart" by waiting on him in prayer and meditation upon His Word? Over and over again *"the man after God's heart,"* King David says to us: *"Wait on The Lord, and again, I say, wait on the Lord."*

The first Bible Story pointed out was concerning Jacob's experiences in the 32nd chapter of Genesis, verse 9 and verses 24-29. In the second Bible Story attention was called to Moses' experience in the war with Amalek. Exodus 17: 8-13. The third Bible Story was in 2nd Kings 2: 9-11 and told how Elisha refused to leave Elijah and was rewarded with the vision of horses and chariot of fire taking Elijah to Heaven in a whirlwind and receiving a double portion of Elijah's Spirit! In each instance, the great blessing came after great physical "endurance to the end." At least three times in the Gospels we find these words of The Lord Jesus

Christ: *"He that endureth to the end shall be saved!"* And in Revelation 2:10 the risen and glorified Christ, Whom when the Apostle John saw he fell at his feet as one dead, said: *"Be thou faithful unto death, and I will give thee a crown of life!"* The personal application the individual Christian should make in fulfilling his vows to God is to exercise yourself in "Searching The Scriptures" to get familiar with "every word that proceedeth out of the mouth of God;" and *"Men ought always to pray and not faint"* -- Luke 18:1 -- and refuse to turn back or stop going on, even as Elisha.

As to a prediction of the results to be expected; would call your attention to these words of Christ in Luke 8:11, etc.: *"Now the parable is this: The seed is the Word of God. Those by the wayside are they that hear, 'Then comes the devil,' and taketh away the Word out of their hearts, lest they should believe and be saved."* "Then comes the devil!" He comes when the Seed is sown. After God sowed the Seed in the 2nd chapter of Genesis, then came the devil in the third chapter and we have the record of the fall and the curse. So, if you set yourself to "get familiar with every Word that proceedeth out of the mouth of God" expect to meet the devil in time. If you do not know that there is a devil, you will surely find it out. It is better to find out now, while you can get deliverance from The Saviour, Jesus Christ, than wait until too late: *"The harvest is past, the summer is ended, and we are not saved"* -- Jeremiah 8:20. Hold on and wrestle like Jacob did, and like Moses, keep your hands up until sundown, and like Elisha, don't stop or turn back, but be there when the horses and chariots of fire appear for our "translation!"

March 8, 1969

†††

General Themes

In Ezekiel 44:24 God says: *"And in controversy they shall stand in my judgments; and they shall judge it according to my judgments; and they shall keep my laws and my statutes in all mine assemblies; and they shall hallow my sabbaths."* Those interested are invited to consider some of God's judgments regarding worship, as there is considerable controversy in this matter these days:

There was a man named Cain. He came to worship God and brought an offering. God did not want what he brought and would not accept it. Cain god mad. Cain killed his brother Abel. The final outcome of Cain's worship was a curse and not a blessing. -- Genesis 4: 3-12.

Nadab and Abihu were invited to make a command appearance before The King of Kings, Lord of Lords, even Almighty God. So with Aaron their father and Moses and seventy of the Elders of Israel they climbed Mount Sinai, and there *"They saw God, and did eat and drink."* After this marvelous and supernatural experience they went into the Tabernacle one day to worship. They made an offering that was unacceptable to God -- an offering of "Strange Fire!" The fire of God leaped on them and burnt both to death. The outcome of their worship on that occasion was a curse, death, and not a blessing. Read about it in Exodus 24: verses 1, 9, 11; and in Leviticus 10: 1-3.

King David, the man after God's heart, in moving the Ark of God had a new cart made and hitched oxen to it. God had commanded that it should be moved only on the shoulders of the priests and Levites. The oxen stumbled! An attendant named Uzza caught hold of it. God struck him dead! 1st Chronicles, 13th chapter. No doubt the intentions of both David and Uzza were good, but profaning of that which was sacred brought a curse instead of a blessing!

King Uzziah was one of Judah's greatest kings. He reigned fifty-two years. He sought to obey and please God and was greatly blessed, together with his people and nation. There was great prosperity, much business and great advancement made in agriculture, and especially military science, inventions and fortifications. He had a great and powerful army that put down all their enemies. His name spread far abroad over the then known world. He was respected and feared. He went into the Temple one day to worship. He forgot his place and undertook to worship in his own way, though warned and withstood by the priests. God struck him there in the Temple in his act of worship. Struck him with leprosy! He was taken out and put in a pest house where his body rotted until life left it! 2nd Chronicles, chapter 26.

Moses met God at the "Burning Bush." God said, *"Put off thy shoes from thy feet, for the place where thou standest is holy."* -- Exodus 3: 1-6. God appeared to Joshua before the city of Jericho and Joshua said: *"What saith my Lord unto His servant?"* The reply was: *"Loose thy shoe from off thy foot; for the place where thou standest is holy."* Joshua 5: 13-15.

The only record we have of Christ striking anyone physically when on the earth in the flesh were those whom He lashed with a whip of cords and drove out of God's House for profaning and misusing the sacred place. John 2: 14-17.

Read Acts 5: 1-11 and learn of another judgment of God upon a man and his wife who tried to enter the Church with ulterior motives, rathern than *"repentance towards God, and faith towards The Lord Jesus Christ"* -- both of them struck dead for *"lying to The Holy Ghost . . . and tempting the Spirit of The Lord."* Peter said it was because Satan had filled their hearts to lie to God!

Jesus Christ was the only one ever born into this world

who could pick His place of birth. He chose an animal stable, the manger, doubtless because the world hated him (John 7:7) and He knew *"there was no room for Him"* and He was not wanted. After speaking in the synagogue of the town where He spent most of His life as a carpenter, they took Him out to throw off a cliff, and later He said: *"Foxes have holes, and the birds of the air nests, but The Son of Man hath not where to lay His head."* In Mark 5:17 we read: *"And they began to pray Him to depart out of their coasts,"* and He got back into the ship and left. He left when asked to! In Luke 14:10 He gives these instructions: *"When thou art bidden, go and sit down in the lowest room."* It appears that Jesus Christ left and stayed away from places where He was not wanted. Romans 8:9 says: *"Now if any man have not the Spirit of Christ, he is none of His."*

John 4:21-24: *"Jesus saith unto her, Woman, believe me, the hour cometh, when ye shall neither in this mountain, nor yet at Jerusalem, worship The Father. Ye worship ye know not what -- but the hour cometh, and now is, when the true worshippers shall worship The Father in spirit and truth; for The Father seeketh such to worship Him. God is a Spirit; and they that worship Him must worship Him in spirit and in truth."*

"Keep thy foot when thou goest to The House of God, lest you offer the sacrifice of fools." Ecclesiastes 5:1.

Beware of going to worship with ulterior motives, any other than repentance towards God, and faith towards The Lord Jesus Christ! Beware of "making an offering of strange fires." Remember Nadab and Abihu!

May 4, 1963

†††

97

Recently there were reports in the papers of the law authorities having trouble somewhere here in Georgia with folks promoting rooster, or cock-fights. This brought to mind a story: Some man had a rooster tooted to be the champion, and willing to meet any and all comers. A great fight was promoted. The arena around the cock-pit overflowed with customers, most of whom bet their money on the highly advertised "champion." At the proper time "champ" was thrown into the cock-pit. He looked his opponent over, and refused to fight. On the contrary, the confound thing went over into a corner, sat down, and "laid an egg!"

The chain reaction following this story made me think of many things, far apart, and very different. Thought of a picture in the newspapers a few days ago, and of a news item I read a few minutes ago, then The President, of Isaiah the Prophet, of Napoleon, of John Wesley, of Hannibal, and one thing Hannibal did made me think of words of Christ, and these words of Christ made me think of Moses, St. Paul, Martin Luther -- but I must stop somewhere. You can judge whether my effort to connect all these together make any sense, or might be profitable.

The picture I saw in the newspapers were some "young roosters" sitting down in the streets around the White House "laying eggs." Eggs of cowardice, saying, "Don't fight, quit!" They were attempting to block the path of The Commander-in-chief of the armies, navies, air force, and other military forces of the nation designed and provided to the protection of our land, lives and liberties! Mr. President in taking charge swore to use them for these purposes. Young roosters, sitting down in the streets laying eggs, snake eggs, viper eggs, scorpion eggs!

Isaiah, the great Prophet, must have looked down the

corridor of time thousands of years and foreseen our day when he wrote: *"They trust in vanity, and speak lies; they conceive mischief and bring forth iniquity. They hatch cocatrice eggs, and weave the spider's web; He that eateth of their eggs dieth. And that which is crushed breaketh out into a viper."* Isaiah 59:4.

Recent riots and mobocracy here, there, yonder, and all around -- mostly the work of "young roosters" who have been stirred up by "old devils" -- caused me to think of Napoleon. He appeared on the scene shortly after the French Revolution during the reign of King Mob and King Anarchy. (King Mob suggests to us some very appropriate thoughts for our day.) If we mistake not, Napoleon first attracted attention in the world by cleaning the streets of King Mob and King Anarchy. He ordered them to disperse. If they obeyed, things went well. If they disobeyed authority he did not have four of his soldiers carry them to prison screaming and kicking with a soldier holding each one's hand and one foot. Rather, he ordered his soldiers to "sweep the streets" with rifle and gunfire, leaving the carcasses to be carried out to the "bone orchard" where they could do as they pleased. In our opinion God raised up Napoleon to scourge and discipline large parts of the world. When he undertook to discipline England, well, God had already raised up and used John Wesley to do that job, so Napoleon met his "Waterloo."

"The lapse of church discipline was a certain sympton of social and political anarchy!" God used Hannibal to scourge the Roman Empire. Said a historian: "To however narrow a compass one may restrict one's selection of the greatest military commanders of all time it is difficult to exclude Hannibal on any casting vote. As a strategist, as a tactician, as a manipulator of men, one is loath to assign any a higher rank. Spurred on by his boyhood vow of undying hostility to Rome, he led an army from Spain, and in spite of all that nature and human foes could do to obstruct his passage, he brought it through terribly thinned, across the Alps into Italy. There, in the heart of the enemy's country, and that enemy the most martial people of history, he maintained his army for years and inflicted on the world conquering Romans defeats so terrible that the names of Cannae and Lake Thrasymene have become synonyms for crushing disaster. A thankless country abandoned him, and finally drove him to exile and suicide to escape the vengeance of the people he so sorely scourged.''

God bestows on some men such great talents and gifts that they stand out like super-men. Consider the feat of Hannibal in bringing an army across the Alps in spite of heights and depths of obstacles, ice, snow, bitter cold, storms, avalanches; plus the resistance of the mountaineers who from high places rolled down great stones and boulders on his soldiers, elephants, horses, and other animals and equipment. Think of his ability to keep most of his men faithful and willing to keep going in spite of the fact that great numbers were perishing nearly every day -- at one time we are told that about ten thousand refused to go on. Instead of trying to persuade or force them to go on, Hannibal gave them permission to return home, saying his army would be stronger when they got rid of those who were afraid and too weak-kneed to go on. This makes one think of what Christ told a man: *"He that puts his hand to the plow and looks back, is not fit for the Kingdom of God."* Luke 9:61-62. Think of Hannibal's will-power and determination that banished discouragement and retreat. Is it not an inspiration to think of this pagan and his accomplishments in view of what John Baptist said in John 3:27: *"A man can receive nothing, except it be given him from above."* When Hannibal was a child, nine years old, he begged his father, General of the Army, to let him go to war with him. The father had to refuse on account of the age of his son, but he did take him to the religious festivities and sacrifices seeking the blessings of their pagan gods on the expedition. There he was permitted and encouraged to take part in the defense of his country by vowing "undying hostility to Rome."

In Psalm 138:2 we are told: *"God magnifies His Word above all His Name."* Surely, the implication is plain and forceful that God blesses in a special way the man who *"magnifies his own word, his own promises, the vows he makes."* Is there anything greater that any man ever does than to make a promise to God Almighty? Is there anything worse that any man ever does than to neglect, break, and reject his vows to God? It could be that the gifts and talents bestowed on Hannibal by God which made him one of the most remarkable men that ever lived, were rewards for faithfulness to the vows he made at nine years of age!

Consider the vows you made to God in joining His Church! Consider the vows that millions of our young people have made to God in joining His Church! "There is a cause" for the condition our nation is in, young and old, clergy, statesmen, educators, etc. "The curse causeless shall not come."

Moses was faithful to his vows: He refused to be called the son of Pharoah's daughter, choosing to suffer affliction with the people of God. He endured, as seeing Him who is invisible. Great gifts, talents, and power he received from Heaven, and what a blessing to mankind!

The Apostle Paul said: *"I was not disobedient unto the Heavenly Vision,"* and how he has blessed the world through the ages! And time would fail to tell of Martin Luther who defied all the powers of the world and devils, ecclesiastical and temporal, in order that he might be faithful to his vow to God.

Surely, you and I would be better off, our community, our

101

country, and our world, if we set in order and keep our promises to God in good order.

April 24, 1965

✝✝✝

"For the wages of sin is death, but the gift of God is eternal life through Jesus Christ our Lord." Romans 6:23.

"And much study is a weariness of the flesh. Let us hear the conclusion of the whole matter: Fear God, and keep His commandments: for this is the whole duty of man. For God shall bring every work into judgment, with every secret thing, whether it be good, or whether it be evil!" Eccles. 12: 12-14.

Whoever shall undertake to write a history of the families that fear not God nor regard the duties they owe to man, but live and riot on the miseries of their kind, will portray to the world an awfully instructive chapter of the retributive justice of God -- many a family that started out in life and formed a family connection under the most auspicious circumstances. They were industrious, enterprising, frugal and seem to have started fair for domestic peace and a happy competence. Yet in an evil hour they yielded to the delusive bait of temptation -- they were in haste to be rich. They turned aside from the paths of honest industry and domestic tranquility and plunged into a dissipating and iniquitious business, which, while it seems to promise wealth and future independence, it was but the sure presuror, to ruin and disgrace; or the same ruinous result was arrived at no less effectively by the violation of The Holy Day! How awfully in the history of families is the truth sometimes illustrated that God will *"Pour out His fury upon the families that call not on His Name." "They that despise me shall be lightly esteemed."* Examples crowd upon us from every quarter;

102

Every neighborhood furnishes them!

In Numbers 32:23 God says: *"Be sure your sins will find you out!"* In Deuteronomy 32:29 God says: *"O that they would consider their latter end!"* "Sin is any want of conformity unto, or transgression of The Law of God." We now quote God's Second Commandment as found in Exodus 20: 4-6:

"Thou shalt not make unto thee any graven image, or any likeness of anything that is in the heaven above, or that is in the earth beneath, or that is in the water under the earth; thou shalt not bow down thyself to them, nor serve them; for I the Lord thy God am a jealous God, visiting the iniquity of the fathers upon the children unto the third and fourth generation of them that hate Me; and showing mercy unto thousands of them that love me, and keep my commandments."

Yes, The God of The Old Testament is a jealous God. Says so Himself in this Commandment! Also in Exodus 34:14: *"For thou shalt worship no other God; for the Lord whose Name is jealous is a jealous God."* And again in Deuteronomy 4:24: *"For the Lord thy God is a consuming fire, even a jealous God!"*

Yes, the God of the New Testament is a jealous God. Jesus Christ said: *"I and My Father are One."* And *"Before Abraham was, I am!"* Even the same as God revealed Himself to Moses at The Burning Bush. In Malachi 3:6 God says: *"I change not!"* Don't stay in His Church and try to change Him. It were better that a mill stone were hung about your neck and you were drowned in the sea! Do not expect the parties to agree who strive to preserve the lives of murderers, rapists, traitors, etc., etc. *"Be sure your sin will find you out . . . . . . O, That they would consider their latter end!"*

Often indeed is the peace and comfort of families

103

blighted, children prove profligate and prodigal, and a series of untoward circumstances blast their prosperity; when if you were permitted to read their history, you would find that sin lay at the door -- some conjugal unfaithfulness -- some previous marriage contract unfilled -- some plighted faith violated -- some youthful trifling with affections -- some grievous indiscretion and guilt to be atoned for. The histories of families not unfrequently furnish the most melancholy illustrations that family sins are visited by family afflictions, defections in parental restraint, by the insubordination and licentiousness of children, and extravagance, intemperance, or skepticism of parents; by immorality and profligacy in children.

Surely by this time those who read this Column have learned the "heathen" are those who set themselves against the Commandments of God Almighty and His Anointed, The Lord Jesus Christ; and that all the heathen are not in the far away places and jungles. Several times friends with the desire to be helpful have suggested a change in the name of this Column. Wonder if unconsciously they too resent the negative of God's *"Thou Shalt Not!"* What use have you for a servant that won't carry out orders? *"Why call ye me Lord, Lord, and do not the things which I say?"* Luke 6:46. True Faith follows after Perfect Obedience.

January 27, 1973

†††

"And though shalt remember all the way the Lord thy God hath led thee these forty years" -- Deuteronomy 8:2. For your consideration: The same Lord God has led our nation these 150 odd years, 1777-1930. Generally speaking, it was in the 1930s our nation and her Government began to turn away from honoring and following after the God of our

fathers, The God of the Bible, His Ways, His Laws, and His Commandments. However, we kept on writing on our money "In God we Trust," and still do, in spite of the fact that we have "cast away the Law of the Lord of Hosts" in many respects: concerning idolatry, profaneness, Sabbath desecration, dishonoring of father and mother, murder, adultery, stealing, false witnessing, and coveteousness -- *"coveteousness is idolatry."*

Christ said of Himself: *"The Son of Man is Lord of the Sabbath Day."* Have we not taken away His Lordship of the sacred Day and turned it over to the Kings of Sport, the world, the flesh, and the devil? Also, do we not almost boast that we have nearly done away with the Death Penalty commanded by The Almighty, and are saving the lives of murderers, rapists, whoremongers, homosexuals, and others whom God commanded His people to put to death and send their spirits back to Him who gave them? We will not take time to speak of our heavy and growing crop of crime, thieves, liars, coveteous, etc.

"Be not deceived; God is not mocked; For whatsoever a man soweth, that shall he also reap. For he that soweth to his flesh reap corruption; but he that soweth to the 'spirit' shall of the 'spirit' reap life everlasting. "Galatians 6: 7-8. Since this Column began, over 600 times it has presented God's question to man in the Second Psalm: "Why Do The Heathen Rage?" together with His statement as to who are the heathen: "People who imagine a vain thing, their kings and rulers," and that their rage is against God Himself, and His Anointed, and for the purpose of getting rid of His Laws and Commandments: *"Let us break their bands asunder, and cast away their cords from us."* In this Psalm God also reveals to us the fruit and harvest of this anarchy will bring the *"Contempt of the Almighty,"* *"He that sitteth in the Heavens shall laugh: The Lord shall have them in derision. Then shall He speak unto them in His wrath, and*

vex them in His sore displeasure.''

During the past thirty years or more have we not been very successful and made a good job of ''breaking God's and Christ's bands asunder and casting away their cords from us?'' Is not the rise of crime, rape, riots, pillage and burning of our cities good evidence that God meant what He said about ''holding in derision and vexing with all adversity'' those who reject His Laws and Commandments?

''And God is angry with the wicked every day -- The wicked shall be turned into hell, and all the 'Nations' that forget God!'' Psalm 7:11 and Psalm 9:17.

''I have not sent these prophets, yet they ran; I have not spoken to them, yet they prophesied. But if they had stood in My counsel, and had caused My people to hear My words, then they should have turned them from their evil way, and from the evil of their doings.'' -- Jeremiah 23: 21-22.

''Of making many books there is no end -- Let us hear the conclusion of the whole matter [of life and death]; Fear God and keep His Commandments: for this is the whole duty of man. For God shall bring every work into judgment, With every secret thing, whether it be good, or whether it be evil.'' Ecclesiastes 12: 12-14.

''Now therefore, fear The Lord, and serve Him in sincerity and truth -- and if it seem evil unto you to serve The Lord, choose ye this day whom ye will serve -- but as for me and my house, we will serve The Lord.'' Joshua 24: 14-15.

August 25, 1963

†††

''So Absolom stole the hearts of the men of Israel!'' 2nd Sam. 15:6.

''But in all Israel there was none to be so much praised as

106

Absolom for his beauty; from the sole of his foot even to the crown of his head, there was no blemish in him. " 2nd Sam. 14:25. But the hearts of the men of Israel belonged to their great King David, the man Sacred Scripture calls "A man after God's heart."

According to our appraisal King David is certainly not a man "after the heart" of most professing Christians. Once upon a time I overheard two friends, both probably considered by others and themselves as "sound in the faith," talking about David. One remarked David did some things that seemed mighty strange to him. On first thought I rather agreed, but on second thought I decided I better keep my thoughts and mouth shut regarding David. Will mention one or two of these second thoughts: When God Almighty turns the light of His Holiness on all my life as His Word does on David's life, on my deeds, actions, thoughts, ambitions, jealousies, coveteousnesses, etc. -- and that time is coming, and might be nearby -- expect David might look at my record and say it seemed to him that I did some "strange things," especially concerning my lack of repentance, restitution, and fruit worthy of repentance!

David would doubtless consider our doings "strange" concerning our lack of courage to fight present day "lions, bears, Goliaths and other Uncircumcised Philistines of apostasy, crime, rape, adultery, sex abnormalities, etc.!" Did you know that? The Bible says that in only "one" thing David turned aside from that which God commanded him? -- 1st Kings 15:5. Probably most of the things David did that seem so strange to us today if we knew and believed God's Word and Judgements, we would understand that he was obeying and carrying out God's orders, which we rage at and reject today!

The hearts of the men of Israel belonged to King David. God raised him up to deliver them from all their enemies.

His great military victories brought them liberty, peace, and prosperity, and made him the idol of the nation. However, they got deceived, believed a lie, with the result of the damnation of civil war and great slaughter among the people.

We call attention to 2nd Thessalonians 2:11-12, where we are told God sent a delusion to folks who loved unrighteousness that they might believe a lie and be damned. *"And for this cause God shall send them strong delusion, that they should believe a lie; That they all might be damned who believed not the truth but had pleasure in unrighteousness."*

Absalom was the third son of The Great King David. He was the best looking man in the whole nation, maybe of men and women.

The Great King's Son, "idol of the eyes," stole the hearts of the men of Israel, deceived them, caused them to believe a lie, and to be damned with civil war! How did he manage to accomplish this stupendous task, and turn the nation against their deliverer and national hero? The 15th chapter of 2nd Samuel tells the story:

The hero's son, winner of all the beauty prizes, idol of the eyes -- especially that "head of hair," got himself horses and chariots, and fifty men to run before him -- imagine that sight and its effect on the "beatles and teenagers!" And he got up early in the morning to "strut his stuff!" He did not "waste his gas" riding about in folly and foolishness. No, indeed. With these fifty men running ahead of his chariot, he charged down to the city gate to make war on "poverty, injustice, and uphold civil rights!" My! How he did love the people, justice, and "what have you!"

When folks came to the Capital City to see The King, he introduced himself -- without needing any, being a Royal Prince, and inquired about their controversy: *"See thy matters are good and right; but there is no man deputed by The King to hear thee. Absalom said moreover, Oh that I were judge in the land, and every man which hath any suit or cause might come unto me, and I would do him justice! And so it was, that when any man came nigh to do him obeisance, he put forth his hand, and took him, and kissed him"* -- imagine getting a kiss from a Royal Prince, and the best looking person in the land, to boot! *"And on this manner did Absalom to all Israel"* -- Jew, Gentile, barbarian, rich and poor. He kept this up for years, stole the hearts of the men of Israel from The Man After God's Heart, and the nation was damned with civil war!

The New Deal, The Fair Deal, The New Frontier, The Great Society, are not new wrinkles! Absalom started a Great Society about 3,000 years ago. So will all Societies end that steal men's hearts from The King of Kings, The Lord Jesus Christ, God's Word and Precepts!

Even Judas Iscariot showed concern about the poor -- the waste of money on ointment for Christ that might have been given to the poor! What effect does our concern for the poor have on our "own" pocketbook and bank account? God is not deceived!

August 31, 1974

†††

One day many years ago a man was riding his mule down the road on a trip to visit a King. This was one of the modes of travel in those days for even great men, and this traveler was indeed a great man, internationally known and famous as a wise man and prophet. Recently the peoples of the world watched and followed with great interest the journeys of the astronaut around the earth in outer space, earth watching a man's journey in the heavens. Those who read

109

this are invited to watch a short trip of a man going along one of earth's roads. "He that sitteth in the heavens" was watching this trip, and was so interested and concerned that He sent down an Angel to be a "roadblock" -- and there is good Scriptural ground for thinking this Angel might have been none other than Christ Himself. See 1st Cor. 10:4 -- Am of the opinion that it will do our world much greater good and benefit to watch this man and his mule on their trip, and so let us go along with them in our mind's eyes.

Man and beast appear to be contented and happy and each occupied with their own thoughts. The great man was probably thinking with much pleasure and anticipation of the great honors, riches and rewards promised him by the King who had invited him to come and do a job, a job that would not tax his physical energies too much, for all that would be required of him would be that he should do some "cussing" -- curse Moses and his people whom God had delivered from the bondage of Egypt and Pharoah, probably the most powerful king of that day and generation.

Have heard a story about the devil going fishing -- imagine it was on The Sabbath, or The Lord's Day -- he baited his hook with a bottle of liquor and soon caught a drunkard; next with a deck of cards, or dice, and shortly had a batch of gamblers; he caught the biggest fish of all when the bait was money, silver, or gold: the covetous, avaricious, the greedy of gain, etc. -- did you know that the Bible says "the greedy of gain" trouble their own house? Often those who are "greedy of gain" excuse or justify themselves on the ground they are seeking to benefit and better provide for their house, home, wife, children, and their future welfare, but God says you are making trouble for your own house. The devil's fishing was just fine until he ran out of bait. He decided to try his luck with no bait on the hook, quickly got a strike, and pulled up a fellow "cussing!" God's Third Commandment says: *"Thou shalt not take the*

Name of The Lord thy God in vain, for the Lord will not hold him guiltless that taketh His Name in vain."

Why do the heathen rage? *"A heathen is one who does not believe in The Lord of The Bible,"* and he rages against The Bands and The Cords of restraint of God's Moral Law and Ten Commandments! Do you ever hear any rage these days against God's Third Commandment? Are you guilty? The devil gets you without bait!

As to the mule, probably his thoughts and anticipation also were very pleasant as she looked forward to visiting royal stables, keeping company with ass royalty and nobility, and with them eating the King's fodder and other fancy feed. Suddenly, however, these happy and contented travelers became upset and greatly disturbed: For no apparent reason the mule became frightened and turned out of the road into the fields. For a long time the master had owned this mule and ridden her on many trips, but she had never acted like this before. He whipped her, and as he was an expert at "cussing" probably used some harsh and bitter words that made the mule's long ears burn to their nethermost tips! He got her back in the road and things went along o.k. for a time, until they came to a place where the road was narrow and a wall or fence on each side. Here the mule became frightened again, and in trying to get out of the road, mashed the rider's foot or leg against the fence! She had to take another beating with the whip, and another lashing from her master's tongue.

They resumed their trip again, but doubtless both man and beast were troubled and their happiness and contentment had departed. They came to a place of one way traffic where the road was so narrow there was no room to turn to the right or left. Here the mule laid down with the rider on her! A third awful flogging with the whip followed, together with more sharp, cutting and choice "cussing," which continued until the ass began to talk with man's voice!

111

If I had been the rider I think I would have gone away from that place, changed my mind about which way to go, and even though I had plenty of time on my hands, would have gone away in a hurry, that is, if I could have without being cut down by the unseen visitor! -- Suddenly the rider quit his beating and cussing the ass and joined him on the ground, falling flat on his face, for he saw what was causing the ass to balk; there standing blocking the road was The Angel of God with His sword drawn. *"The Lord opened the eyes of Balaam, and he saw the Angel of The Lord standing in the way, and His sword drawn in His hand; and he bowed his head and fell flat on his face. And The Angel of The Lord said unto him, Wherefore hast thou smitten thine ass three times? Behold, I went out to withstand thee, because thy way is perverse before Me; and the ass saw Me, and turned from Me these three times; unless she had turned from Me, surely also I had slain thee, and saved her alive."* Numbers 22: 31-33.

The Book of Numbers, chapter 22 through 24 give the record concerning Balaam. It was Mark Twain, I think, who said it was not the things in The Bible that he did not understand that troubled him, but it was those he did understand. The New Testament tells us in 2nd Peter 2:15-16 that Balaam *"loved the wages of unrighteousness; but was rebuked for his iniquity; the dumb ass speaking with man's voice forbade the madness of the prophet."* And in the Book of Jude, verse 11: *"Woe unto them! for they have gone in the way of Cain, and ran greedily after the error of Balaam for reward."* Is it not very clear and easy to understand from this passage of God's Word, His Revelation of Himself to man, God's attitude and action against avarice, the covetous and greedy of gain?

The Tenth Commandment: *"Thou shalt not covet thy neighbor's house, thou shalt not covet thy neighbor's wife, nor his man servant, nor his maid servant, nor his ox, nor his ass, nor anything that is thy neighbor's.* "Obedience to this commandment would bring blessing and peace to our land in quick order. A genuine Christian is one who has had this Commandment written in his heart by The Spirit of God! Genuine Christianity will do away with stealing, cheating, swindling, graft, race troubles, strikes, and various and sundry assortments of evil and devilment, for at the bottom of them all is "coveting" that which God in His Providence has given to someone else. "Is your life a channel of blessing," or it a curse on account of being "greedy of gain" and thereby troubling your own house, your own community, your state, your country, your world? Here we have the account of Heaven watching the journey of a man on earth, and opening the mouth of a dumb ass to resist and rebuke him! Remember the words of The Angel: *"I went out to withstand you, because thy way is perverse before Me; And the ass saw Me, and turned Me these three times; less she had turned from Me, surely also now I had slain thee, and saved her alive." "Beware of covetousness,"* warned Christ in Luke 12:15, etc.

How will it be with you, with me, when our eyes are opened and we see an Angel of God? Surely that experience is just ahead for us all when we have to move out of this "house of clay," this body! *"The Angel of The Lord encampeth around about them that fear Him, and delivereth them."* Psalm 34:7. Contrast this verse, however, with that of Psalm 78:49: *"He cast upon them the fierceness of His anger, wrath and indignation, and trouble, by sending evil angels among them."* It appears that the way our day and generation rage against The Laws of God that we have qualified ourselves for "evil angels!"

June 15, 1963

†††

Are you concerned and troubled about the great increase in lawlessness? Violent hold-ups, stealing, cheating, swindling, murder, rape, adultery, and other kinds of violence and anarchy! At times these things strike mighty close to our homes, loved ones, and friends. And they will get closer unless some change is made.

In the days of Noah God destroyed the earth and everything wherein was the breath of life excepting the eight members of Noah's family, and the animals he kept alive in the Ark according to God's orders. The cause of this judgment was for causes similar to the ones that exist today: "Man corrupted God's way on the earth, and the earth was filled with violence." With good reasoning and logic, it has been estimated there might have been four hundred and eighty billion people that perished -- over a hundred times as many as now living on the earth! (We digress again to suggest in this column man had better leave the matter of "birth control" in the hands of The Almighty, where it belongs, lest He say of us what He did of one man: *"It had been good for that man if he had not been born!"* Matthew 26:24. We remind you that God says in His Word "If we fear God, and keep His Commandments, the whole duty of man," God has engaged Himself to bless the "fruit of the womb" and take away sickness; also, to bless the fruit of the ground in order there might be plenty to eat. Hear the words of the Man after God's Heart: *"I have been young, and now am old; yet have I not seen the righteous forsaken, nor his seed begging bread."* Psalm 37:25. Of course, however, unbelief and disobedience makes null and void these precious promises. It appears there is very little confidence in them today, with most of us!)

"My Spirit shall not always strive with man --" The Almighty announced in the days of Noah, and sent the flood. Gen. 6:3. It may be the time has about arrived when His Spirit will quit striving with you and me. Until that time comes we would do well to remember that Christ told us to do some striving: *"Strive to enter in at the strait gate: for many, I say unto you, will seek to enter in, and shall not be able!"* Luke 13:24. We can strive to be "faithful unto death"

114

to the vows made to God in joining His Church -- *"When thou vowest a vow unto God, defer not to pay it; for He hath no pleasure in fools; pay that which thou hast vowed."* Eccles. 5:4. We should strive to be faithful in our testimony that The Bible is the Word of God, and be careful not to get in the "road way" of unbelief of those who both in and out of the Church attack the Bible. We should strive to be faithful in our testimony that the Ten Commandments reveal the morality, righteousness, and very character of God; and strive to be workers together with His Holy Spirit in writing these Commandments in our hearts to the end we may accomplish the whole duty of man, which is *"To fear God, and keep His Commandments."*

We call attention to another judgment and visitation of God upon corruption and violence. This was by means of a vision, probably foretelling things shortly to come about in the city of Jerusalem. In the 9th chapter of Ezekiel, we read: *"And the Lord said unto him, go through the midst of the city, through the midst of Jerusalem, and set a mark upon the foreheads of the men that sigh and cry for all the abominations that be done in the midst thereof. And to the others [those with destroying weapons] He said in mine hearing, Go ye after him through the city, and smite: Let not your eye spare, neither have ye pity; slay utterly old and young, both maids and little children, and women; but come not near any upon whom is the mark; and begin at my sanctuary. Then they began at the ancient men which were before the house."* Pay day, some day is coming.

Concerning God's judgements and slaughter of the wicked, the writer has had Divines, or Dry Vines, say to him: "God is not like that!" Permit this comment on that: Consider the slaughter, death, and suffering going on all the time in all the world; surely as the Scripture says: "The whole creation groaneth and travaileth in pain and death even until now." Think of the death, suffering, and sorrow in our own city, in our own generation, and the wars of former generations, history, and antiquity. If your god doesn't control all these things, then surely your god must have lost control. Surely you need to seek and find the God who has not lost control, even the true Christian's God -- not one sparrow falls to the ground without His permission. He explains why all this death, slaughter, suffering: The cause is sin: Disobedience to His Laws and Commandments: *"For the wages of sin is death!"* But, But, *"But the gift of God is eternal life through our Lord Jesus Christ -- for God so loved the world, that He gave His only begotten Son, that whosoever believeth in Him should not perish, but have everlasting life."* John 3:16.

In closing, we quote two passages of Scripture in which God tells us how we can get rid of evil:

First is from Isaiah 26:9-10: *"When God's judgements are in the earth, the inhabitants of the world will learn righteousness. Let favor be showed to the wicked, yet will he not learn righteousness:In the land of uprightness will He deal unjustly --"* This is meant especially for those who have God ordained authority to keep law and order, and put away evil. Of course, there is no hope here when such authorities are themselves in rebellion against the judgements of The Almighty!

The Second is from Jeremiah 23:21 where God says if the prophets, even though He did not call them to prophecy, would stand in His Counsel and cause His People to hear My Words: *"Then they should have turned them from their evil way, and from the evil of their doings."* The application here is especially for the clergy, preachers, teachers, parents, and all who claim to be Christian. Who is to blame when wickedness grows and abounds, becomes rampant and worldwide, and the stench of man's vileness mounts up to heaven!

March 13, 1965

†††

"For such a time as this!" To how many who claim to be Protestant Christians does this quote mean anything? Maybe we are unduly critical and pessimistic but doubt if one in ten know its Scriptural setting and context. Jews ought to know. Could hardly expect Catholics to know, since their spiritual food is not only rationed, but also predigested. If you want to eat that way, it is your privilege in this land of freedom, and in some other countries, but think it is "command food" in parts of the world today.

In the centuries past we are told that great numbers of martyrs perished for refusing to eat "command food!" *"Daniel purposed in his heart that he would not defile himself with the portion of the king's meat, and with the wine which he drank."* Daniel ate that which God told him to eat, and it surely "paid off." The great world dictator King fell on his face before Daniel and worshipped him, and at another time he made a decree that if any people, nation, language spoke anything amiss against The God of The Hebrew children they should be cut in pieces, and their houses made a dunghill.

Another King clothed Daniel in scarlet, put a chain of gold about his neck, and proclaimed him third ruler in the kingdom. The great King Darius made him President of the 120 Princes that were over the whole kingdom. Daniel spent the night in a lion's den in company with an angel of God who made the lions as harmless as kittens! During his life time great world rulers rose and fell, one went crazy and lived the life of a beast for a time -- we got a lot of folks like that all about now -- others were slain, but *"Daniel continued even until the first year of King Cyrus."* Daniel's influence and faith continue still to bless all generations of mankind who have learned of him and to trust his God.

It is not too big a job to get to know him today, just get familiar with the first six chapters of The Book of Daniel. Get the facts in your mind, so you can think on them after you close the book. For the present, maybe you better not spend too much time on the last six chapters or you might get in water over your head and drown! Read them, but be careful about interpreting until you grow a little more. Martin Luther speaking of Predestination, advised not to "fly too high" into the Celestial mysteries of God lest you fall and break your neck, for it is better to abide by the "swaddling clothes" of the manger until you grow a little more strong in faith and knowledge. The "diet of Daniel" together with his steadfastness of purpose was the secret of his great success, aside from the fact that "*The Lord had laid His hands on him*" and he was a chosen vessel.

Martin Luther chose the "diet of Daniel." He tells of how some years after he became a monk he found a Bible. He devoured it, reading it over and over again. His fellow monks told him he would be worth much more to their order if he would quit reading that Book so much, get a sack and go out in the city, and beg food and others gifts for the monastery. -- Thank God they were not able to pull him away from "The Book," for his life and testimony changed the course of history, and has done more to bring liberty to the individual and nations than probably any other one thing since the days of the Apostles!

Some historian has truly said that we are all a different people and living in a different world because of his teaching and testimony. The noted French historian, Michelet, though a Catholic, was a great admirer of Luther, and he acknowledges in the preface of his "Life of Luther" that he was indebted to him for the liberty he enjoyed of writing as he wanted to. 445 years ago next Wednesday, Oct. 31st, Luther nailed some papers to The Church door challenging the religious "status quo" of his day. He was judged a heretic by The Church and tried. The unusual punishment for the condemned unless they recanted was death by fire at the stake. At the Diet of Worms -- this does not mean the eating of worms, but here diet means a great deliberate Assembly, and Worms was the name of the city where it was held -- at this Diet, Luther was tried and condemned. "There were present at the Diet, besides the Emperor, six electors (governors), one archduke, two landgraves, five margraves, 27 dukes, and numbers of counts, archbishops, bishops, etc., in all 206 persons. (Surely the Supreme Court were all there, just called by some other name at that time. You boys who "tear your shirt" these days when one questions or resists its judgements should take note of this).

Expecting to have to go to the stake and burn alive, Luther stood his ground against the whole bunch -- he had some friends in the crowd. He said to The Emperor and the rest of the crowd: "It is not safe to go against The Word of God and conscience. Here I stand. I can do no other, God help me." God did help him, and delivered him, and they failed to get him to the fiery stake! He has spoken to all generations since in his great song "A Mighty Fortress;" "Let goods and kindred go, this mortal life also; the body they may kill; God's truth abideth still; His Kingdom is forever." We who call ourselves Protestants are supposed to "follow in his trail!"

The first recorded words of Christ after His baptism were: *"Man shall not live by bread alone, but by every word that proceedeth out of the mouth of God."* Matthew and Luke 4:4. The Creator of life, The Preserver of Life, The Redeemer of life, ought to know that which is essential for man to live, is it not so? Towards the close of His ministry, Jesus said to The Church and national leaders: *"Ye do err, but not knowing the Scriptures, nor The Power of God." There are 1440 minutes in every 24 hours. If we were to spend 40 minutes a day reading our Bible consecutively we*

119

could look at "every word that proceedeth out of the mouth of God" two or three times every year, and still have 1400 minutes of every twenty-four hours to do other things. There is no good excuse for the Christian not to know what is in The Bible. Forty minutes a day spent in reading God's Word is a season definitely spent in the presence of God Almighty, if we are sincere.

You will doubtless soon have trouble in this exercise for the devil will fight to break it up, and he may get you in the "lions's den," but it will be well worth it to have a visit from the Angel of God: *"The angel of God encampeth round about them that fear Him, and delivereth them --* Psalms 34:7. The Apostle Paul told Governor Felix: *"And herein do I exercise myself, to have always a conscience void of offence toward God, and toward men."* (It is the writer's conviction that this New Bible has the poison of unbelief in it, and would advise you to hold on the the King James version. A few obsolete words and phrases here and there are not going to poison you, but passages produced by unbelief are dangerous, for *"Faith cometh by hearing, and hearing by The Word of God"*).

Did not get to comment on "Such a time as this" in particular. You can find it in its setting and context in the 4th chapter of The Book of Esther.

October 27, 1962

†††

"The fundamentals of vice are sensuality, pride and ambition, and avarice." Sensuality is "the doctrine that gratification of the senses is the highest good, indulgence of bodily appetites, carnal gratification." Are we not in this great and blessed country, now building on these foundations, and have rejected "The Firm Foundation laid for The Saints of The Lord in His Excellent Word?'' If so, we had better look out for the "lightning to strike!''

"The dread foes of man are not belligerent circumstances, but the riotous passions -- the leopard of incontinence, the lion of violence, and the wolf of avarice -- after food she is hungrier than before!''

The Leopard of Incontinence: The dictionary says incontinence means "Lack of restraint, especially undue indulgence of sexual passions; licentiousness, etc.'' How many great nations and empires of history have for this cause rotted from within, fallen in decay, perished! Is that not largely true of our great land today! "Chastity is driven away as an enemy by all men, like a snake!''

The Lion of Violence: Riot, rebellion, rape, murder and violence of all sorts and description stalk the globe in our days! Some of the most miserable and hypocritical violence of the present and recent times has dressed itself up in the garb of "Non-Violence,'' and even taken the name of God in vain and calls itself "Christian!'' And many, if not the majority, of the great men of our government, our educational and ecclesiastical institutions, are lending their support and power and influence. *That which is highly esteemed among men is abomination in the sight of God.* '' so said Jesus Christ, God, just before telling of the dead rich man's trip to hell and his reception there! We *do err, not knowing the Scriptures, nor the Power of God!* '' Do we even know the ABC's of Christianity? Here they are, consider them? "A -- Abandon self. "B'' -- Bear the Cross. "C'' -- Come after me, Jesus Christ, God!

"A'' -- Abandon Self: The first thing the would be follower of Christ is called upon to do is to *"deny self.''* *"Foxes have holes, and the birds of the air have nests, but the Son of Man hath not where to lay his head.''* and with these words Jesus turned back one follower. Another said:

121

"Lord, I will follow Thee, but first let me go home and bury my father." The answer he got was: *"Let the dead bury the dead, but go thou and preach the Kingdom of God."* And to still another who said he wanted to follow after he had attended to some other affairs: "He that putteth his hand to the plow and looketh back is not fit for the Kingdom of Heaven." Someone has written and expressed himself as believing that most of our present-day "revivals" are a farce! There are grounds for such an attitude; we call folks to join the church, accept Christ, without teaching and impressing upon them the ABC's of The Faith. "Break up your fallow ground; sow not among thorns; sow to yourselves in righteousness, reap in mercy!"

"B" -- Bear the Cross: Cross-bearing does not mean just patiently enduring the aches and pains and disappointments and losses more or less common to all men in the flesh, but rather the Cross of Christ means the rejection and suffering at the hands of an evil world, men, and devils because of their hatred and rage against the righteousness and holiness of God, His Word, Moral Law, Ten Commandments, the Bands, the Cords of restraint He has placed to hold us back from His wrath and the pit of hell! In John 7:7 Jesus said: *"The world hates Me, because I testify of it, that the works thereof are evil."* Have we forgotten, or did we never know it, that when Jesus began His ministry and went back to His home town of Nazareth what He said made the folks so mad that they took Him out of town to throw off a precipice? But they did not know who they were fooling with, and He just walked away and left them! Do we know Who we are dealing with in our churchanity? We think we believe in Christ! Test it out with the question He asked in John 5:44: *"How can ye believe, which receive honour of one another, and seek not the honour that cometh from God only?"*

"C" -- Come After Me -- If we have not learned the C's in the ABC's of Christianity, it is because we never really

122

learned the B's; and if we never learned the B's, it is because we failed to learn the A's -- abandon, deny self. In The Sermon on The Mount Jesus said: *"Not every one that saith unto Me, Lord, Lord, shall enter the Kingdom of Heaven, but he that doeth the will of My Father which is in heaven. Many will say unto Me in that day, Lord, Lord, have we not prophesied in Thy Name? and in Thy Name cast out devils? and in Thy Name done many wonderful works? And then will I profess unto them, I never knew you; depart from me, ye that work iniquity."*

How many of us church members are definitely and deliberately making effort day by day to learn of and to know Him, Whom to know is life eternal? If one does "the will of The Heavenly Father" and neglects The Bible, The Word of God, The Day of God, The House of God, the Prayer Life, he does even more than Jesus Himself did. In view of the fact that our land, our cities, and our lives are filled with sin, rebellion, and rage against The Almighty, and in view of the fact that the nuclear bombs hang heavy, heavy, heavy over our heads, would it not be wise to take up and learn or brush up on the ABC's of Christianity?

Daniel interpreted King Nebuchadnezzar's dream recorded in the second chapter of The Book of Daniel. He told him that he and his kingdom were the "head of gold" of the great image he saw in his dream. Probably that put the notion in the king's noodle to make the great image of gold we are told about in the third chapter, and to gather all the great ones of his empire to its dedication, and demand that they all fall down and worship it when "the band began to play." There were three men present, friends of Daniel -- Shadrach, Meshach, and Abednego, who refused to disobey their God and bow down to the king's idol, although warned if they did not they would be thrown into a furnace of fire! But let them speak as "they said to the king, O Nebuchadnezzar, we are not careful to answer thee in this matter. If it be so, our God is able to deliver us from the burning fiery furnace, and He will deliver us out of thine hand, O king. But if not, be it known unto thee, O king, we will not serve thy gods, nor worship the golden image which thou hast set up. Then was Nebuchadnezzar full of fury -- he commanded that they should heat the furnace seven times more than it was wont to be heated. And he commanded the most mighty men that were in his army to bind S.M., and A. and cast them into the midst of the burning fiery furnance -- and these three men -- fell down bound into the midst of the burning fiery furnace.

"Then Nebuchadnezzar the king was astonished, and rose up in haste, and said unto his counsellors, did not we cast three men bound into the midst of the fire? They answered and said unto the king, True, O king. He answered and said, Lo, I see four men loose, walking in the midst of the fire, and they have no hurt; and the form of the fourth is like The Son of God. Then Nebuchadnezzar came near to the mouth of the burning fiery furnace, and spake, and said, Shadrach, Meshach and Abednego, ye servants of the most high God, come forth, and come hither. Then S., M., and A. came forth out of the midst of the fire. And the princes, governors, and captains, and the king's counsellors being gathered together saw these men upon whose bodies the fire had no power, nor was a hair of their head singed, neither were their coats changed, nor the smell of fire had passed on them!" That was a pretty good crowd of witnesses to a mighty good bomb and fallout shelter, is it not so?

"Let us hear the conclusion of the whole matter: Fear God and keep His Commandments; for this is the whole duty of man. For God shall bring every work into judgment, with every secret thing, whether it be good, or whether it be evil." Eccles. 12: 13-14.

November 10, 1962

†††

124

Second Psalm & Acts 4:25

Why Do the Heathen Rage?

Vol. 2

A compilation of newspaper columns which appeared in leading newspapers across the nation from 1962 to 1981.

The Authority Of
The Scriptures

Division One

"Why do the heathen rage, and the people imagine a vain thing?"

The question is the first clause of the first sentence of the Second Psalm of God Almighty's Book! God Himself is quite an Author! Quite an Editor! Quite a Columnist! He is "King of Kings, Lord of Lords - Where the word of a king is there is power - The Word of God is quick and powerful." He spake and the worlds came into existence, including Milky Ways and Galaxies millions of "light years" distance. We like to hear that great song *How Great Thou Art,* but how is it that we don't like to read His Book and hear all He has to say, and learn of Him whom to know is Eternal Life?

In the Old Testament there are approximately seventeen hundred and fifty passages (1750) prefaced by *"Thus saith the Lord,"* *"God spake,"* or kindred words that indicate God Himself is speaking. But our generation has but little, if any, time for all that talk: "The Ancient of Days is out of date." Is it not so, Mr. Modernist, D.D.? Nevertheless, He holds the whole world in His Hand! He holds the tiny baby in His Hand!

7

In commenting on Jesus' statement regarding the little children: *"Of such is the Kingdom of Heaven,"* someone has observed that after the little children appear on the scene as a "little bundle from heaven," dwell and are in the hands of parents, school teachers, preachers, etc., whose hearts are *"deceitful, above all things and desperately wicked,"* and never find it out, that of many of these children after a few years it might truly be said, *"Of such is the kingdom of hell and devil!"* Where is the sincere grown person that doesn't feel ashamed and responsible that there are grounds for such an observation?

Yes, God is quite an Author; He used about forty different secretaries over a period of about 1500 years to produce His Book, The Bible, and in the closing words warned men not to meddle with it by taking from, or adding to! Martin Luther was quite an intellectual giant, and a very learned man. Hear what he said regarding some of the great of the earth who have raged against The God of The Bible: "Infinite potentates have raged against This Book, and have sought to destroy and uproot it - King Alexander the Great, the Princes of Egypt and Babylon, the monarchs of Persia, of Greece, and of Rome, the Emperors Julius and Augustus - but they nothing prevailed; they are all gone and vanished, while the Book remains, and will remain for ever and ever, perfect and entire, as it was declared at first." Take heed, Modernists, New Translators, Scorners and Scoffers, you, too, will all soon be gone and vanish, but The Book will remain because God is its Author. Jesus Christ said of it: *"The Scriptures cannot be broken."* Take courage and rejoice fundamentalists. John Wesley was called a "Bible Bigot" in mockery. But where are the mockers?

Consider this Great Author and His Book scribes and writers of various and sundry kinds and assortments, all the way from the respected preachers, editors, columnists, etc. down to the miserable wretches that vomit and puke forth their vile and obscene filth that corrupts and perverts the sacredness of marriage vows and God ordained sex relations, affecting perversely even the unborn generation - if God permits another one to arrive. The God of The Bible in ordering the utter destruction of the Canaanites said they were so vile that the land itself vomited them out - maybe our time is near!

There is a definite connection between high grade and low grade scribes mentioned above, in that when the ''highs'' neglect or reject the ''Wisdom that comes from above,'' savor of the things that be of men and not those of God, then the door is gradually opened for the devil to enter with his cohorts and men and society sink lower and lower. The Great Author says in His Book that every idle word that men speak they shall have to give account of in the day of judgment. Look to yourselves! Look at that great stack of stuff on file of your verbal effusions your mind has manufactured for the pulpil, for the newspapers, for magazines, etc., to feed the minds of men, women, and children. It may be that some writers don't keep a file of their writing, but as soon as they get their check burn the junk and laugh at the ''suckers.'' But God has it all on file in your record and He says He will bring every secret thing into judgment, whether it be good, or whether it be evil.

Here is a suggestion if you are interested in having a vital and successful Christian experience: Consider and meditate on Joshua 1:8, and Daniel 1:8, and Galatians 1:8. Sincere meditation on God's Law will show you that you are a lost soul, and point you to the Saviour. Purpose to obey Him and stick to your purpose like Ruth did to Naomi (Ruth 1:16 and 17); and like Daniel did to his purpose, and he and his friends gained the victory in the fiery furnace and in the lions den. Then hold fast to Galatians 1:8 and the apostates, the false prophets, the false preachers, and the devil won't be able to get you.

Don't rage against God and His Moral Law and Ten Commandments like the rebellious in The Second Psalm and get in line for the wrath and curse. Rather, go back to the First Psalm, depart from evil counsel, evil ways, the seat of the scornful, and meditate day and night in The Law of The Lord with the prayer that you will come to delight in it. If this never happens would you enjoy heaven even were you to get there? Judging from the way many church members stay away from The House of God, it is surely going to be a heavy strain on them to have to *"dwell in the House of the Lord forever"* - if they get the chance.

March 17, 1962

† † †

The Second Psalm tells us who the heathen are, why they rage, and the results of this rage, which is a pretty good blueprint of the conditions of the world today. God also tells us the way out, and gives and urges upon us the acceptance of His invitation to come out of adversity, vexation, and confusion into peace and blessedness. However, it appears that we prefer to continue to rage! Someone wrote us and said they had a friend who said if someone did not tell him "what in the hell" this column was raving about he was "going crazy." We replied that we hoped the friend had not as yet gone crazy, but please tell him the object of our raving was to keep him and others "out of hell" rather than "in hell."

We quote from another letter received from one who does a splendid job of "sitting in the seat of the scornful," witness: "The Holy Bible which you call The Word of God is one of the most obscene books published and it is surprising someone hasn't used its pornography commercially. The entire history of the Christian religion is one of violence, crime, and sin." If this party as a result of the teaching of a Godly mother, or father, or friends, joined some Protestant Christian Church in years gone by, we certainly hope he has had the honesty and sincerity to resign and get out and ask that his name be taken off the Church roll!

We wish to comment on this since we believe that this is

not a rare and isolated case, but is shared by great numbers today, even by many who remain in the church to share in its benefits and influence, and especially by some who have attained to high and leading positions in the ecclesiastical world. For example, in recent years a Bishop who was honored by one of the largest Protestant denominations by being promoted to the highest office his church could give, wrote that The God of the Old Testament was a "dirty bully." And another who was advanced to the top position of his great Protestant denomination likened God to Hitler. Of course, these men were generally approved and supported by the majority of the preachers and church authorities under them or they would never have reached such high positiions.

Dante, in his trip through the infernal regions tells of seeing a man in hell whom he knew to be still alive on earth. Asking for an explanation, the "shade" told him that he got to be so "low down" while on the earth that his soul was carried down to hell even before his death, and a demon took possession of his body, and animates it on earth until its time ran its course - a demon had taken its place in the body that walks and sleeps, and drinks and puts on clothes! If after taking the solemn vows of the Protestant Christian Church, and especially those of one of its officials, and then instead of resigning and getting out I remained in my position, accepting a good salary and used it to corrupt and destroy and fight the doctrines of its Confessions of Faith, I fear I would have fallen so low that I deserved the punishment of the man that the poet saw in hell!

But as said above, the object of this column is to keep out of hell ourself, and every other one by the grace of God we possibly can. So, in God's Name we call on all who "Sit in the seat of the scornful" to repent, and bring forth fruit meet for repentance, or else resign and get out of the church. You will be safer and better off, for *"Whosoever shall fall on this stone shall be broken; but on whomsoever it shall fall, it will grind him to powder."* These are the words of the "Gentle

11

Jesus" in Matthew 21:44, and in Luke 20:18. It doesn't pay to rage against the Almighty!

We replied to the "sitter in the seat of the scornful" quoted above that our reaction to his views concerning God's book, The Bible, might be illustrated as follows: Suppose here is a man who finds a nest of polecats under his home. In cleaning them out he is defiled with their awful odor, and for a time if folks did not see him but only smelled him they would think he was a polecat. But he is not one, but on the contrary, deserves to be honored for suffering a while in order to make his home and the abode of his family and loved ones decent and free from the horrible stench. The unpleasant things in the Bible the *"sitters in the seat of the scornful"* mock at, appear in order to reveal to all men that the natural man in the eyes of the "Holy, Holy, Holy, Lord God Almighty" are as "spiritual polecats" - read Psalm 14:3 noting the margin translation for "filthy," also Romans 1:21-32 - and the only way to get clean from our vileness and avoid being cast into the fires of eternal hell, is by being washed in the atoning blood of the Lord Jesus Christ, shed on Calvary, the blood of the one Clean and Perfect Man, the Second Adam.

"There is a fountain filled with blood, drawn from Immanuel's veins, and sinners plunged beneath that flood lose all their guilty stains." This is the Gospel of the Grace of God in Christ Jesus. Don't reject it! *"In Christ's stead, I beseech you, be ye reconciled to God."*

† † †

Webster says a heathen is "one who does not believe in the God of the Bible." They rage to get rid of God's Word, The Bible, its Laws and Commandments for men. An easy and sure way to get rid of The Bible is to neglect, quit reading and remain ignorant! Christ said: *"To him that hath*

12

shall be given, but from him that hath not shall be taken away that which he seemeth to have!"

Fail to use your possessions and opportunities and lose them! Doubtless this explains the loss of the Bible, The Ten Commandments, and The Lord's Prayer from our schools. It is not just the fault of The Supreme Court and others in high authority, but also on account of the neglect and resulting ignorance of probably a large percent of the about 75 million of our citizens that call themselves Christians: *"Be sure your sin will find you out."* Numbers 32:23. And in Hosea 4:6 we read: *"My people are destroyed for lack of knowledge; because thou hast rejected knowledge, I will also reject thee - seeing thou has forgotten the Law of thy God, I will also forget thy children!"* Another explanation why God's Book has been taken away from the public schools. *"Jesus answered and said unto them, ye do err, not knowing the Scriptures, nor the Power of God."* Matthew 22:29.

"I have esteemed the words of thy mouth more than my necessary food," said Job 23:12. The first verse of this Book says of him: *"And that man was perfect and upright, and one that feared God, and eschewed evil."*

If you could stand on some high place and look down a line of men that included all that have lived since Adam, those who stand out as giants and tower over the multitudes because of being of great blessing to their fellows are the ones who like Job and had faith to *"Esteem the words of God more than their necessary food."* Noah heard God's Word, and moved with fear prepared an Ark to the saving of his house, and the race! There tower up Abraham, Moses, David, - read the 119th Psalm and learn of David's attitude towards God's Law, Statutes, Commandments, Precepts, etc. Jesus Christ was The Word of God made flesh. The life and ministry of The Apostle Paul has blessed mankind for about two thousand years, and is still doing so. The secret of Luther's great life and power was the result of finding the Word of God and "esteeming it more than his necessary food," indeed, he offered his body to be burned in order to be obedient!

13

Luther said: "That the Bible is God's Word and book, I prove thus: All things that have been and are in the world, and the manner of their being, are described in the first book of Moses on the Creation. Even as God made and shaped the world, so does it stand to this day. Infinite potentates have raged against this book, and sought to destroy and uproot it - King Alexander the Great, The Princes of Egypt and Babylon, The Monarchs of Persia, of Greece, and of Rome, the Emperors Julius and Augustus. But then nothing prevailed; they are gone and vanished, while the Book remains and will remain forever and ever, perfect and entire, as it was declared at first. Who has thus helped it - Who has thus protected it against such mighty forces? No one, surely, but God himself, who is master of all things and 'tis no small miracle how God has so long preserved and protected this book; for the devil and the world are sore foes to it. I believe that the devil has destroyed many good books of the church, as, aforetime, he killed and crushed many holy persons, the memory of whom has passed away; but the Bible he was fain to leave subsisting."

Do you fear that unbelievers, scholars, false prophets, etc., will be able to do what such great men and powers have failed to do over such long periods of time? The late George Stuart likened those who fight against The Bible to a fool that went out to overturn Lookout Mountain with a crowbar; and those who feared The Bible would be destroyed to the bigger fool who put his shoulder against the other side of the mountain to keep it from being overturned!

John Wesley said: "I beg leave to propose a short, clear and strong argument to prove the divine inspiration of the Holy Scriptures. The Bible must be the invention of good men or angels, bad men or devils, or of God.

1. It could not be the invention of good men or angels, for they could not make a book and tell lies all the time they were writing it, saying, 'Thus saith the Lord,' when it was their own invention.

14

2. It could not be the invention of bad men or devils, for they could not make a book which commands all duty, forbids all sin, and condemns their own souls to 'Hell for all eternity!'

3. Therefore, draw the conclusion that the Bible must be given by Divine Inspiration!''

Ecclesiastes 12:12-14: *"And further, by these, my son, be admonished; of making many books there is no end; and much study is a weariness of the flesh. Let us hear the conclusion of the whole matter: fear God and keep His Commandments; for this is the whole duty of man, for God shall bring every work into judgment with every secret thing, whether it be good, or whether it be evil."*

How long has your favorite author or columnist or commentator been living, writing, or talking? How much longer do you think he will live? How long do you suppose his notions, ideas, and writings will survive? Will they upset and overthrow one "jot or tittle" of God's Word? Christ said it would be easier for heaven and earth to pass away. Would it not be wise for you, me, and all of us like Job to *"Esteem the Words of God's Mouth more than our necessary food. Lay it up in our hearts that we might not sin against Him?*

July 19, 1975

† † †

Did you ever hear tell of "the mark of the beast?" We are not talking about some rancher's mark or brand "burnt into the hide" of his beasts - cows, horses, livestock - in order to identify and protect his own property and assets. The "mark of the beast" we are talking about is the mark or brand the devil puts on his beasts and livestock - men and women who reject God's Government and Laws for their lives, His King and Ruler, the Lord Jesus Christ. The Book of Life, God's Word, the Bible, tells about this "Mark of the Beast." In Revelation 13:16, 17, we read: *"And he caused all, both small and great, rich and poor, free and bond, to receive a mark in their right hand, or in their foreheads: and that no man might buy or sell, save he that had the mark, or the name of the beast, or the number of his name."* Our attention has been directed to this Scripture text on account of the laws of about thirty of our states, and the effort being made to include all others, that make it illegal for a man to hold his job without some mark of a labor union to which he pays tribute.

There is much that is mystical in this great last book of the Bible. However, we are trying to avoid "meddling with this mystical" and confine ourselves to the literal facts as stated. In order not to take this text out of its context, we are undertaking to present an overall picture, what might be called a "bird's-eye view" of the whole Book of Revelation.

Try and visualize and get your mind's eye on four articles: A Candlestick, a Book, a Trumpet, and a Vial (vase or bowl). Associate the number seven with each of these: A Candlestick with seven candles, a Book with seven seals. A Trumpet in the hand of each of Seven Angels, and a Vial in the hands of each Seven Angels.

There are at least two great revelations or visions of the "risen from the dead" and glorified Lord Jesus Christ: He is shown walking in the midst of the seven candles, or churches, or their ministers, giving each one a message, mostly warnings. (When I meditate on these messages and warnings I don't hesitate to advise folks to "get out of the church, or get right with God," and stay right and be faithful unto death!) The second great vision or revelation shows Christ on the Throne of God, standing at His right hand with a Book in His hand that is sealed with Seven Seals. If you get His messages to the Churches, and then learn what takes place in earth, heaven or hell as each of the Seals are broken, then you will be well informed as to the literal contents of this Book. Get the literal facts in mind, meditate upon them if you are seeking to do the will of God - without which being done no one can enter Heaven - and whatever of the mystical you may need in order to do your job will be revealed when needed.

When the last Seal of the Book is broken, there appear Seven Angels each with a Trumpet. Each in turn blows his trumpet. After the Seventh Angel blew his trumpet, another Seven Angels appear each holding a Vial "filled with the wrath of God." One by one these pour out their "Vial filled with the wrath of God" upon the earth, the sea, or air, and then we are told of God's final judgments upon the devil, his angels, and the men who have received "the mark of the beast" upon them - In the first two chapters of the Bible, sin has not entered, and is not mentioned; and in the last two chapters of the Bible, sin has been judged and put away, and sin is not mentioned nor appears in the New Heavens and the New Earth.

However, our special concern in this article is to locate in the above concerning the facts presented, the why, the what, and whereof of "The Mark of the Beast!" In Revelation 11:15 is recorded that the Seventh Angel sounded his trumpet. After this, and before the appearance of the Seven Angels with the Vials of the seven last plagues, the Apostle John was shown a great wonder in heaven: *"A woman clothed with the sun, and the moon under her feet, and upon her head a crown of twelve stars, travailing in child-birth."* Before her stood a great Red Dragon ready to devour the child as soon as born. This child was destined to rule all nations with a rod of iron, and was caught up unto God and His Throne. The woman fled into the wilderness. There was war in heaven, and the Dragon and his angels were cast out: *"And the Dragon was wroth with the woman, and went to make war with the remnant of her seed, 'which keep the Commandments of God, and have the Testimony of Jesus Christ.'"* (It appears that many today who "have the testimony of Jesus Christ," or claim to have, have mighty little regard for "keeping the commandments of God," which is the whole duty of man: *"To fear God and keep His Commandments."* Probably this accounts for the lapse of Church discipline, and the resultant anarchy in social and political life, and the great victories the devil and raging heathen seem to be gaining over the people of God.) The 13th chapter of Revelation tells of the strategy of the dragon in this warfare against the remnant of the seed of the woman: He produces two great beasts, one comes up out of the sea, and the other comes up out of the earth. They both have great power to work miracles and do wonders that deceive men and turn them away from God. The beast that comes out of the earth causes an idol to be made to which he gives life so that it can speak, and has power to kill. His special method of killing appears to be by putting "The Mark of the Beast" on all his and the devil's livestock so that none can buy or sell without it!

Can you see any resemblance between this revelation of God, and the spirit of men, great or small, rich or poor, bond or free, who use, or seek to usurp power in order to force their fellows to do and go their way? This temporal life is like an hand-spread, as a vapor that appears for a moment and then gone. The great concern for the Christian and child of God should not be about losing his job, or going hungry, but rather that we and none of our fellow human beings get marked and branded the devil's property. Consider their end as found in chapter 20:10-15: *"And the devil that deceived them was cast into the lake of fire and brimstone, where the beast and the false prophet are, and shall be tormented day and night for ever and ever - and death and hell were cast into the lake of fire . . . and whosoever was not found written in the Book of Life was cast into the lake of fire!"*

We used to often sing a song in Sunday School and Church entitled: "Is my name written there, on the page white and fair?" The first verse ran: "Lord, I care not for riches, neither silver nor gold, I would make sure of heaven, I would enter the fold: Is my name written there?" Once a visiting preacher was in the Church for a Revival Service. He gave out the number of the above hymn with this comment: "Let us skip that verse, there is no use singing that lie and telling the Lord we care not for silver and gold!"

When you consider sincerely the message of the Book of Revelation, as well as many other Scriptures, would we not do well and wisely to pray God to work a work in our hearts and lives regardless of the temporal and time cost, to the end we should truthfully and faithfully *"Seek first the Kingdom of God, and His righteousness that all these other things might be added."*

July 11, 1970

† † †

On March 3, 1962, there appeared in the two Atlanta papers the first article of this column. With the exception of the following Saturday, an article has been submitted every week. Several have been rejected, and a number sorely censored. As much, or probably more than any other verses quoted from the Bible have been Ecclesiastes 12:12-14:

"Of making many books there is no end; and much study is a weariness of the flesh. Let us hear the conclusion of the whole matter: 'Fear God and keep His Commandments: for this is the whole duty of man.' For God shall bring every work into judgment, 'With every secret thing,' whether it be evil, or whether it be good."

During these years the object and aim of every article for the most part has been to present and urge upon men this message from God Almighty, their Creator.

Much of the following is quoted from that first article: in the Second Psalm God asks this question, and then answers it. He tells who the heathen are, why they rage, His reaction and the consequences of their rage. God also gives instruction, and warning, and an invitation. Webster says a heathen is "one who does not believe in the God of the Bible." This definition fits in with what God says in the Psalm: *"The kings of the earth - and the rulers"* and *"the people [who] imagine a vain thing"* and support their

19

leaders as they *"take council together, against the Lord, and His anointed."*

Why do the heathen rage? What is the cause? They want to "break the bands - cast away the cords," and get rid of the restraints, the fences, the roadblocks and the Almighty has thrown across our paths to hold us back from damning ourselves, our children, and our posterity in time and in eternity. In other words, they rage to get rid of God's Ten Commandments, God's Moral Law. It appears our generation is making good headway performing this job!

Next, God tells us in this Psalm the consequences of this rebellion and raging: *"He that sitteth in the Heavens shall laugh, the Lord shall have them in derision: then shall He speak unto them in his wrath, and vex them in His sore displeasure." "He poureth contempt upon princes,"* we read in Job 12:21; and in Isaiah 40:23, *"He bringeth the princes of the earth to nothing; He maketh the judges of the earth as vanity."*

In our day and generation has not God laughed at, held in derision, spoken in His wrath, and poured contempt upon many a king, prince and ruler? Where is the late Czar and Stalin and Khrushchev of Russia, the late Kaiser and Hitler of Germany, Mussolini and others who attained great power, but now gone? And in this visitation of the Almighty has not most of the nations had to drink the "wine cup of His wrath and indignation?" We blame this man and that, this nation and that, but the blame according to this message from God lays at the door of those who rebel and rage against His Commandments to keep from obeying!

In Luke 18:1-5, in speaking of men whose blood Pilate had shed, and men who died as the result of a tower falling, Christ passed up talking of Pilate's responsibility, or the responsibility of the tower engineers, and made the application personal to His hearers: *"Do you think these men were sinners above all other men? I tell you, Nay; but, except ye repent, ye shall all likewise perish!"* Elijah, the

20

man taken to heaven without dying, bypassing the grave, said to King Ahab, *"I have not troubled Israel, but thou, and thy father's house, in that ye have forsaken the Commandments of God!"* *"There is no peace, saith my God, to the wicked!"* Yet we cry, Peace, Peace, and then make very little, if any, effort to cut out our personal wickedness and indifference, or to rise up and put away the lawlessness and crime about and around.

"The lapse of Church Discipline was a certain symptom of Political and Social Anarchy," said a great English Historian as he looked across the centuries of their experiences! Generally speaking, our churches have just about "junked" discipline. Seem to think it unchristian, regardless of the fact that God says *"Judgment must begin at the House of God."* The devil himself can join most any of our churches, provided he dresses decently and tells a big profane lie - which is no hindrance to him of whom Christ said was the *"father of lies."* Someone has said that the best of us in the churches are so dirty and weak we have neither the will nor strength to "bathe the balance." Things get mighty bad and offensive when people quit bathing! Soon smell worse than goats! In the Judgment Scene the goats were put on the left! Are you a leftist? I sure want to be on the extreme right in that day!

Our trouble, the world's trouble, is that we have a corrupt form of Christianity! A Christianity that has been shoved off its base, the Law of God! *"Let us hear the conclusion of the whole matter: Fear God and keep His Commandments, for this is the whole duty of man. For God shall bring every work into judgment, with every secret thing, whether it be good, or whether it be evil."*

In 1st John 5:3, *"For this is the love of God, that we keep His Commandments."* Revelation 22:14, *"Blessed are they that do His Commandments, that they might have a right to the tree of life, and may enter in through the gates into the city."*

March 4, 1967

† † †

21

General Themes

Division Two

The word "Ah" is "an exclamatory expression of surprise," so says the dictionary. We are trying to make an "acrostic" out of "Ah-h." We understand an acrostic is where the letters of a word are taken in order to form a composition, phrase, motto, name, or word. So let "A" stand for Apostacy; "H" for Heresy; and the second "H" for Hypocrisy. Think of them in connection with yourself rather than the other fellow. The other fellow will probably neither know or care whether or not you apply them to him, but if honest and sincere, it will sure benefit an individual, and might produce concerning his own condition an "Ah-h" - an exclamatory expression of surprise! God's Word says: *"For if we would judge ourselves we should not be judged"* 1st Corinthians 11:31.

Apostacy is "the forsaking, or abandonment of what one has hitherto professed, or adhered to, as faith, principle, or party." In order to try to be helpful to any who want to

23

"judge self," we suggest that you consider whether or not that when you joined the Church or hitherto, you professed and adhered to the faith that The Bible was the infallible Word of God Almighty, and "the only rule of faith and practice whereby to be directed to honor and glorify God?" Or, did you once profess and adhere to God's Fourth Commandment: *"Remember the Sabbath Day to Keep it Holy;"* believing that man should do no work on that Day except for mercy and necessity, and that the Day should be spent with the aim of increasing our knowledge of God and seeking His pleasure and honor, rather than our own? See Isaiah 58: 13, 14.

If I have forsaken or abandoned these beliefs, then I am apostate so far as these matters are concerned. These are only two of many other ways by which one may check himself regarding apostacy. If there be any such thing as an "honorable apostate," maybe I can deserve that honor by asking the Church to erase my name from the rolls!

Heresy: I understand this word comes from one meaning "to make choice." "It is an opinion or doctrine which is at variance with fundamental truths commonly received as orthodox, especially leading to divisions; religious opinion at variance with fundamental truths commonly received as orthodox, especially leading to divisions; religious opinion at variance with authorized standards." The fundamental truths commonly received as orthodox among Protestant Christians are found in the great **"Thirty-Nine Articles of the Church of England,"** and in the **"Westminster Confessions of Faith,"** which, if we mistake not, are in full agreement on all essential doctrines of the Protestant Faith. To choose opinions and doctrines at variance is heresy. If there be such a thing as "an honorable heretic," probably it is that person who reveals his unbelief and withdraws from the Church.

Hypocrisy: "A feigning to be what one is not; dissimulation; false profession." If I am apostate, if I am heretic, and fail to get out of a Protestant Church, there is no doubt but what I am a hypocrite regardless of what the authorities and doctors may say: *"For if we should judge ourselves we should not be judged!"* The devil and man's natural corrupt nature will cause him doubts, fears, uncertainty, at times, but if he gets to the place where he gives precedence to his doubts above the orthodox doctrines on which his church was founded, preaches or teaches them without first resigning and getting out, surely he has earned the title of hypocrite!

"Ah-h!" Consider what great danger such folks are in! God's Word testifies and warns! John Bunyan's *Pilgrim's Progress* has lived, endured, and blessed mankind for about 200 years. Shortly after Christian and Hopeful escaped from Doubting Castle and the clutches of Giant Despair, they came to the Delectable Mountains where they find four Shepherds: Knowledge, Experience, Watchful, and Sincere. They are shown and taught many wonderful things which greatly encourage them, but also some terrible sights and lessons of warnings. They were carried to a place in a bottom, where a door was on the side of a hill; and they opened the door, and bid them look in. It was very dark and smoky; they also thought they heard a rumbling noise, as of fire, and a cry of some tormented, and they thought they smelt the scent of brimstone! Then said Christian, "What means this?" The Shepherds told them, "This is a by-way to hell, a way Hypocrits go in at, namely, such as sell their birthright, with Esau; such as sell their masters, with Judas; such as blaspheme the Gospel, with Alexander, and that lie and dissemble, with Ananias and Saphirra his wife!"

Hopeful asked the Shepherds if all these did not make a show of being pilgrims, or Christians? Yes, they replied, and they held on to their show for a long time before the truth of them was known. Some go even farther down the true road than Christian and Hopeful had reached, and proof of this was seen: "They entered into a dark lane, where they met a man when seven devils had bound him with seven strong cords and were carrying him back to the door they saw in the side of the hill - "The By-Way to Hell!"

Good Christian and Hopeful began to tremble. As the devils led away the man, Christian looked to see if he knew the man, and he thought it might be one **Turnaway, that dwelt in the Town of Apostacy.** But he did not perfectly see his face, for he did hang his head like a thief that is found; but being past, Hopeful looked after him, and espied on his back a paper with this inscription: "Wanton Professor, and Damnable Apostate." Then said Christian and Hopeful one to another: "We have need to cry to the strong for strength." And the Shepherds said: "Yea, and you will have need to use it when you have it, too!"

Dante, telling of his trip through hell and the infernal regions, when at the pit where heretics were punished, describes the stench at this place of his journey as something awful. The morning newspaper carried a story of one who had stolen a large sum of money and buried it for safe keeping. But when dug up, part of it stunk so bad that he threw away about two thousand dollars of it. He loved money dearly, but could not stand its stink.

Beware, heretics, you may love your own choice of beliefs more than the revelations of God Almighty, but the day of accounting is nearby! Isaiah foretold of the time when some would cast their silver and gold to the moles and bats. Judas Iscariot did not enjoy the money that he valued above The Sun of Righteousness!

"Look to yourselves -" 2nd John 8. It would be the part of wisdom for us to use David's prayer in the last two verses of Psalm 139 as follows: *"Search me, Oh God, and know my heart, try me, and know my thoughts; and see if there be any apostacy, any heresy, any hypocrisy in me, and lead me in the way everlasting."* "Ah-h!" - an exclamatory expression of surprise!

January 22, 1972

† † †

26

On a certain day two sermons had been preached, one by Martin Luther and the other by a friend and his co-laborer we will call Doctor B. Luther said to his friend: "You preached a good sermon, but I liked mine better than yours." "Well, Doctor, I will acknowledge your superiority." "No," replied Luther, "that is not it; the reason I liked mine better than yours is that every child and illiterate servant present could understand mine and knew what I was talking about, but much of yours was only understood by the learned and the scholars."

Some years ago there was a prominent politician in this State who had some oratorical ability along with a "flowery gift of gab." After one of his speeches two farmers met and one asked the other if he had heard the speech, and on learning that he had not he said: "Man, you don't know what you missed. Believe that was the finest speech I ever heard. He sure 'went to town'!" "What did he talk about?" asked his friend. After hesitating a little: "I don't know, he never did say what he was talking about!"

On a number of occasions letters have come asking the objective of this column, which probably is another way of asking "what are you talking about?" Our first article appeared on the first Saturday of March, 1962, and with the exception of the following week, there has been one in every Saturday paper, and in the first one and in all the following ones, directly or indirectly, we have talked about the fact that generally speaking The Church is corrupt and has junked discipline, and the results of "corrupting God's way in the earth" will mean in the end, and the end might be near, the visitation of the wrath and curse of God upon us as individuals, our nation, and the world, calling attention to the fact that this was the cause of the destruction of the world in the days of Noah, the cause of the visitation of the wrath and curse of God upon the Jewish people down through the centuries, the cause of the disappearance from the face of the earth of great cities and nations and kingdoms of antiquity, and the cause of all the disasters, troubles, etc., of mankind including the calamities we read about in every day's newspaper!

The "heathen rage" to get rid of God's Moral Law, Ten Commandments, and The Almighty holds them in derision, laughs, and vexes them with all adversity. We have also in these articles continually talked about the fact that God sent His Son to the earth to keep His Commandments perfectly, and that He will impute that perfect righteousness to every soul that sincerely accepts and believes on Jesus Christ, and will write His Commandments in their hearts, or in other words, fix them up where they will want to "obey God, and keep His Commandments, which is the whole duty of man."

"It is singular how long the rotten will hold together, provided you do not handle it roughly." Picture a rotten apple hanging on a tree, or elsewhere, it holds together a long time unless it falls or is handled a little roughly, and then you have "rotten apple sauce." One meaning of "corruption" is "rottenness." The earth became corrupt, or rotten, in the days of Noah. God handled it rather roughly; it went to pieces and there was none left except the man who found grace in God's sight, the man who feared God, and obeyed Him!

Some have estimated there might have been 480 billions of people in the earth when the flood came! The Jewish nation as a whole became corrupt, rotten; God has handled them roughly through the centuries and behold their history, suffering, and how they have been scattered. There is much rottenness and corruption in the home and family life of our nation; there is much rottenness and corruption in the political life of our nation; the main cause of the corruption and rottenness in the family and governmental life of our nation can be traced to corruption and rottenness in our Protestant Christian Church life, and every one of us who have taken such vows are especially responsible!

Did not God handle us roughly when He permitted our President to be assassinated? No doubt in our mind but that this "permissive providence" of The Almighty is a rebuke to the entire nation! Generally speaking, The Church refuses to "get rough" with its own rottenness of unbelief, apostacy, rejection of God's Laws and Word, and so the corruption holds together and increases: the civil powers of government refuse to "get rough" with murder, robbery, vile immorality - have heard it said time and again that the City of Washington, the seat of the great power of this nation is the worst "sink of sin and cesspool of iniquity" of such crimes in all this great land, and therefore, corruption and rottenness "hold together."

What can one man do? He can do the "one thing needful," read what it is in Luke 10:41,42: *"And Jesus answered and said unto her, Martha, Martha, thou art careful and troubled about many things: But 'one thing is needful'; and Mary hath chosen 'that good part,' which shall not be taken away from her."* The good part Mary chose was to "sit at the feet of Jesus and hear His Word." Go and do likewise, get rid of corruption and rottenness, become "good fruit by the power of God!"

December 7, 1963

† † †

"Ye that love the Lord, hate evil! - Take thou away from me the noise of thy songs; for I will not hear the melody of thy viols. But let judgment run down as waters, and righteousness as a mighty stream!" Psalm 97:10, and Amos 5:23 and 24.

One may love the great hymns and music of the Church, but if one does not "hate evil" it appears God doesn't appreciate the music, and it is unacceptable.

Here is a story, an incident that happened many years ago in a Church located near one of Atlanta's large cotton mills: There was a Deacon in this Church who was noted for his "long and loud" prayers. There was in this community a

29

little store operated by a Widow, that thus supported herself and children. Brother Deacon and Sister Widow were both at prayer meeting one Wednesday night. Brother Deacon was offering a prayer, either having been called on to pray, or having begun spontaneously and voluntarily. At any rate he was in extra good form on this night, for he seemed to "mount the wind and ride the clouds;" on and on he rode with the wind getting more boisterous. Sister Widow was not enjoying it a little bit, and could not join in the chorus of "amens." In fact, her indignation reached the explosion point, and suddenly she jumped up and shouted so that she could be heard above the "windstorm"; "Aw, the devil, there ain't nothing to all that, that rascal has been toting rations out of my store for a long time, and eating them, but he won't pay his bill!" To say the least, "the wind" was taken out of Brother Deacon's "sails."

"Ye that love the Lord, hate evil - Let judgment run down as waters, and righteousness as a mighty stream!"

Last week as a man ate breakfast in a cafe, he looked out of the window and saw a very fine specimen of physical manhood, one who weighed about 200 lbs., well-proportioned and good looking. This fine looking young man, made in the image of God, picked up a newspaper without putting any money in the box, brought it inside, and looked at it while he ate, and went out leaving it on his table or seat. Maybe he was just absent-minded and did not realize what he had done. Or, maybe he was in some mental strain, business trouble, or trouble at home and his wife had to whip him before he left. Possibly the previous morning he did not have the right change and had put a dime in the box and the box owed him a paper. Or maybe, although greatly blessed of God physically and apparently well able to "pay his own way" he had opened his mind and heart for the devil to enter in and he considered himself more important than the Law of God Almighty that says *"Thou shalt not steal,"* and more important than the laws of county, state, and nation, as well as the right of his fellowman to his own property!

"Ye that love the Lord, hate evil - Let judgment run down as waters, and righteousness as a mighty stream!"

"Deacon Johnson was preaching to his flock at a big Camp Meeting one day, when a brother sitting over in the "amen corner" got angry and was forced to say: "Jasper Johnson, shame on you, you don't preach and rob us, too. You don't buy no fowls at no 2 a.m. I want all the people here to find you out so they can all stand up and shout: 'Shame on You!'""

Are there any voices being lifted today crying Shame on you, you thief, you liar, you adulterer, you fornicator, you Sabbath desecrator, you murderer, you profane and covetous wretch? How many individuals do you know, how many Churches do you know, whose "Love for God" is made known and manifested by their "Hatred of evil?" What just complaint have we if The Almighty withdraws His restraining Hand and lets our enemies rain down "Hell-bombs" on our home, cities and fair land!

"Thy throne, O God, is forever and ever: the scepter of thy kingdom is a right scepter. Thou lovest righteousness, and hatest wickedness; therefore, God, thy God, hath anointed Thee with the oil of gladness above thy fellows." Psalm 45: 6, 7.

"But unto The Son he saith, Thy Throne, O God, is forever and ever: a scepter of righteousness is the scepter of thy kingdom. Thou has loved righteousness and hated iniquity; therefore, God, even thy God, hath anointed Thee with the oil of gladness above thy fellows." Heb. 1:8,9. *"He that hath not The Spirit of Christ is none of His."* Do we who claim to be "born again" and that "Christ is within us" manifest in our witness bearing any real "hatred of evil?" Or, do we not often "make apology for the devil that dwells within" and tolerate evil and unrighteousness! The late Dwight L. Moody said: "If Christianity doesn't straighten out a man's character, it is not worth 'the snap of your

finger'!''

"Ye that love the Lord, hate evil - Let judgment run down as waters, and righteousness as a mighty stream!"

June 16, 1962

† † †

The object of this article is to try to stir you up to give more attention to reading the Bible itself, for yourself, with the aim of getting familiar with all of it. If you have neglected doing so for many years, or throughout a long life, and feel it is too late now, remember that an endless Eternity stretches out before you. *"The world passeth away, and the lust thereof, but he that doeth the will of God abideth forever."*

As long as you live, keep up learning of God: *"Learn of Me."* said Jesus in Matthew 11:29. *"The word of our God shall stand forever!"* Consider the context of Scripture in which this last quote appears: *"All flesh is grass, and all the goodliness thereof is as the flower of the field; the grass withereth, the flower fadeth; because the Spirit of God bloweth upon it; surely the people is grass. The grass withereth, the flower fadeth, but the word of our God shall stand forever!"* Isaiah 40:6-8. (Note the emphasis by repetition). Lay up God's Word in your heart, be obedient, and you, too, will stand forever!

The first recorded words of Christ after His baptism are: *"It is written, man shall not live by bread alone, but by every word that proceedeth out of the mouth of God."* This quotation is found in both Matthew and Luke, 4:4. Christ called Peter, Satan, ordered him to get behind Him, he being offensive to Christ because he savored not of the things that be of God, but those that be of men - in other words Peter through ignorance or unbelief rejected revealed Truth concerning Christ. *"Of making many books there is no end; and much study is a weariness of the flesh. Let us hear*

32

the conclusion of the whole matter; Fear God and keep His Commandments, for this is the whole duty of man. "Eccles. 12: 12, 13. Much of the study and book-makings of the clergy and scholars is not only weariness to the flesh to wade through, but also a dreadful curse to mankind in every particular wherein they *"savor not of the things of God, but those that be of men."* *"Cursed be the man that trusteth in man, and maketh flesh his arm, and whose heart departeth from the Lord - blessed is the man that trusteth in the Lord, and whose hope the Lord is."* Jeremiah 17:5-7.

Most professed Christians feel and believe they can get more profit from the Bible by reading some men's comments on it. This may be good and helpful in case the commentator is a true and faithful man of God. However, if one substitutes the reading of commentators to the neglect of a direct contact with The Almighty and His experience of having, and knowing, "God has touched his heart." Or, as the Spiritual Song puts it: "I know the Lord has laid His hands on me!" Christ said, *"My words are Spirit, and they are life!"*

Recently heard a man say if he had to listen to a preacher whom he believed was speaking for himself and not representing God, he felt like retiring down into the "fall-out shelter," which many of our churches have now provided. The after effects of a nuclear explosion are as nothing, being only physical and temporal, in comparison with the after effects of the explosions of false prophets, as such are spiritual and for Eternity! In 2nd Corinthians 11:13, 14 we are warned of the time when the devil would get in the House of God, in the pulpit, and deceive men into believing he was an Angel of Light! This party said, however, he thought it his duty to deny himself the comfort and protection of the "fall-out shelter," and stay on the job of listening, learning of the enemy, and praying for all unconverted, especially the preacher!

In urging you to read the Bible, we mean the King James Version, or one translated by men and scholars who believe the Old and New Testaments to be the infallible Word of God. Martin Luther said no other kind were capable of making a faithful translation for the simple reason they undertake the work with blinded eyes, minds, and hearts, lacking the Wisdom and Light of God's Holy Spirit. In Acts 5:32 the Apostle Peter speaking of the Holy Spirit said: *"Whom God hath given to them that obey Him."* Doubtless there are other true and faithful translations in addition to the King James version. We are not familiar with them. We do know that for nearly 400 years God has mightily used the King James Version for blessing mankind and the establishment of the great Protestant denominations.

As for the Bible recently translated called the Revised Standard Version, the testimony of this column is, and has been: "Beware of it!" The main reason for this is that this version drops the word "virgin" in Isaiah 7:14, and puts in its place "young women!" Here, and a number of places in the New Testament the deity of Christ is subtly attacked! *"A little leaven leaveneth the whole lump!"* Christ put His approval on "the whole lump" when He said *"The scriptures cannot be broken!"*

It would be better for a church to liquidate its assets and go out of business, rather than preach, teach, and promote doctrine that denies the Virgin Birth and the Deity of the Lord Jesus Christ! There is a "Massive Attack upon the Word of God," coming from many directions in these days; the atheists, the communists, many of the clergy and educational institutions of great denominations, schools, colleges, and it appears recently their position is being supported by some great instruments of national and international news media. We believe this situation, an exceedingly dangerous one, is the result of Christian people of our nation miserably falling down on the vows they took to serve and obey God.

Much more is at stake than our national safety and preservation: The welfare of our souls throughout an endless eternity is at stake, and that of the young people and children of the coming generation.

In the Gospel of Luke, 12:23, etc., there is the account of one asking Christ, *"Lord, are there few that can be saved? And he said unto them, 'Strive to enter in at the straight gate; for many, I say unto you, will seek to enter in, and shall not be able!'"* Christ then goes on to tell how many will be greatly disappointed in finding they were unprepared for entering heaven, had believed a lie and were shut out for eternity!

We suggest one way, maybe the most important, as to how to "strive" to enter in at the strait gate: Strive to get familiar with God's Book, the Bible, *"every word that proceedeth out of the mouth of God."* The enemy is coming in like a flood and for the most part, the people of God have not the only weapon with which to withstand him: *"The Sword of the Spirit, which is the word of God!"* The Apostle Paul said at one of his trials after the enemy had imprisoned him: *"And herein do I exercise myself to have always a conscience void of offense towards God and towards men."* Acts 24:16. Exercise yourself in "Searching the Scriptures," in order to always have a conscience "void of offense towards God, and towards men," lest you be found aiding and abetting the enemy of your soul, instead of withstanding him!

January 23, 1965

† † †

The 90th Psalm is "A Prayer of Moses the Man of God." It is especially appropriate for New Years, birthdays, and funerals. The Eternity of the Almighty is contrasted with the brevity, shortness, frailty and evil of man's life. *"Before the mountains were brought forth, or ever Thou hadst formed the earth and the world, even from Everlasting to Everlasting, Thou art God."* God has not created us with minds capable of comprehending that which has no beginning, nor end. Why "kick against the pricks?" Why not acknowledge our limitations? It could be the preparation needed to learn to *"Trust in the Lord with all our heart, and lean not to our own understanding."* -Prov. 3:5.

Man's time and days are *"As a sleep; like grass which groweth up; in the morning it flourisheth and groweth up, and in the evening it is cut down, and withereth."* God *"turns man to destruction, and sayeth, Return, ye children of men."* Return to dust. *"Return unto the ground . . . For dust thou art, and unto dust shalt thou return."* -Genesis 3:19. God's Word is being fulfilled unto Adam whom He warned not to disobey orders regarding eating the Forbidden Fruit!

Five times in three verses - 7, 9, 11 - Moses mentions the anger and wrath of God because of His countenance!" This Psalm is frequently read at funerals, or parts of it, for often these verses are skipped that reveal the real cause of death. Would it not be more appropriate to constantly remind ourselves of the anger and wrath of God against the "iniquities and secret sins of men," and then rejoice because Christ took our place and endured the wrath and curse that we might be saved? And might it not stir us up who believe with a greater zeal to win the lost to the Saviour? He came *"to seek and save that which is lost."* - If you do not believe these things, or take part of God's Word for "myth," you certainly are out of place in a Protestant Christian Church! Mr. Unbeliever, is it "myth" that men return to dust? Do you expect to escape such an experience? Is Genesis 3:16 a "myth" where we read: *"Unto the woman He [God] said: I will greatly multiply thy sorrow and conception; in sorrow shalt thou bring forth children?"* Ask any, or ask all women who have travailed in childbirth if this statement of God in Genesis is "myth"!

"If I only could, I surely would, stand on the rock where Moses stood." Think these words are from a Spiritual. Probably the basis is the passage in Exodus 33:19-23 where

God placed Moses in the "cleft of a rock" and covered him with His hand, as His glory passed by. Doubtless it is also the basis of the beloved song, *"Rock of Ages, cleft for me, let me hide myself in Thee."* It is bad, it is too bad, it is two thousand and more bad, that some of our modern clergy are telling us that "The Rock of Ages" is out of date! From the way I read God's Word, even the words of The Gentle Jesus, it would be a favor done such prophets if *"a millstone were hanged about their neck, and they were thrown into the sea!"*

Imagine you stood where Moses did and watched The Almighty *"turn man to destruction and return him to dust."* Think of the Hebrew male babies destroyed by Pharoah's command, which destruction Moses himself only escaped as by a miracle; and the numbers of his own people that perished as their lives were ground out in bitter and cruel bondage and slavery; and those who died as a result of the ten plagues, especially the firstborn of all that were not protected by "blood on the doorposts;" his eyes beheld the destruction and return to dust of Pharoah's army that were drowned in the Red Sea, and of many of the Amalakites, and other pagan tribes that fought against Israel in the wilderness; his eyes also beheld large numbers of his own people returned to dust as they raged against God in various rebellions, murmurings, and complainings at the providences of God sent to test them, and indeed the return to dust of the entire generation of over 500,000 men who wasted away in the wilderness and failed to make it into the Promised Land!

Even Moses himself "returned to dust" outside of that good land! (The heart in your bosom is a "muffled drum" beating out a march for us to the cemetery, and dust.) Surely, Moses knew what he was talking about when he said in this Psalm *"Thou carriest them away as with a flood . . . for we are consumed by Thine anger, and by Thy wrath are we troubled . . . Thou hast set our iniquities before Thee, our secret sins in the light of Thy countenance . . . All our days are passed away in Thy wrath . . . Who knoweth the power of Thine anger? Even according to Thy fear, so is Thy wrath , , The days of our years are threescore and ten; and if by reason of strength they be fourscore years, yet is their strength labor and sorrow; for it is soon cut off, and we fly away."*

With the background of these experiences in his mind's eye, and having confessed them in the first part of his prayer, he then prays to God in the 12th verse:

"So teach us to number our days, that we may apply our hearts unto wisdom." Note he asks God to be their Teacher to the end that they might have wisdom for the use of their swift passing days. *"The fear of the Lord is the beginning of wisdom."* John Bunyan commented that he that had not the "beginning" had neither the "middle" nor the "end"!

God had said "Return to dust." Now Moses prays God to "Return" to them with forgiveness and blessing: *"Return, O Lord, how long? and let it repent Thee concerning Thy servants, O satisfy us early with Thy mercy; that we may rejoice and be glad all our days. Make us glad according to the days wherein Thou has afflicted us, and the years wherein we have seen evil. Let Thy work appear unto Thy servants, and Thy glory unto their children. And let the beauty to The Lord our God be upon us; and establish Thou the works of our hands upon us, yea, the work of our hands establish Thou it."*

We digressed from the original intention of this article. It was to seek to stress the importance and wisdom of so numbering our days as to give honor to God on His Day, the Christian Sabbath.

"O day of rest and gladness, O day of joy and light, O balm of care and sadness, most beautiful, most bright: On Thee the high and lowly, Through ages joined in tune. Sing 'Holy, Holy, Holy,' to the great God Tri-une.

"On Thee, at the creation, The light first had its birth; On Thee, for our salvation, Christ rose from the depths of the earth; On Thee, our Lord, Victorious, The Spirit sent from heaven; thus on Thee, most glorious, A triple light was given.

"Today on weary nations, the heavenly manna falls: To holy convocations, The Silver Trumpet calls. Where Gospel light is glowing, With pure and radiant beams, and living waters flowing, With soul refreshing streams."

January 5, 1963

† † †

A heathen is one who does not believe in the God of the Bible." He rages to break the bands and cast away the cords of restraint of God's Moral Law, His Ten Commandments. See Second Psalm.

"Believe it or not" some articles in this column have traveled to our largest city, New York! Who would have thought it! Arriving in the great city, they found their way to the national headquarters of a well-known organization, into the office of one of the top men. This great man condescended to write us a letter, greeting us thusly: "Dear religious liar and bigot!" Other compliments were: "Your ad is a despicable piece of nonsense - you are a religious crank - not fit to shine the shoes of Voltaire or Thomas Paine." Then as an afterthought he added by postscript: "You are a contemptible and reprehensible cur!" - Otherwise we hope we are O.K.

Don't believe this fellow likes us - am hard to fool. Further, we figure the "big boy" has been wounded, painfully hurt, for his roarings and threatenings are frightening! He makes us think of the fierce fellow who *"scratched his head with the lightning, and soothed himself to slumber with the thunder!"* Also, his letter made us think of a Scripture passage, Ephesians 6:12: *"For we wrestle not against flesh and blood, but against principalities, against powers, against the rulers of the darkness of this world,*

39

against spiritual wickedness in high places." However, this prince, this king, "his majesty," does not use wise strategy in trying to "capture the cur"; he should have approached the job under the cover of kindness - "nice doggie" - until he could lay hands on it, for he ought to have sense enough to know that to approach breathing threatenings, thunder, and lightning would terrify the little animal and make him harder to catch! It is too late now to apply for the job of shining Voltaire and Tom Paine's shoes, but if it were not, I might be willing to make application in order to get the opportunity to tell them of Jesus: The Light of the World, the Mighty to save. Have read that Voltaire on his death bed complained that God and man had abandoned him, and in despair he often cried out, "O Christ, O Jesus Christ!"

Concerning comparisons, would like to express the opinion that the members of the organization do not do as much damage to true Christianity as those apostates who have "crept in unawares" and are in so many pulpits denying The Virgin Birth, the Miracles, and Deity of Christ. His literal Resurrection and Ascension, the Authority and Infallibility of the entire Bible, etc. Have read that Luther, the great Reformer, bestowed a degree of D.D.D. on some preachers - Doctor of Divinity Devils! If he were alive today am persuaded he would award this degree to great numbers of our modern clergy.

On the back of the letter from this organization were quotations from about fifteen well-known Americans of the past. Whether these quotes were taken out of context and used differently from the purpose their authors had in mind, is indeed a question in some instances. However, if knowledge, time and space were at hand, many hundreds of other great and prominent Americans could be called upon to show that these people are very "unreasonable with their reasons." Their arguments are based on "natural reasons" - the only ones at their command. "Nature is pagan," says no less an authority than the great Reformer Luther. You "nature worshippers" would do well to consider this:

"Nature is pagan." Is not art involved to some extent?

To the organization and its members, whether you hear or forbear, may we call your attention to Words of the Great God who created you, in Whose hand is your breath, and Who shortly will close that Hand and bring you into judgment - "the heart in your bosom is a 'muffled drum" beating a march for you to the cemetery." *"It is appointed unto men once to die, and after this the judgment."* Repent while it is called today!

"Seest thou a man wise in his own conceit? There is more hope of a fool than of him." Prov. 26:12. *"He that trusteth in his own heart is a fool; but who walketh wisely, he shall be delivered."* Prov. 28:26.

"Cursed be the man that trusteth in man, and maketh flesh his arm, and whose heart departeth from the Lord, for he shall be like the heath in the desert, and shall not see when good cometh; but shall inhabit the parched places in the wilderness, in a salt land and not inhabited. Blessed in the man that trusteth in the Lord, and whose hope The Lord is, for he shall be like a tree planted by the waters, and that spreadeth out her roots by the river, and shall not see when heat cometh, but her leaf shall be green; and shall not be careful in the year of drought, neither shall cease from yielding fruit. The heart is deceitful above all things, and desperately wicked; who can know it? I, the Lord, search the heart, I try the reins, even to give every man according to his ways, and according to the fruit of his doings. As the partridge sitteth on eggs, and hatcheth them not, so is he that getteth riches, and not by right shall leave them in the midst of his days, and at his end shall be a fool." Jeremiah 17:5-11.

Christians, pray for the heathen; those who do not believe in the God of the Bible. Pray that God will give them to His Son, that their unbelief, pride, arrogance, covetousness, etc. might be "broken with a rod of iron, and dashed in pieces like a potter's vessel," and instead there might be.

"Repentance toward God, and faith in the Lord Jesus Christ."

November 27, 1963

† † †

The question is the opening words of the Second Psalm of the Bible, God Almighty's revelation of Himself to man. "The heathen are those who do not believe in the God of the Bible." They rage against God, and His Kingdom, seeking to overthrow their Kingdom by doing away with its Laws and Commandments. No kingdom or government can endure long when its laws are neglected, rejected, and not enforced. But God's Kingdom is an Everlasting Kingdom that shall not pass away, and men and devils who rage against it sooner or later are *"broken as with a rod of iron, and dashed in pieces like a potter's vessel!"*

"He that sitteth in the heavens shall laugh. The Lord shall have them in derision: then shall He speak unto them in His wrath, and vex them in His sore displeasure." Psalm 2:4, 5.

"He poureth contempt upon princes." Job 12:21, Psalm 107:40, and Daniel 4:17.

"He . . . bringeth the princes of the earth to nothing; He maketh the judges of the earth as vanity." Isaiah 40:23.

In our day and century, has not God laughted at, held in derision, spoken in His wrath, and poured contempt upon many a king, prince, or ruler? What about the late Czar and Stalin of Russia, the late Kaiser and Hitler of Germany, Mussolini, and other? And in this visitation has not most of the nations, including our own, had to drink of *"the wine cup of His wrath and indignation?"* We blame this man, and that, this nation and that, but the blame according to this message from God, lays at the door of those who rebel against His Commandments, seeking to get rid of their restraint! Elijah, the man taken to heaven without dying,

42

by-passing the grave, said to King Ahab: *"I have not troubled Israel; but thou, and thy father's house, in that ye have forsaken the Commandments of God. . ." "There is no peace to the wicked, saith my God!"*

There are some who are offended because this column calls attention to these truths from God's Book. "What do we have to do to stop these extreme ads?" writes some churchman, sending one of his own church ads that cries Peace, Peace, but takes no notice of the evil all around about to swamp us! "Extreme conditions" require "Extreme measures!" You can't catch and capture a lion that is loose with a net made to catch butterflies!

We suggest two ways effort might be made to stop these extreme ads: One is that you face squarely their contents, refuting and showing where they are wrong and in error. Flip the switch in a dark room, and instantly the light drives out the darkness. *"The lip of truth shall be established forever; but a lying tongue is but for a moment."* -Prov. 12:19. If there be untruth and lies in these articles you will do us and the public a noble service to expose them. Surely, you are not in favor of doing away with freedom of speech so long as it is carried on in a responsible way, with valid and authoritative reasons given for the opinions expressed. To silence one by force instead of debate and argument would be oppression! God's Word says: *"Surely oppression makes a wise man mad!"* Eccles. 7:7.

Hope you do not object to the assumption, or presumption, that you are a wise man? The other suggestion as to what to do to get these extreme ads stopped, is that you pray and call on your god for help! We think your god and ours is not the same! In the 18th chapter of 1st Kings there is the account of the testing of our God and another god, and we will still cling to Elijah's God!

Another letter has just come bitterly attacking this scribe for cowardice and other "little things" that are not likely to enhance our vanity. There is too much truth in this charge

43

for comfort. But we are ashamed of our entire "crop of cowardice," and sincerely hope to overcome and get rid of all of it. We confess to being afraid of "the faces of folks," more or less. In Jeremiah 1:8-17, and in Ezekiel 2:6, God warns the prophets against this kind of fear, and demands that they speak His Word to the people, *"whether they will hear, or whether they will forbear."* Christ speaking in Luke 12:4, 5 says: *"And I say unto you, my friends, be not afraid of them that kill the body, and after that have no more that they can do. But I will forewarn you whom ye shall fear: Fear Him which after He hath killed hath power to cast into hell; yea, I say unto you, Fear Him!"*

No doubt, when God told the prophets not to be afraid of "the faces of men," He also meant the "faces of women." Jeremiah being a bachelor, it is likely that the "faces of women" were a "greater fright" to him than those of the men! Some years ago I knew a man who owned and lived on "Cat Island" out from Charleston. He said the Island got its name from a man who named it in honor of his wife - he himself was a bachelor. The Bible does not say so, but tradition does, so I have heard, that the Prophet Isaiah was put to death by his own people by sticking him in a hollow log and then sawing it up in short pieces!

Someone has suggested that if this were true, the execution might have been devised by the ladies, after hearing his sermon regarding their pride, vanity, sin, and God's judgment upon them as recorded in Isaiah, chapter 3: 16-36. Due to lack of space, and cowardice, this sermon will not be quoted here, but suggest that you read it out of your own Bible, and Hear the Word of the Lord! In this connection, would also like to call attention to Deuteronomy 22:5, and suggest that this message of the Almighty come to you directly out of His Holy Book, and that you carefully consider Who is speaking and what He says, rather than the reception His Words get from men, and the "run of the mine" church members! This message is not part of the Jewish ceremonial law, but it has a permanent message in God's purpose concerning the distinguishing of the sexes, and the purity of the sexes for the protection and blessing of the home and family.

March 2, 1963

† † †

44

"Thus saith the Lord: Cursed be the man that trusteth in man, and maketh flesh his arm, and whose heart departeth from the Lord. For he shall be like the heathen in the desert, and shall not see when good cometh; but shall inherit the parched places in the wilderness in a salt land and not inhabited.

"Blessed is the man that trusteth in the Lord, and whose hope the Lord is. For he shall be as a tree planted by the waters, and that sreadeth out her roots by the river, and shall not see when heat cometh, but her leaf shall be green; and shall not be careful in the year of drought, neither shall cease from yielding fruit.

"The heart is deceitful above all things, and desperately wicked: who can know it? I the Lord search the heart, I try the reins, even to give every man according to his ways, and according to the fruit of his doings. As the partridge sitteth on eggs, and hatcheth them not; so he that getteth riches, and not by right, shall leave them in the midst of his days, and at his end shall be a fool." Jeremiah 17:5-11.

In the above we are told of the horrible wilderness and salt land of the "man who trusteth in man!" But below we are told of the blessing and happiness of those who "come out of the wilderness" - the would that truly "trusteth in the Lord, and whose hope the Lord is."

One Sunday morning over 40 years ago the gates of a jail in Atlanta, The Old Tower, opened up and the writer walked in - believe it or not, he went in voluntarily, oh, yes, he did! He went in with others to conduct a religious service for the guests, large numbers of whom registered the Saturday night just passed. Heard of a Doctor who was mending and sewing up some Colored patients who had been broken and cut up in a Saturday night party. He remonstrated with them about their violent and savage conduct, and got this reply: "Doctor, if you could be a 'nigger' just one Saturday night, you would not want to be "white folks" no more." Were much surprised to see how well dressed and refined looking

45

were many of the white guests, especially women and girls - Were you there?

Out of respect for The Creator's Acts and Providences, one part of this "hotel" was reserved for White guests and another part for Colored. One service was held for the White, and another for the Black. If this appraisal is correct, there was a much better spirit of worship in the Colored service than there was in the White. We figured this was accounted for by such Scriptures as *"God resisteth the proud, but giveth Grace to the humble,"* and *"He that humbleth himself shall be exalted, and he that exalteth himself shall be abased."* Just as the speaker finished his message to the Colored people, voluntarily and spontaneously someone in the audience "raised the song": "Didn't you feel happy when you come out of the wilderness leaning on the Lord who died on Calvary." As we recall, some of the words in this song were:

"Didn't you feel happy when you come out of the wilderness, come out of the wilderness leaning on the Lord? I'm leaning on the Lord, I'm leaning on the Lord, who died on Calvary. My hands looked new, when I come out of the wilderness, my feets looked new, when I come out of the wilderness a leaning on the Lord. I'm leaning on the Lord, I'm leaning on the Lord, didn't you feel happy when you come out of the wilderness leaning on the Lord who died on Calvary."

One of the party said that hearing those several hundred humble people sing that song was one of the most inspiring experiences of his life. Some might call it all emotion, but we judged it to be motion stirred up by the Spirit of God fulfilling His promise to give Grace to the humble, as they seemed to be moved by that spirit of the Publican who would not so much as lift up his eyes to heaven, but smote upon his breast crying: *"God be merciful to me a sinner."* No telling how many of those souls are now among "The Cloud of Witnesses" accompany about those who in faith and humility are waiting on the Lord for their "Advancement," and "fighting the good fight of faith," those who "got good religion and can truthfully sing "I'm going to trust in the Lord till I die."

It may be that song was born during slavery time in the heart and experience of some poor slave - but he got to be rich - who had a cruel master that "sold him down the river." In his bonds he heard the Gospel, The Good News of the Lord Jesus Christ who said:

"Come unto me, all ye that labour and are heavy laden, and I will give you rest. Take my yoke upon you, and learn of me; for I am meek and lowly in heart; and ye shall find rest unto your souls, for my yoke is easy and my burden is light."

As he heard and listened "The trumpet of the Lord sounded in his soul," and he said to himself: "I ain't got long to stay here, so steal away, steal away to Jesus." He did "steal away to Jesus," quit stealing from his master and others and kept on "stealing away to Jesus" until he came forth singing "Didn't you feel happy when you came out of the wilderness a leaning on the Lord who died on Calvary." Doubtless, he did not know his own background enough to realize just what a wilderness the Lord has used his temporary slavery to bring him out of: the "wilderness" of his former condition in the jungles of Africa with its frightful nightmare of darkness, ignorance, superstition, oppression, cruelty, and witchdoctor led devil worship. His relatively short period of physical suffering and slavery, even if he had a cruel master, was mighty small pay to be delivered from all that natural and spiritual darkness into the happiness of sins forgiven and some knowledge of God and His Son, the Saviour Jesus Christ, and the good hope of everlasting life where *"eye hath not seen, ear hath not heard, neither have entered into the heart of man the good things God hath prepared for them that wait for Him."*

God marvelously and miraculously delivered His people out of the slavery and oppression of the Egyptians, yet afterwards he permitted them to suffer hunger and thirst

47

and many privations to test and discipline them, and to teach them that *"Man cannot live by bread alone, but by every word that proceedeth out of the mouth of God."* When they continued to murmur and complain He became angry, and all that generation died "in the wilderness" and failed to get in the "promised land" except two, Joshua and Caleb. Murmurings and complainings at the Providences of God are great sins, especially for those who claim to be trusting Him and say:

"God is our refuge and strength, a very present help in time of trouble." However, if your hope for advancement is in man, man made governments and laws and organizations, etc., you might as well go ahead complaining when things don't go to suit you, grumble, and growl, and bite the hand God has provided for near a hundred years to feed you in providing work and a means of making a living. Get all the help you can and advance yourself as much as you can. God permitted the rich man destined for hell to be *"clothed in purple and fine linen and to fare sumptuously every day."*

This closing word is one I have heard from the Colored people: "You better mind, you better mind, God is going to set your sins before you some of these days." You better mind and leave it to the Almighty to correct and handle those whom you think do you wrong!

April 18, 1968

 † † †

Respecting God's Law

Division Three

Fox Book of Martyrs and John Bunyan's *Pilgrim's Progress* doubtless are second only to God's Book, *The Bible,* in producing and developing the greatness and blessings of the English speaking peoples. Bunyan advised his children to spend at least a few minutes every day in thinking of their own funeral - not to make them morbid or sad but rather that they might "be ready when it comes," and be able to look forward to it as a time of great victory. Many of those Martyrs that Fox tells us about found it so - we are told that some went even to cruel deaths rejoicing.

By the way, the weekly *DeKalb Tribune* recently has had answers regarding funerals from one of our County Funeral Homes. A few days ago the writer met a friend who operates a Funeral Home: Said I, "How many funerals will there be all over our nation today?" Said He: "About five thousand." "How many all over the world?" "Don't know, but a lot of folks!" Far be it from me to offend, but the thought occurred that in view of what is happening every day the folks that don't believe in the "death penalty" must be "crazy as a bed-bug!" - think that is much more considerate of them to say they are "crazy" than to tell such they are "devilish" - it was Satan, the Devil, you know, that told Mother Eve: *"Ye shall not surely die,"* Genesis 3:4.

If you want to get rid of the death penalty, capital punishment, may we suggest you do not fight it by passing human laws. God Almighty announced and established these laws in The Garden of Eden in the event of disobedience. Fight by announcing and preaching the atoning death of the Lord Jesus Christ. Face the facts concerning death. Adam and all men until the time of Noah lived about 900 years, or more, but they all died and returned to dust - one exception was a man named Enoch got to walking around with God Almighty and when 365 years old, one day he walked on off to Heaven with God. With the exception of Elijah, who was carried in a chariot of fire to Heaven in a whirl-wind, all the men of the following generations have died, including the names of those in today's papers! Fear I would be guilty of "Presumption" to try to get rid of the death penalty other than in the way God has provided. This writer interprets Deuteronomy 29:19-21 as saying God's Anger and Jealousy "shall smoke" against "presumptuous spirit."

The article in this column last week called attention to the judgment of God upon the nation of Israel, and King Saul's family, because of a "breach of promise," or broken vow: three years of famine, and the hanging of seven of Saul's sons! In the same Saturday it happened that the writer came across a true story about a hanging that will be profitable to those seeking to know "the will of God" and please Him regarding the controversy of "Capital punishment." It might be well for those who feel that their own present opinion is the "last word" in the matter to skip reading the following. It is quoted from the life story of the late Dr. R.A. Forrest, the founder and developer of Toccoa Falls Institute.

When Dr. Forrest was a teen-age boy he attended the

funeral of a neighbor boy several years older than he. On his return his grandmother called him to her rocker and asked him to sit down. "I want to tell you a story," she said, "and I don't want you to forget it." This is the story she told:

"A number of years ago a child was born to a young couple. They loved this baby boy dearly; in fact, the mother almost worshipped him. But when the child was still a baby, he grew very ill. In spite of all that the doctor could do, the fever continued to mount until he despaired of the baby's life. A Christian man, he called the young mother to him and said, 'I think God wants your baby.' 'What do you mean?' the Mother screamed. 'Do you mean my baby is going to die? I won't let him die! God can't have my baby!" 'Now, now,' the doctor reasoned, 'you should be very careful what you say. God knows better than we do. If it's His will that your baby die - Well, God's will should be done.' The woman turned blazing eyes to him, then looked down at the still form of her babe. Already the child seemed to be gasping his last breath. Suddenly she grabbed her baby out of his crib, held him up towards heaven, and shook him violently as she defied God: 'You can't have my baby! I won't let you have him! He's mine! He's mine! He will stay alive. I'm going to keep him!' Again she shook the child violently. Later the doctor said he didn't know whether it was the furious shaking, or what, but the baby began to breathe again, and from that moment was on the road to recovery. Richard, you have just come from that boy's funeral. He has always been an outlaw. He has broken his mother's heart again and again. He was hanged for murder on his twenty-first birthday!"

There is no telling how much influence this had upon Dr. Forrest's life. He was mightily used of God in his ministry to youth, teaching them "God wants your life," and urging them to "let Him have it." Great numbers responded to his call, and today many of them are scattered over this and other nations, telling this message to young and old: "God wants your heart, your life." The trouble with a lot of us is that we have promised Him our lives, but have never in reality "delivered the goods!"

If God wants the soul of the murderer sent back to Him, should we refuse and not let Him have it? Can't we trust Him with it? Christians are called to be "workers together with God." If God wants the soul of the child old enough to know the difference between right and wrong sent back to Him, if he murders, should we resist and rage against Him? *"Wilt thou disannul my judgment? Wilt thou condemn Me, that thou mayest be righteous?"* Job 40:8, *"He that seeks to save his life shall lose it, but he that will lose his life for righteousness sake shall save it"* so said The Lord Jesus Christ.

"Let judgment run down as waters, and righteousness a mighty stream." -Amos 5:24. God's judgment upon the murderer is the death penalty, and no satisfaction taken for his escape. Blood pollutes and defiles the land in God's sight, and it can be cleansed only by the blood of the one who shed it. Failure to carry out His command in this matter will cause the judgment to be transferred to another, and maybe "another!" *"Wherefore, sirs. . .I believe God, that it shall be even as it was told me."* -Acts 27:25.

The heathen rage because they are the enemies of The Kingdom of Heaven, the King of Eternity! *"O God, the heathen are come into Thine inheritance; Thy holy temple have they defiled. . ."* -Psalm 79:1. They can sing and pray "Hallowed be Thy Name, Thy Kingdom come, Thy will be done on earth as it is in heaven," and apparently enjoy doing so, and think they mean it. However, when it comes to literally obeying and establishing The Heavenly Kingdom Laws, The Moral Law, The Ten Commandments, and observing them in our daily conduct and commerce, frequently, if not most of the time, men are aroused to raging against them! God is not pleased with such an offering of worship! *"I hate, I despise your feast days . . . Take thou away from Me the noise of thy songs; for I will not hear the melody of the violes. But let judgment run down as waters, and righteousness as a mighty stream."* Amos 5:21-24.

"Why call ye me, Lord, Lord, and do not the things which I say?" Luke 6:46. Martin Luther, the great man of God of the 16th Century, said that if he had the gift of miracles, yet it were better to testify of his faith by obedience, than by working miracles! To avoid any confusion in the minds of some, please note the Martin Luther here referred to is the "mighty man of God" of the 16th century. There are men in more nations than one, and of more races than one, who have that name, or part of it, of whom it might be more appropriate to designate as "witch-doctors" rather than "doctors of divinity." - and we don't think this idle talk, but it can be backed up with many Scriptures from God Almighty's Book, *The Bible,* His infallible revelation of Himself to all men for all ages.

"The great desideratum in the council-chamber of the infernal king has always been how man's innate religious feeling should be satisfied, and yet God not be served. How could the heart be kept from God, the clamors of conscience be silenced, and yet the demands of any instinctive religious feeling be answered? The arch enemy of man's immortal hopes solved the problem. The solution appears in the cunning devices he has sought out to beguile unwary souls. He has varied his plans to suit times and circumstances, the condition of man, the progress of society, the character of human governments, and the condition of the human mind." Whoever it was that said that surely "knew his way around" in the spiritual world, in "The things of the Spirit." And he goes on to point out the devil's strategy down through the ages in solving this problem with remarkable success until he gets to the place where God says: *"Thus far, but no further."* But that is quite another story, and "The things of the Spirit are foolishness to the natural man."

"At that time Jesus answered and said, I thank Thee, O Father, Lord of heaven and earth, because Thou hast hid

53

these things from the wise and prudent, and hast revealed them unto babes. Even so, Father: for so it seemed good in Thy sight. All things are delivered unto Me of My Father: and no man knoweth the Son, but The Father: neither knowest any man The Father, save The Son, and he to whomsoever the Son will reveal him. Come unto me, all ye that labour and are heavy laden, and I will give you rest. Take my yoke upon you, and learn of me, for I am meek and lowly in heart: and ye shall find rest unto your souls, for my yoke is easy, and my burden is light." -Matthew 11:25-30.

August 2, 1969

† † †

"Man, when left to himself, is half fiend and half brute!" Bishop Hall.

"Man, when left to himself, is a motley mixture of the beast and the devil!" William Law.

The dread foes of man are not belligerent circumstances, but the riotous passions - the leopard of incontinence, the lion of violence, the wolf of avarice. Incontinence means "lack of restraint, especially undue indulgence of sexual passions; licentiousness, etc." Great nations and empires of history, as a result of this sin have rotted from within, decayed, perished. Is not our great land in danger of the same curse? "Chastity is driven away as an enemy by all men, like a snake!" Is not the "lion of violence" and the "wolf of avarice" back of and the cause of riots, strikes, etc.? It is said that a wolf is hungrier after food than before!

A man may foretell as plainly as can be what will become of us, if we grow indifferent and lukewarm in repressing evil. Make it a shame to see men bold in profaneness, and God will bless you. Be confident that our liberty and prosperity depend upon reformation - if not, what difference is there between a man and a beast?

Beware of making laws in the face of God - telling The

54

Almighty you will meet all His Dispensations, and stay things, whether He will, or no.

"God will curse me if I put personal interests above duty!" - Oliver Cromwell. (Consider this last statement, remembering Pontius Pilate: *"Suffered under Pontius Pilate"* because of conflict of interest!)

Devoutly thankful ought we to be for the gift of great and good men. They are God's noblest work - For nothing should the people of God more devoutly pray than that their great men may be good men. (If we had been doing that during the past few decades, do you reckon we would today have a Supreme Court such as is, one that has taken away from our schools and children God's Book, the Bible, and the Lord's Prayer? I think not. Or, we would have such men in authority over us that let them get by with it? I think not.) One honest statesman - one great, sanctified, devout Christian man in the Senate or Cabinet of a nation, or at its head - is worth more to a nation than all the riches of El Dorado, and is a surer defense than all her armies and navies!

Every young man should strive by the best possible improvement of his talents and opportunities, to make himself a great and a good man. This is a true and noble ambition. A great and a good man is the noblest work of God . . . strive then, my young friend, to fit yourself for the times in which you live.

God gives us preachers, teachers, and students that put "The study of their own hearts" above the study of their books. *"Search the Scriptures,"* for it is the mirror by which God reveals to us our hearts; *"For the Lord seeth not as man seeth; for man looketh on the outward appearance, but the Lord looketh on the heart,"* 1st Samuel 16:7.

"For all flesh is as grass, and all the glory of man as the flower of the grass. The grass withereth, and the flower thereof falleth away; but the Word of the Lord endureth forever. And this is the Word which by the Gospel is preached unto you." 1st Peter 1:24, 25.

"For all that is in the world, the lust of the flesh, and the lust of the eyes, and the pride of life, is not of the Father, but is of the world, and the world passeth away, and the lust thereof: but he that doeth the will of God abideth forever." 1st John 2:16, 17.

November 20, 1971

† † †

In the First Psalm He says the man is blessed that departs from evil in his walk, his stand, his sitting, and *"his delight is in the Law of The Lord; and in His Law doth he meditate day and night."* Have we a right to be heard and blessed on account of our efforts to meet and fulfill these conditions?

In John 6:44, etc., Jesus said, *"No man come come to me, except The Father which hath sent me draw him . . . And they shall all be taught of God. Every man therefore that hath heard, and hath learned of The Father, cometh unto me."* Have we put ourselves in position to be "taught of God" by Searching The Scriptures and meditating on His Word? It appears we are always "passing the buck" to The Almighty while in reality His Word "passes it to us!"

The Law is our School-master to bring us to Christ. The reason our Churches are so full of "dead wood and excess baggage" of folks who don't know what it is to be convicted of sin and made to see their lost condition by the power of The Holy Spirit, is that they are drawn into the Church and to Christ, as they think, by the precepts of men, the devices and wiles of the devil, and not by The School-master so "teaching them of the Father" that they are drawn by His power to The Son!

In the Second Psalm there is the opposite picture of the "Blessed Man." It shows us men raging and rebelling against God, and His Anointed, in order to break the bands and cast away the cords of His *"Thou shalt nots,"* His Moral

56

Law and Ten Commandments. So, instead of being blessed men and nations, we have God's curse poured out upon us; His laughter and derision, His wrath and displeasure that sorely vexes mankind.

A few hours ago we heard a broadcast telling of how our nation was becoming the laughing-stock of much of the world, which may indirectly reflect the laughter of The Almighty! *"He maketh the judges fool . . . He poureth contempt upon princes, and weakeneth the strength of the mighty."* Job 12:17, 21. And there are numbers of other such passages which reveal God's attitude and actions toward men and nations that forget His Laws!

We blame this man and that, this nation and that, but according to God's message here the blame lies at the door of all who refuse to depart from evil but choose to rage against The Almighty. Read Luke 13:1-5, and make the application. Elijah, the man taken to heaven without dying, bypassing the grave, said to King Ahab: *"I have not troubled Israel, but thou, and thy father's house, in that ye have forsaken the Commandments of God . . ."* 1st Kings 18:18.

"There is no peace, saith my God, to the wicked. Cry aloud, spare not, lift up thy voice like a trumpet, and show my people their transgression, and the house of Jacob their sin" - This is the last verse of the 57th Chapter of Isaiah, and the first verse of the 58th. We suggest you read the last two verses of this chapter, 13th and 14th, and consider whether there is any rage today against God's Fourth Commandment: *"Remember the Sabbath Day to keep it holy, etc."* Does it give any justification of those who claim to be of the Spiritual "House of Jacob" to use the Day for sports, working and making others work when not a case of necessity and mercy, traveling about the world, etc.?

Several years ago the writer was in a Sunday School class that had an "Open Forum" session and discussed the Observance of The Sabbath. The first man up expressed himself as in favor of Sunday baseball, thought it was o.k. with the Almighty, and so he attended. The second man up said if his brother wanted to rebel against the plain Command of God and his own Church, and stand up in the House of God on the Lord's Day and advocate rebellion, then go ahead, *"eat, drink and be merry, for tomorrow we die!"* As we recall this rather threw a "chill" on things and the discussion was discontinued.

A striking and impressive after-math of the affair was that the man "died on the morrow," figuratively speaking, for in two or three years he was in his grave! Have just stated the facts concerning the incident - you can take it on from here! Whether you consider Saturday or Sunday the right Sabbath, we would urge you to strive to observe it in obedience to and the spirit of these two verses, the last two of Isaiah 58. Especially note the marvelous promise of God: *"Then shalt thou delight thyself in The Lord; and I will cause thee to ride upon the high places of the earth, and feed thee with the heritage of Jacob thy father; for the mouth of The Lord hath spoken it."* "When the mists have rolled away, and we know as we are known," see if the reason America is now "riding upon the high places of the earth" is not because our fathers up to about 1920 honored God by a more or less strict observance of The Lord's Day, and we are enjoying the fulfillment of the above promise. However, we are now wasting and dissipating our rich heritage, "riding for a fall," and "great will be that fall" unless we repent, and *"bring forth fruit meet for repentance."*

In Colossians 2:16 God's Word says: *"Let no man judge you . . . of the Sabbath days."* We suggest that we "let God be the judge" and consider *"every word that proceedeth out of the mouth of God"* concerning The Sabbath. It seems that many have taken the above passage from Colossians, made a bat out of it, slugged and knocked out of the way about all the other passages in The Bible regarding the Sabbath! Jesus told the devil when the devil quoted one Scripture to destroy another Scripture he was "tempting God." Consider

58

the context of the passage, look back at verse 8 and you will observe that the Apostle is not striking at the Fourth Commandment, for if you break one of them you break them all, but he is warning us to *"Beware lest any man spoil you through philosophy and vain deceit, after the traditions of men, after the rudiments of the world, and not after Christ."* The Fourth Commandment is not after the philosophy of men and vain deceit, neither after the traditions of men, nor after the rudiments of the world, but it is after Christ, after God who spoke it audibly out of the fire at Mt. Sinai, and further put it on a table of stone, *"written with the finger of God."*

When the Apostle John had his wonderful and supernatural vison on the Isle of Patmos, he said: *"I was in the Spirit on The Lord's Day."* Likely he would have never had that vision if he had been "in swimming on the Lord's Day"; or had he been fishing on the Lord's Day - and he was a fisherman when he met Jesus; - or on the golf links, at the baseball game, sightseeing around the island, or maybe working the garden, trimming the lawn, hedges, etc. There is a time for these things, but it is not on the Lord's Day when we should major in *"sitting at the feet of Jesus and hearing His Words,"* and obeying His command: *"Learn of Me,"* or seeking to be *"taught of God"* that we might be *"drawn to Christ."*

"And this is life eternal, that they might know Thee the only true God, and Jesus Christ, whom Thou hast sent." John 17:3.

"Behold, I stand at the door, and knock; if any man hear my voice, and open the door, I will come in to him, and will sup with him, and he with Me." Rev. 3:20.

October 13, 1962

† † †

Concerning heathenish raging against morality and God's Seventh Commandment: *"Thou shalt not commit adultery:"*

In the first few verses of the eighth chapter of The Gospel of John we are told that Jesus early in the morning came into The Temple, sat down, began teaching the people when the scribes and Pharisees brought before Him a woman taken in the act of adultery, saying that Moses in The Law said such should be stoned, but what did He say? Jesus did not answer them, but stooped down and began writing on the ground, but when they continued asking He stood up and answered them and then stooped down again to write while the scribes and Pharisees left for a "cooler climate," their own consciences having made "that spot too hot!"

We are not told what the writing was and naturally, there has been much speculation about it, which probably is all right if done in reverence and for profit for The Scriptures say *"It is the glory of God to conceal a matter, but the honor of kings to search it out."* A good guess as to what was written might be: "Where is the man? Did you not say she was taken in the act?" Their saying that Moses said she should be stoned was only half of the story, for The Law said: *"they shall both of them die, both the man that lay with the woman, and the woman; so shalt thou put away evil from Israel."* Deut. 22:22 and Leviticus 20:10.

If we prefer the evil to the remedy it is because of ignorance, blindness, and unbelief of the eternal judgment and justice of The Almighty! Of course, Jesus, being God as well as man, knew where and who the man was: *"Thou God, seest me! . . . The eyes of God are in every place, beholding the evil, and the good."* So, Mr. Adulterer, Mrs. and Miss Adulteress, God knows who you are and where you are, whether the scribes and pharisees find you, or not: every one of us must give account of ourselves unto God! Beware, lest you "wrest" this Scripture passage and think Jesus indifferent to immorality and adultery! He did not abrogate God's Law of severity by saying to the woman *"Neither do I condemn thee, go and sin no more,"* but on the contrary,

He magnified the Law and made it honorable by taking upon Himself the woman's death penalty, and shortly afterwards, died a much more horrible death than stoning - crucifixion! It surely cost Him to say *"Neither do I condemn thee, go and sin no more!"*

"Where is the man?" might have been what Jesus wrote on the ground. Last week this column told a story about three men, A, B, and C, and how Mr. B had an illigitimate child in an Orphans' Home he failed to support. Mr. C said the Orphans' Home Superintendent was a friend of his and told him about this, not in gossip, but it came out as he was telling of some of his operational problems, and the information was kept confidential and not made the subject of gossip. However, after it was too late, Mr. C said there was one party he should have told about his knowledge of the affair, and that was the guilty party; he should have gone to him as a friend and tried to persuade him to correct his wrong, repent, make restitution as far as possible and support or help support the child, for God's Word says: *"If any provide not for his own, and especially those of his own house, he hath denied the faith and is worse than an infidel!"*

With The Almighty, it is Restitution, if possible, or Retribution! If you don't know the meaning of those words, it would be well for you to learn and meditate upon them! *"The Word of the Lord came unto me, saying, Son of man, hear the word at My mouth, and give warning from Me. When I say unto the wicked, Thou shalt surely die; and thou givest him not warning, nor speakest to warn the wicked from his wicked way, he shall die in his iniquity, but his blood will I require at thine hand. Yet, if thou warn the wicked, and he return not from his wicked way, he shall die in his iniquity; but thou hast delivered thy soul!"* Ezekiel 3:16-19.

Mr. Paul Smith had several fine cows and sold his preacher neighbor milk and butter. The preacher told his son to go over between Sunday School and Church time and get some butter for dinner. The boy loafed and killed time and his father was already preaching when he got back to Church, and the preacher being warmed up to his subject happened to cry out in his exhortation just as his son entered: *"What did Paul say?"* He said you were not going to eat any more of his butter until you paid for what you done got!''

Preachers, pay your debts, especially the debt due all the people due to your solemn Ordination Vows to proclaim The Word of God, and keep on telling us more of "what Paul said" such as *"He that don't provide for his own has denied the faith and is worse than an infidel."* We need to hear a lot more of that kind that affects our every day conduct; but also, don't forget to tell us what Ezekiel and the other prophets declared in *"Thus saith The Lord."* The first recorded words Christ spoke after His baptism were: *"Man shall not live by bread alone, but by every word that proceedeth out of the mouth of God"* - Matthew and Luke 4:4. It appears that we and our nation are in danger of losing our lives! In Jeremiah 23:21, 22 we read: *"I have not sent these prophets, yet they ran; I have not spoken to them, yet they prophesied. But if they had stood in My counsel, and had caused My people to hear My Words, then they should have turned them from their evil way, and from the evil of their doings."* First Timothy 5:8: *"But if any provide not for his own, and especially those of his own house, he hath denied the faith, and is worse than an infidel."*

What about failing to "provide for those of your own body!" Mr. C says he warned his friend B indirectly of his evil and profane ways but he don't feel comfortable about it since he may have failed to do his whole duty because he did not tell him he knew of this particular and awful sin in his life, and strive to get him to repent and make what restitution he could, at least to help in the support of the child. If he failed, he might make amends somewhat by warning you, if guilty.

We hear a great deal about our government supporting,

and probably thereby encouraging illegitimacy! Where are the men? If you are responsible for one or more of such children, you better hear "What Paul said," speaking for God Almighty, look them up and make as much Restitution as possible! The Law of God says *"both the man and the woman shall die!"*

Mr. Adulterer, Mrs. and Miss Adulteress, have you "Come to Jesus" for forgiveness, cleansing, and grace to *"go and sin no more!"* Christians, if the woman brought to Jesus by His and her enemies, got saved, how much more might some of the multitudes of guilty all about get saved and cleansed if brought to Jesus by the testimony and prayers of His and the sinners friends - *"Ye are my friends, if you do whatsoever I have commanded you."*

September 14, 1963

† † †

"Chastity is driven away by all men, like a snake!" Think this quote was spoken of the generation of Dante's times. There is cause to fear that it is fearfully true and applicable to our day and generation. Sitting on the "high seat" and "handling the reins" in this "drive," it appears there are some highly esteemed Clergymen and Educators! According to the statement of The Lord Jesus Christ, such should have *"a millstone tied about their neck and drowned in the depth of the sea!"* - And I would comment there ought to be apologies made to all maritime life in the sea for so Polluting Their Water!

The past few articles in this column have dealt with how Abraham, Friend of God, was the means of delivering some of his kinfolk out of Sodom just before the judgment of God fell, fire and brimstone falling from heaven, consuming the city and the inhabitants! Sins of sex obsession was one of the causes of the terrible judgment. The account of these things are written for our admonition and warning! And how we need to take heed to this warning! Being plagued with sex obsession sins and in danger of the curse of God falling upon our nation.

"Chastity is driven away by all men, like a snake!" The following is the historical testimony of a beautiful Christian young woman whose "chastity" all men failed to drive away: "Her chastity was impregnable" and she testified by life, suffering and death "Virtue alone could procure true happiness!"

In the year 249 A.D. Decius was the Roman Emperor. He became angered and enraged because of the amazing increase of Christianity which caused the heathen temples to be forsaken and the Christian Churches thronged. For these reasons he attempted the very extirpation of the name Christian. In general, his subjects, raging heathen, were ambitious to enforce the imperial decrees, and looked upon the murder of Christians as a merit to themselves. At that time under such conditions, there lived in Sicily a lady by the name of Agatha. She was remarkable for personal and acquired endowments, but most of all, for Christian consecration and piety. On account of her great beauty, the governor of Sicily, Quintian, fell in love with her, and made many attempts upon her chastity without success. In order to gratify his passion with greater convenience, he put the virtuous lady in the hands of Aphrodica, a very infamous and licentious woman. This wretch tried every artifice she could to win her to the desired prostitution; but found there was "nothing doing," for her chastity was impregnable, and she well knew that virtue alone could procure true happiness.

Aphrodica reported to the Governor the failure of all her efforts, who, enraged at being foiled in his design, changed his lust into resentment. When Agatha confessed she was a Christian, the Governor, being encouraged and supported by the Emperor's effort to wipe out Christianity, determined to gratify his revenge, as he could not his passion. Agatha was scourged, burnt with red hot irons, and torn with sharp hooks. She bore these torments with admirable fortitude.

Next, she was laid naked upon live coals, intermingled with glass, and then being carried back to her prison, she there died on Feb. 5th, 251 A.D. She lost her life, but not her virtue: "Her chastity was impregnable!"

October 25, 1969

† † †

This question is the opening words of The Second Psalm of The Bible, God Almighty's Book revealing Himself to man. "A heathen is one who does not believe in The God of The Bible." Is that you? If so, we suggest you "Search the Scriptures," asking God to reveal Himself to you personally. If you do so in sincerity and promise obedience *"in due season you will reap, if you faint not."*

The heathen that rage are identified as people who *"imagine a vain thing"* and support kings and rulers in their purpose and efforts to get rid of God's Moral Law and Ten Commandments, to break the Bands and cast away The Cords of restraint. The results of this rage: *"He that sitteth in the heavens shall laugh: The Lord shall have them in derision. Then shall He speak unto them in His wrath, and vex them in His sore displeasure."* Even if you have not *"the fear of The Lord"* in your heart and are without faith, can you think of any better explanation and reason for the present world conditions of crime, violence, rebellion, immorality, etc. than that the Creator is angry with His creatures for their evil and is vexing them in sore displeasure, and *"delivering them unto Satan for the destruction of the flesh,"* and we hope for their salvation?

"God is angry with the wicked every day . . . The wicked shall be turned into hell, and all the nations that forget God" -Psalms 7:11 and 9:17. Are you one of those offended by so much talk of the curse and judgments of God? If so, consider the verses in the 1st Psalm just before the question *"Why do the heathen rage?"* is asked: *"Blessed is the man that walketh not in the counsel of the ungodly, nor standeth in*

65

the way of sinners, nor sitteth in the seat of the scornful. But his delight is in the law of the Lord; and in his law doth he meditate day and night. And he shall be like a tree planted by the rivers of water, that bringeth forth his fruit in his season; his leaf also shall not wither; and whatsoever he doeth shall prosper. The ungodly are not so . . ."

In these first two of the Psalms God is saying again to man what He said to Moses: *"Behold, I set this day before you a blessing and a curse; A blessing, if ye obey the commandments of The Lord your God, which I command you this day; and a curse, if ye will not obey the commandments of The Lord your God . . . I call heaven and earth to record this day against you, that I have set before you life and death, blessing and cursing; therefore, choose life, that both thou and thy seed may live."* -Deut. 11:26-28 and 30:19.

Consider this, all of you who "delight in the Law of The Lord," and may we suggest that you meditate upon the following "day and night?" That respect and obedience to God's Tenth Commandment would bring a blessing to our land in quick order, and would do away with stealing, cheating, swindling, and graft; and respect and obedience to this Tenth Commandment would blot out race trouble, strikes, and various and sundry other assortments of strife, ill will, and devilment, for at the bottom of all these is "Coveting," that which God in His Providence has given to another, and therefore unbelief and rejection of promises of blessings, advancement, and prosperity in His own good time to those *"who fear God and keep His Commandments, which is the whole duty of man."*

Maybe you don't know what God's Tenth Commandment is? Quote: *"Thou shalt not covet thy neighbor's house, thou shalt not covet thy neighbor's wife, nor his manservant, nor his maidservant, nor his ox, nor his ass, nor anything that is thy neighbor's."* We submit for your meditation that it is The Church's business to teach men that "Coveteousness is idolatry," and that no coveteous person hath inheritance in the Kingdom of God, or in other words, according to the plain and often repeated teaching of The Bible they are lost and headed for hell and damnation! We further submit for your meditation that a genuine Christian is one who has entered into The New Covenant with God and The Spirit of God has written into his heart God's Commandments, including this Tenth: *"Thou shalt not covet anything that is thy neighbor's."*

Friend, maybe you need to go to an old-fashioned meeting where you have the opportunity to go up to the altar, kneel, pray, and ask God's people to pray for you for *"Repentance towards God, and faith towards The Lord Jesus Christ!"*

"Son of man, I have made thee a watchman unto the house of Israel; therefore, hear the word at my mouth and give them warning from Me. When I say unto the wicked, Thou shalt surely die; and thou givest him not warning, nor speakest to warn the wicked from his wicked way, to save his life; the same wicked man shall die in his iniquity; but his blood will I require at thine hand. Yet if thou warn the wicked, and he turn not from his wickedness, nor from his wicked way, he shall die in his iniquity, but thou hast delivered thy soul." Ezekiel 3:17-10.

"I have not sent these prophets, yet they ran; I have not spoken to them, yet they prophesied. But if they had stood in My counsel, and had caused My people to hear My words, then they should have turned them from their evil way, and the evil of their doings." Jeremiah 23:21, 22.

If you wish in your meditation on "coveteousness" to do a little home work, read Joshua 7th chapter, and note the terrible judgment of God upon the man, his family, and even his dumb animals, the man who confessed: *"I saw . . . I coveted . . . I took . . . I hid!' . . . And that man perished not alone in his iniquity."* Joshua 22:20. Or, you might meditate on the results to King Ahab and his wife of coveting and taking that which God had given to another; The dogs licked up the blood of the King, and the dogs ate the carcass of

Jezebel! 1st Kings 21. *"Take heed, and beware of covetousness,"* is the warning of Christ - Luke 12:15, etc.

May 25, 1963

† † †

The information herein concerning President Zachary Taylor is from the National Geographic magazine of January, 1965. He became President in 1849, but died after being in office only about a year and a half. He was the first Professional Soldier to occupy the White House. He lacked political experience, and never voted - probably a wise thing to do when you do not know what you are doing. Here is a man that never voted, and yet his fellow citizens voted him the highest office the country could give. He was so honored because of his ability, character, integrity and devotion to duty in the defense and protection of his country. U.S. Grant, who served under him, said years later: "No soldier could face danger or responsibility more calmly than he. These are qualities more rarely found than genius or physical courage."

Taylor treated bullets as trifles and never lost a battle. In the battle of Buena Vista, February 1847, General Taylor with 4,700 inexperienced invaders defeated the Mexican Army of 15,000 troops, and became a national hero. In February 1850, President Taylor held a stormy conference with several southern leaders who threatened secession. Taylor told the southerners that to enforce the law he would lead the army in person, and if they were taken "in rebellion against the Union," he would hang them with less reluctance than he had hanged deserters and spies in Mexico." It is believed that this unwavering stand delayed the Civil War 11 years. Ironically, his only son, Richard, served as a general in the Confederate Army.

"Never bothered to vote." We do not mention this to suggest that you do likewise, unless you do not know what

68

you are doing, but rather to point out that it is not the right to vote that exalts a man, but rather character, integrity, ability and performance. Or, to put it in Scriptural language: *"Righteousness exalteth a nation; but sin is a reproach to any people."* Proberbs 14:34. And surely this applies to the individual.

It has been said, and doubtless very true, that mobs are seldom or never guilty of atrocities till they are deluded and misled. Do we not need intelligent and principled voters? Are we striving to produce them? Can it be done by removing prayer and Bible reading from our public schools? And teaching that God is dead? *"Whatsoever a man soweth, that shall he reap!"* We have seen time and again of the communists announced plans to delude and mislead some of the most ignorant and immoral of our citizens into mobocracy in order to rend our government apart, and it appears they won the support of many of our "highly esteemed" in the government and colleges, churches, etc.

"For that which is highly esteemed among men is abomination in the sight of God!" We submit that the highly esteemed slogan: "Vote as you please, but please vote," falls in the category of things abominable to God; for if it pleases a man to vote for that which is evil, regardless of whether his pleasure is due to ignorance, coveteousness, immorality, lust, dishonesty, lack of integrity, or any other evil, the result in the long run will be a curse to the man, his family, state and nation: For he is responsible to God Almighty for his motives, acts, words, thought, and he will bring you into judgment to *"require your soul of you!"* In the 17th chapter of Jeremiah God hath spoken: *"I the Lord search the heart . . . even to give every man according to his ways, and according to the fruit of his doings."*

The right to vote has been won at exceeding great cost and sacrifice down through the centuries. The price paid is far above gold, silver, precious stones, etc. To hand this treasure over to the ignorant, immoral, dishonest, lacking character and integrity, might be likened to *"giving that*

which is holy to the dogs and casting pearls before swine!"
In the Sermon on the Mount, Christ said: *"Give not that which is holy to the dogs, neither cast ye your pearls before swine, lest they trample them under their feet, and turn again and rend you."* It appears that this Scripture has been largely fulfilled in our great nation by removing just about all good qualifications to protect the ballot and turning it over to the ignorant and immoral in many instances, and even to children in some states. And there are many records of some of them turning against the government to rend it apart.

Did you ever hear of the experiences of some of Atlanta's citizens; we refer to one whose place of business, a cafe, was "miserably messed up," and another being deprived of his business which had taken many years to build up? And these abominations were permitted, if not encouraged, or winked at, or "passed by on the other side" by many of our "highly esteemed" authorities in the political, educational, ecclesiastical and editorial world - highly esteemed Priests, Levites, Reverends (?), and Doctor Divines (?). The Bible says, *"Whatsoever things are pure, true, of good report . . . Think on these things."* God grant that some of these guilty "highly esteemed" may think on these things, turn, repent, and make what restitution possible, lest they be found abominable in the sight of God *"When He cometh to make up His Jewels,"* and require of men their souls! Is it well with your soul?

"To them that have shall be given," said Christ, *"But from them that hath not shall be taken away that which they have!"* If we fail to use and protect the right to vote, it will be taken away from us! Has it not already been taken away from many of the people of the world? They vote, but with instructions who to vote for!

May 28, 1966

† † †

70

The article in this column a week ago opened and closed with the request: "Please page Phineas." Doubtless all know the meaning of "page" in this instance is to find, locate and call for the whereabouts of an unknown party.

Phineas was a man who picked up a javelin and thrust it through the belly of a woman and a man - killing them both - who boldly and brazenly put on the sex act of adultery, regardless of its publicity - even before the rulers and highest authority of the nation!

Note God Almighty's reaction! Due to the nation's open and general disregard of God's Seventh Commandment, *"Thou shalt not commit adultery,"* God sent a plague upon the people and great numbers were dying. After 24,000 were dead, suddenly the plague stopped; it was immediately after Phineas used his javelin in judgment.

Hear what God said about this act, and of him:

"And the Lord spake unto Moses saying, Phineas the son of Eleazer, the son of Aaron the Priest, hath turned away my wrath from the children of Israel while he was zealous for My sake among them that I consumed them not in My jealousy, wherefore say, behold, I give unto him My covenant of peace; and he shall have it and his seed after him, even the covenant of an everlasting Priesthood, because he was zealous for his God, and made an atonement for the children of Israel." Numbers 25:10-13.

The terrible sins: of adultery, whoredom, fornication, homosexuality, etc. strike at the very source of life. The Home from which proceed society, the state, the nation, governments, and the Church! These great and horrible sins and enemies of mankind have brought down, destroyed and caused to perish many a great man, many a great nation, and great empire! The Bible is the Book of Life! God Almighty is its Author! Men and nations and churches who reject its message *"Perish!"* Consider God's message to mankind at the hand of Phineas: *"God was with him!"*

The writer is deliberately making this article short,

relatively speaking, with the hope and prayer that all who claim to be Christian will give much serious consideration to "What is written!" Have you done anything about "Paging Phineas" since this request was publicly presented to you? Has it caused you to give any serious thought to your own conduct, your own dress, your own eternal welfare, as well as that of your family, loved ones, the Church of God, our Eternal welfare - note and consider that portion of The Sermon on The Mount recorded in Matthew 5:27-30.

"Ye have heard that it was said by them of old time, 'Thou shalt not commit adultery; but I say unto you, that whosoever looketh on a woman to lust after her hath committed adultery with her already in his heart. And if thy right eye offend thee, pluck it out, and cast it from thee; for it is profitable to thee that one of thy members should perish, and not that thy whole body should be cast into hell, and if thy right hand offend thee, cut it off, and cast it from thee; for it is profitable for thee that one of thy members should perish, and not that thy whole body should be cast into hell.'"

Comment: Am quoting Revelation chapter 1, verse 5: *"And from Jesus Christ, Who is the faithful witness. . ."* In view of the immorality and unchastity and uncleanliness showing up every way one looks, and in view of the fact that I take it upon myself to be a Columnist claiming to "Preach the Word of God," do I not need to check upon: "My faithfulness as a witness?" *"Pray ye the Lord of the harvest, He will send forth laborers into his harvest."*

December 22, 1973

† † †

It appears that there are renewed and persistent efforts on the part of many to do away with God's Commandments for the disposition of murderers. In spite of the terrible and shameful record of the number of murders all over our land, yet there seems to be a great effort to make the country safe for the life of the murderer. It appears the promoters think they are doing God a service by rebelling against His plain and often-repeated commands in both The Old and New Testaments.

In John 8:44 Jesus Christ said the devil was a murderer from the beginning, and the father of lies! To pass judgment on myself: in view of the fact that Christ, God, said the devil was a murderer from the beginning, and that God commanded the murderer to be put to death at the hands of his fellow-man, if I were in favor of abolishing this Commandment of Almighty God, am inclined to believe the cause would be because it is also true of me what He said in the first clause of this same verse: *"Ye are of your father, the devil, and the lusts of your father ye will do,"* and I just can't bear the thought of "dear old dad" being hung or executed! Surely, natural affection would demand this attitude. But then you can figure out your own measure of devotion to this "old dad."

In our opinion there is a way one may probe into a fellow and find out if the devil is at home within: Just tell him his offering and worship are displeasing and not acceptable to God his Creator and if the devil is in "that old house," there is liable to be a flash of hell fire, maybe murder! There are a great number of incidents in the Bible upon which to base this opinion, and we will mention several prominent ones.

In the 4th Chapter of Genesis, we find God told Cain his offering was unacceptable, sin was the cause, and Cain got mighty mad, and *"his countenance fell!"* *"And Cain talked with Abel his brother; and it came to pass, when they were in the field, that Cain rose up against his brother, and slew him!"* The implication appears plain that Abel must have touched on the sore subject, Cain's unacceptable offering, and it cost him his life, he was murdered!

The Bible records a number of prophets that were killed by a King, or his agents, because the prophet told him his offering was sinful and unacceptable to God. Note the exception in the case of King David: The Prophet Nathan had to utter terrible denunciations against David: *"Thou art the man"* who committed adultery, murdered, broke up a home, etc.! Did David get angry and threaten to kill the Prophet? Rather, he expected death himself at the hands of God for his sins, and doubtless would have had, had he not been a man after God's heart in the way he repented and came clean! How is your score on repenting and making restitution? There comes to mind the names of several prominent men of whom it was reported they became angry when some of their fellow-churchmen undertook to show them their manner of life was offensive to both God and man, became angry and ran them out of their office or home!

Jesus Christ told the church and secular leaders of His nation: *"The publicans and harlots will get to heaven before you."* This message revealed the fact that the devil was in them, and he came forth roaring to crucify! Myriads of martyrs have had the same experience through the ages.

However, it was necessary for Abel to talk to Cain about his unacceptable offering in order to bear faithful witness: *"By faith Abel offered unto God a more excellent sacrifice than Cain, by which he obtained witness that he was righteous, God testifying of his gifts; and by it he being dead yet speaketh."* Hebrews 11:4. It was necessary for the prophets to cry out against the sins of the kings and people, even though some were killed; it was necessary for Nathan to denounce King David in order to lead him to repentance, life; it was necessary for The Lord Jesus Christ to tell the rulers of Church and State of their hypocrisy, false worship, blindness, etc., in order that all men might come to know *"the way, the truth, and the life,"* accept it and be saved.

All God's soldiers are not champions, said John Bunyan. However, if you truly are in God's Army, you are backing up with prayer and sympathy those who *"Cry aloud, spare not, lift up their voice like a trumpet, and show the people of God their transgressions and sins - that the wicked are like the troubled sea, when it cannot rest, whose waters cast up mire and dirt. There is no peace,"* saith my God, to the wicked. Isaiah 57:21, etc. If it were not such a dangerous thing, think I would tell all those seeking to abolish God Almighty's Commandment concerning disposition of murderers; your offering to God along this line is displeasing and unacceptable, and will bring a curse instead of a blessing! *"For I am the Lord, I change not; therefore, ye sons of Jacob are not consumed."* Malachi 3:6.

June 26, 1965

† † †

We quote excerpts from a letter received from a young lady - and I mean lady - from over in Alabama:

"I am a sixteen year old girl who reads your column every week in our local newspaper. It does me good to see someone who is strong and sure in his Christian faith to write such straight-forward articles in a time when the world has suddenly become so 'free' and lenient. In this letter, I'd like to show my reverence, fear and love in God and His Laws.

"I hardly know where to start. I guess the best way to start is to state the topic of my letter: sex. That's not surprising when you consider that that's about all that anyone talks about these days. First, let me say I am not a 'prude.' In fact, I consider myself a liberal Baptist. I am fed up and literally enraged at the events taking place in our world.

"Today, sex seems to be some kind of idol that demands worship. No longer is sex a private, personal gift from God. It is displayed and exhibited everywhere a person turns. Today, the young people say they have sexual 'freedom.' What they need to realize is that this 'freedom' is really the enslaving bonds of the devil.

"Young people no longer respect, fear, or obey God's rules concerning sex. They insist that as long as they are sincere, pre-marital sex is a beautiful experience. And

75

society is beginning to condone it. Today, people say that marriage is a terrible thing which destroys that relationship they have and marriage is not necessary. They feel that if they live together before, their marriage will be better. Sure, marriage is rough sometimes. But God will help if people will only obey Him and ask Him. If I remember correctly, God gave us marriage for the purpose that a couple could avoid fornication. Today the true, sacred meaning of marriage has been disregarded, because it is 'irrelevant.' To me, sex before marriage is sin, and no beautiful gentle words can mask that fact.

"And today, homosexuals are being treated like 'heroes.' I heard a man on television claim that just because a person is a homosexual, that doesn't mean that he can't be a Christian; in fact, many homosexuals are professed Christians. Where does this man get his Scripture to support his views? I get mine from Leviticus 20:13: *'If a man also lie with mankind, as he lieth with a woman, both of them have committed an abomination; they shall surely be put to death; their blood shall be upon them.'* With these words, I will drop dead in my tracks before I'll respect one of these people.

The young lady then comments quite a bit on the 'movies.' Have to say it has been so many years since I have been to one, am not in a position to comment.

"It is my opinion that all this sexual 'freedom,'' honest movies, and 'beautiful' rock festivals is part of a plan to ruin our country. By making claims that certain 'abominations' are now all right, and doing them, and then calling themselves the children of God, Communists are persuading others to fall into the devil's hands. I only hope that any fellow citizens will realize God's Laws and obey them.

"Thank you for taking time to consider my views. Sincerely."

"Where there is no vision, the people perish!" It appears that God has touched the heart of this young girl, and given her a true vision of the curse of sex corruption that has destroyed in the past multitudes of nations and civilizations; and now has brought our nation mighty low. Would God that

76

the rulers of our religious life, educational life, political life, business life, and all life had the vision granted this young lady! Where is that verse of Scripture - have forgotten where it is and will not stop to look it up now - that says: *"And a little child shall lead them!"* This is the eleventh month, and the eleventh time in this year 1970 that this column has called attention to what God says in Deuteronomy 17: 18-20: "Get yourself a Bible, keep it with you. Read in it all the days of your life that you may learn to fear the Lord your God and keep pride out of your heart, causing you to think you are better than your brethren; to keep from turning to the right hand or to the left from His Commandments and Statutes, to the end you and your children might live a long life and a blessed life in the land God gives you."

The young lady's letter inspires the writer to call attention to many, many Scriptures that support her position. Permit one further comment: In spite of the corruption every way one looks, she hears what God says in Leviticus 20:13: *"If a man lie with mankind, as he lieth with a woman, both have committed an abomination; 'they shall surely be put to death; their blood shall surely be upon them.'* With these words I will drop dead in my tracks before I will respect one of these people!"

Don't forget that the gentle Jesus Christ made a whip of cords and lashed some folks out of His Father's House; and in Mathew 23rd chapter, He called some others fools and fluid, *"Ye serpents, ye generation of vipers, how can ye escape the damnation of hell?!"*

December 3, 1970

Government /Rulers

Division Four

"There is no right to strike against the public safety by anyone, anytime!" Massachusetts' Governor Calvin Coolidge, and later United States' President Calvin Coolidge. Permit the writer to say that again, and another again!: "There is no right to strike against public safety by anyone, anytime!" Amen and Amen!

"Ye are My witnesses," saith the Lord God Almighty to His people in both the Old and New Testaments! Amen and Amen!

The writer found the above quotation in March 26 *DeKalb New Era* in the column *The Passing Scene,* written by Mr. Joseph H. Baird: Thank you, sir!

Other information found in this Column is about as follows: Governor Coolidge called out the Massachusetts militia to maintain peace and order in Boston, and the police strike was ended quickly. Shortly afterward the 1920 National Convention nominated him as their Vice-President

Candidate. The death of President Warren G. Harding in the summer of 1923 opened the doors of the White House to Coolidge, and he remained there until March 4, 1929, having refused for another term by his famous "I do not choose to run" statement.

We suggest you get Mr. Baird's Column, read and meditate upon it. We quote about a couple of paragraphs from the middle of the Column: "So the basic question is whether Calvin Coolidge was right when he declared "There is no right to strike against the public safety by anyone, anytime." It is this Columnist's personal conviction that he was right!" Amen, and Amen!

The first article in this column in January, in February, in March, and in April of this year calls your attention to a message from God to His People in the last part of the 17th chapter of Deuteronomy. It was spoken to the Ruler - and we suggest it is very appropriate and applicable to everyone that sincerely strives to rule himself; rule his family and children; rule his servants; and whoever and whereever he has duty and responsibility. In plain and simple language here is what the Almighty says: Get yourself a Bible. Keep it with you. Read in it all the days of your life in order to learn to *"fear then Lord your God;"* to keep pride out of your heart and thinking you are better than your brethren; to keeping you from turning aside from God's Commandments and statutes to the right or left; and to the end you and your children might live a long time in the earth. How did you do with these orders the first three months? Try and do better during April.

The object of this article is to call your attention to what The Almighty says to us: His Creatures! If you do not believe in the "death penalty" you sure are "out of place" in a genuine Protestant Church! Would advise such to get out and resign without delay! Among the first things God said to Adam and Eve in the beginning was *"Obey, or Die! Perish!"* In the days of Noah everybody on the Earth perished except Noah and family! Inasmuch as most folks up to Noah's time lived about 900 years, it has been estimated that there might have been around two hundred billion people that perished in the flood! Consider Sodom and those who perished by fire, and multitudes of other great cities and civilizations - and today's funeral notices!

In closing, let me call your attention to a passage in God's Word that this writer believes foretells the death of "strikers!" It is the 13th chapter of the book of Romans: Consider its message: It is spoken to "Every Soul" as you will notice in the word number two and three in the first verse of this 13th chapter, it warns of resisting and not being "subject to the higher power," Government Powers Ordained of God, Ordinances of God: *"And they that resist shall receive to themselves damnation!"* This writer does not want to hinder you from getting more money and better pay, but he sure does want to see you avoid Eternal Hell!

"And when the King came in to see the guests, he saw there was a man which had not on a wedding garment: and he said unto him, Friend, how camest thou in hither not having a wedding garment? 'And he was speechless.' Then said the king to the servants, bind him, hand and foot, and take him away, and cast him into outer darkness: there shall be weeping and gnashing of teeth, for many are called, but few chosen!" Matthew 22:11-14.

February 20, 1971

† † †

"The Lord is well pleased for His righteousness' sake; He will magnify the law and make it honorable." So spake the Prophet Isaiah when in vision "he looked afar off" and saw the Glory of Christ's Kingdom, chapter 42:21. God was well pleased for His Righteousness sake, and that righteousness was manifested and revealed by Magnifying and making Honorable God's Law.

"How forcible are right words," said Job in chapter 6:25.

81

Consider the Right and Forcible words in the following concerning "Authority!"

"What is the meaning of Authority? By Authority we mean an unquestionable, unconditional power. An Authority is Absolute! When we stand before it there is no possible appeal! To speak of 'relative authority' is like speaking of a 'square circle!' It is a contradiction of terms. There is no appeal from authority; it demands unqualified obedience!

"From this it follows: that there can be only one authority, the authority of God! God created the world and man and He rules in sovereignty over all: *The Most High ruleth in the kingdom of men, and giveth it to whomsoever he will.*" Daniel 4:17. His holy will is the law of human life.

"But the Bible also teaches that God has delegated some of His Authority to certain men - first to parents; then to magistrates. When they exercise their Authority under obedience to God, they represent God Himself, and to obey them is to obey God. It would be easy to set forth that this is the teaching of The Bible . . ."

"The teaching of The Bible with regard to parental and majesterial authority throws light on the fact that authority is given and cannot be chosen. We do not choose our parents; we do not choose the country in which we are born. When we are born into the world, our parents, our country and its rulers are given to us and cannot be evaded or avoided." Dr. David Hedegard.

With this introduction of the subject of Authority, we are quoting from the Article that was in this Column on May 9, 1966: Last week's article in this Column reported that a letter came asking: "Why do you rage? Why do you revile? Why do you spread hatred and discord?" And, another letter came from our great seat of learning, Athens, likening the writer to Hitler. It could be very profitable to all of us to give consideration to whatever it is that inspires speech, writing, conduct and manners of life. Love for Lucifer's dear daughters, Pride, Avarice, Fraud, Lust, Simony and others doubtless inspire the natural man whose heart has not been "touched by God." Do you seek to "Draw near to God" as He invites us to do, and strive to get close enough for Him to "touch your heart?"

There was a picture on the front page of *The Atlanta Constitution* for March 29th showing two policemen bodily carrying out of one of the Government buildings a "demonstrator." That was in Washington, seat of doubtless the most powerful Government in the world. I thought I saw in that picture "unmitigated anarchy!" My reaction was one of shame, shame for my country, shame for our Government, and those in authority, and shame for all our citizens as they and the rest of the world behold the spectacle of one man running over the majesty and power of this great and God blessed nation of near two hundred million people. Ought not the voice of authority of this great nation been sufficient to move the man out of a government building without having to call upon two policemen to pick him up and carry out to get obedience! Not only did the man defy and make himself more important than the majesty and power and law of this great nation, but also his acts tended to lift himself up and be more important than God Almighty Himself, who has commanded us to submit and obey the laws of human governments which He has ordained that there might be law and order and not confusion here below! We are permitted to disobey only in cases where we are called upon to disobey God Himself; but even then we are to submit to the consequences - consider Christ Jesus and His crucifixion! We are permitted to flee the consequences if we can: *"When they persecute you in one city, flee to another."*

The man who likened this writer to Hitler has put a notion in my head upon which I will comment: How would I handle "demonstrators" who defy the law of a city, county, state, or nation? I would see to it that they understood how and where they could petition the government to seek redress of what they considered wrongs, if done in a quiet and orderly way. I would also see to it that they understood rejection and

83

disregard of Authority, orders of government representatives, police, judges, etc., would not be tolerated. If a man was ordered by the police or some government authority to move on and move out, and he refused and defied the order, he would be given a minute or so to obey. If he remained in rebellion orders would be to shoot him as if a mad dog, and when he is dead, bury him in the dog pound - unless the dogs raised too big a howl, for decent dogs should not have dirty dogs shoved on them. If the decent dogs raised too big a howl, would see what could be done in the "ass cemetery." Remember, I am supposing that I had the power in this land that Hitler exercised in Germany for many years - have been accused of being like Hitler! Are we not now putting up more and more with the vile and devilish criminals usurping individual or gang authority to steal, kill, rape, and no telling what else? There is a God in the Heavens. There is a Heaven, and there is a Hell, and after this life we will go to one place or the other: *"Blessed are they that do his commandments, that they may have a right to the tree of life, and may enter in through the gates of the city. For without are dogs, and sorcerers, and whore-mongers [better check up on your sex conduct], and idolaters, and whosoever loveth and maketh a lie"* - so speaks the Risen and Glorified Christ Jesus in Revelation 22: 14, 15.

May 11, 1967

† † †

Concerning "Police Brutality!" Every good citizen should be much concerned and do all he can to put a stop to it. We are of the opinion it would be stopped or there would be very little, if any, if a lot of folks would cut out acting like "brutes" and "beasts." Bishop Hall and William Law were great, and good, and learned Christians of about the time of the Wesley's and Whitfield. The former said: "Man, when left to himself is half fiend and half brute," and the latter said: "Man, when left to himself is a motley mixture of the beast and the devil!"

It is the duty of the police to round up and handle brutes, beasts, and other wild animals that get loose and endanger the life and possessions of law-abiding citizens. Folks, who in their conduct and relations with their fellow-men act like gentlemen and ladies probably have only a 100 to 1 chance of experiencing "police brutality." Even if one is not a gentleman or a lady, in this case it might be advisable and pay off to be hypocritical and try to act the part.

Hear what God Almighty says in 1st Peter 4:15-19: *"But let none of you suffer as a murderer, or as a thief, or as an evildoer, 'as a busybody in other men's matters.' Yet, if any man suffer as a Christian, let him not be ashamed; but let him glorify God on this behalf. Wherefore let them that suffer, according to the will of God commit the keeping of their souls to Him in 'Well doing,' as unto a faithful Creator."* Be careful not to act "beastly and brutish." Whatsoever a man soweth that shall he also reap."

"A man may foretell as plainly as can be what will become of us, if we grow indifferent and lukewarm in repressing evil. Make it a shame to see men bold in rebellion and disregard of law and order, and God will bless you. Be confident that our liberty and prosperity depend upon reformation - if not, what difference is there between a man and a beast?"

"Because sentence against an evil work is not executed speedily, therefore the heart of the sons of men is fully set in them to do evil!" Ecclesiastes 8:11.

The great Protestant Christian Evangelist of the past generation, Billy Sunday, in one of his sermons told this story about a "speedy execution:" "I'll tell you, I was never more interested in my life than in reading the story of an old Confederate Colonel who was a stickler for martial discipline. One day he had a trifling case of insubordination. He ordered his men to halt, he had the offender shot. They dug the grave and he gave the command to march, and they had stopped three minutes by the clock!'' Speedy - is it not so? My guess would be that there was no more trifling or serious insubordination in his command. Any kind of insubordination might result in the loss of a battle, the loss of the war, the loss of liberty, and slavery in its place. Is it not frightening that today we behold the spectacle of our police officers, who represent the "majesty of the law,'' not only being resisted, stoned, etc., but a year or so ago several were hand-cuffed and murdered? *"Because sentence against an evil work is not executed speedily, therefore the heart of the sons of men is fully set in them to do evil."* Isaiah 42:21 prophesying of Christ says: *"He shall magnify the Law, and make it honorable."* It appears to us the old Confederate Colonel had that attitude towards law and discipline.

Mr. Sunday's sermon in which he told this story, was concerning the victorious Syrian General Naaman, found in the 5th chapter of 2nd Kings. The text was: *"He was a mighty man of valor, but he was a leper."* Thinking we need some preaching today like Mr. Sunday's, we quote: "Leprosy is infectious. And so is sin . . . Some men ought to be hurled out of society; they ought to be kicked out of lodges; they ought to be kicked out of churches, and out of politics, and every other place where decent men live and associate . . . listen to me! Bad as it is to be afflicted with physical leprosy, moral leprosy is ten thousand times worse. I don't care if you are the richest man in town, and the biggest tax-payer in the county, the biggest politician in the district, or the state. I don't care a rap if you carry the political votes of Pennsylvania in your vest pocket, and if you can change the vote from Democratic to Republican in the convention - if after your worldly career is closed my text would make a fitting epitaph for your tombstone and obituary notice in the papers, then what difference would it make what you had done - "He was a great politician, but 'He was a leper!' What difference would it make?''

Looking across the centuries of the experiences of The English peoples, the Historian, Terry said: "The lapse of church discipline was a certain symptom of social and political anarchy." It appears that we now have church, social, political, and just about all other kinds of anarchy!

Generally speaking, the churches of today are not going to discipline you: Do it yourself, the soul you save may be your own, or the souls of your family and loved ones. In view of the vows you made to God when you joined His Church, judge your own self as to the manner you have neglected or failed to keep them. Sentence yourself to "Repentance towards God, and faith towards The Lord Jesus Christ." Execute the sentence "speedily!" Ten righteous people would have turned aside the storm of fire and brimstone that fell upon Sodom and Gomorrah!

September 17, 1966

† † †

God's message to us in the Second Psalm says the heathen are the kings, the rulers, and people who imagine a vain thing and support them in their effort and rage to get rid of the restraints of His Moral Law and Ten Commandments placed upon man in order to keep him from destruction in time, and in eternity. The Psalm also reveals that such folks are held in "Contempt of Court" by "The Judge of all the earth." Punishment in this life results in "Divine Contempt" for man: *"He poureth contempt upon princes - maketh the judges fools."* Job 12:21, 27. The results of The Divine Contempt upon princes and judges for the people and the nations are vexation, confusion, fear, crime, violence, robbery, rape, etc. and more or less anarchy in our most important institutions: The Home, the source of human life; The State, whose duty it is to keep the peace, law and order; and The Church, whose duty it is to teach morals, instruct in wisdom and righteousness, and "The fear of The Lord." Are there any evidences of Divine

Contempt in our country and world today? Unless we be converted, turn, repent and bring forth fruit worthy of repentance, punishment for Divine Contempt in the life to come is the wrath and curse of God eternally. The barren and unfruitful tree was cursed, it withered, and doubtless cut down for the fire. Thank God we don't have to wait for the Church to repent, for Christ said: *"Behold, I stand at the door, and knock; if any man hear my voice, and open the door, I will come in to him, and will sup with him, and he with me."* Rev. 3:20. What goes on round about us in the Church need not affect our individual relations with God. Neither do we have to wait for the home folks, and the state, to repent, for it is an individual matter and responsibility. "No man lives to himself," however, and what we do or fail to do affects others.

What favorable response there has been to the articles in this column have had mostly one common note running through them. They seem to say in one way or another: "Keep it up." May we urge and suggest that all who approve of them generally, or can say "Amen" that they please pray earnestly, regularly, definitely, and persistently, that God would convert the heathen. In this Psalm after saying: *"Yet have I set My King upon My holy hill of Zion,"* God also says: *"Ask of me, and I shall give Thee the heathen for Thine inheritance."* Pray especially for the "Unbelieving heathen" and clergy who have gotten into God's inheritance, The Church, "crept in unawares;" those attacking The Word of God, The Deity of Christ, His Virgin Birth, Miracles, The Resurrection, etc. - "The woods are full of them!" Such heathen have just about usurped the top positions and authority in our great and beloved Protestant Denominations, and The Church is in captivity again, another Babylonian captivity! *"For the leaders of this people cause them to err; and they that are led of them are destroyed."* Isaiah 9:16. (Verse 17 following says: *"Therefore The Lord shall have no joy in their young men."*

Have just read in the papers of a young man in a nearby

town who shot to death his foster mother, who had been "too good to him." Have you ever read in God's Word where He told His people to "get rough" with old and young two-legged devils. The devil "was a murderer from the beginning," so said the Lord Jesus Christ in John 8:44. And it was in this place where He told the Church leaders of that day "the devil was their father!" If we don't break these criminals, they will break us, our homes, our state, and our nation! God makes us men! "Search the Scriptures" and you will find that one reason, if not the main one, that God at times "cuts off the righteous with the wicked" is because the righteous refuse to resist and fight the devil and put evil away from us! *"Curse ye Meroz,"* said the angel of the *Lord, curse ye bitterly the inhabitants thereof; because they came not to the help of the Lord, to the help of The Lord against the mighty."* Judges 5:23.

Also, in the last chapter of the Book of Judges, there is the account of most of the inhabitants of a city being cut off because they refused, or neglected, going to war to put down and avenge the evil of adultery and rape!) Pray, all you who can sincerely do so, that God would give to His King in true repentance these apostate clergy and heathen mentioned above, to the end that their unbelief might be *"dashed in pieces like a potters vessel, broken as with a rod of iron, kings and rulers will be wise, the judges of the earth instructed to Serve the Lord with fear, rejoice with trembling; kiss the Son lest He be angry, and perish from the way when His wrath is kindled but a little."*

Consider the striking contrast in the last few verses of the 8th chapter of Romans with the first few of the 9th. In the former The Apostle Paul seems exalted to heaven in his rejoicing in Christ for himself and the faithful Christians; and then almost immediately he plunges into the depths of sorrow and grief: *"I say the truth in Christ, I lie not, my conscience also bearing me witness in the Holy Ghost; that I have great heaviness, and continual sorrow in mine heart. For I could wish myself accursed from Christ for my brethren, my kinsmen according to the flesh . . .* "It is awful, it is terrible, it is horrible to even meditate upon those *"highly esteemed among men being an abomination"* to the Almighty, and headed for His wrath and curse - and the time so short - in the fires prepared for the devil and his angels, weeping, and wailing, gnashing of teeth, and no rest day or night eternally!

"Men ought always pray, and not to faint." - Luke 18:1.

"I said not unto the house of Jacob, seek ye me in vain." Isaish 45:19.

"The effectual fervent prayer of a righteous man availeth much . . . Brethren, if any of you do err from the truth, and one convert him; let him know, that he which converteth the sinner from the error of his way, shall save a soul from death, and shall hide a multitude of sins." James 5: 16, 19, 20.

February 16, 1963

† † †

God In History

Division Five

(The following quotation is from *The War Cry*, Salvation Army paper. Do not know the date, but think it was in the early 1940's. We are taking the liberty of quoting it on account of the statement at the close of the piece: "Translated for, 'All the World' by Major Clara Becker.")

"One of the strangest experiences in my life is connected with the war," says Nordenberg, an eminent engineer in Finland. I offered my services to the government and was appointed an officer in Gen. Mannerhelm's army. It was a terrible time. We besieged the town. It had been taken by the Red Army and we re-took it. A number of Red prisoners were under my guard. Seven of them were to be shot at dawn on Monday. I shall never forget the preceding Sunday. The seven doomed men were kept in the basement of the town hall. In the passage my men stood at attention with their rifles.

The atmosphere was filled with hatred. My soldiers were drunk with victory and taunted their prisoners, who swore as much as they could and beat the walls with their bloody, bleeding fists. Others called for their wives and children who were far away. At dawn they were all to die. We had the victory; that was true enough, but the value of this seemed to diminish as the night advanced. I began to wonder whether there did not rest a curse on arms whichever side used them. Then something happened; one of the men doomed to death began to sing! 'He is mad!' was everybody's first thought. But I had noticed this man, Koshkinen, had not raved and cursed like the others. Quietly he had sat on his bench, a picture of utter despair. Nobody said anything to him - each was carrying his burden in his own way and Koshkinen sang, rather waveringly at first, then his voice grew stronger and filled out, and became natural and free. All the prisoners turned and looked at the singer who now seemed to be in his element!

> Safe in the arms of Jesus, safe on His
>   Gentle breast.
> There by His love o'er shadowed,
>   Sweetly my soul shall rest.
> Hark, 'Tis the voice of angels, borne in
>   A song to me,
> Over the fields of glory, over the
> jasper sea.

Over and over again Koskinen sang that verse and when he finished everyone was quiet for a few minutes until a wild-looking individual broke out with "Where did you get that, you fool? Are you trying to make us religious?" Koshkinen looked at his comrades and his eyes filled with tears. Then he asked quietly: 'Comrades, will you listen to me for a minutes? You asked me where I got this song? It was from the Salvation Army. I heard it there three weeks ago. At first I laughed at this song, but it got me. It is cowardly to hide your beliefs; the God my mother believed in has now become my God also. I cannot tell you how it happened, but I know it has happened. I lay awake last night and suddenly I felt that I had to find The Saviour and to hide in Him. Then I prayed - like the thief on the Cross - that Christ would forgive me and cleanse my sinful soul, and make me ready to stand before Him whom I should meet soon. It was a strange night,' continued Koshkinen. ''There were times when everything seemed to shine around me. Verses from The Bible and The Song Book came to my mind. They brought a message of the crucified Saviour and the blood that cleanses from sin and of the Home He has prepared for us. I thanked Him, accepted it, and since then this verse has been sounding inside me. It was God's answer to my prayer. I could no longer keep it to myself! Within a few hours I shall be with The Lord, saved by His grace.'

''Koshkinen's face shone as by an inward light. His comrades sat there quietly. He himself stood there transfixed. My soldiers were listening to what this Red revolutionary had to say, 'You are right, Koshkinen,' said one of his comrades at last. 'If only I knew that there is mercy for me, too! But these hands of mine have shed blood and I have reviled God and trampled on all that is holy. Now I realize that there is a hell and it is the proper place for me.' He sank to the ground with despair depicted on his face. 'Pray for me, Koshkinen,' he groaned, 'Tomorrow I shall die and my soul will be in the hands of the devil!' And there these two Red soldiers went down on their knees and prayed for each other. It was no long prayer, but it opened heaven for both, and we who listened to it forgot our hatred. It melted in the light from heaven, for here two men who were soon to die sought reconciliation with God. A door leading into the invisible stood ajar and we were entranced by the sight. Let me tell shortly that by the time it was four o'clock all Koshkinen's comrades had followed his example and had begun to pray. The change in the atmosphere was indescribable. Some of them sat on the floor, others talked of spiritual things. The night had almost gone and day was dawning. No one had had a moment's sleep. 'Sing the song once more for us, Koshkinen,' said one of them. And you should have heard them sing! Not only that song but verses and choruses long forgotten came forth in their memories as buds in the sunshine. The soldiers on guard united their voices with them.

The town clock struck six. How I wished I could have begged for grace for these men, but I knew this was impossible. Between two rows of soldiers they marched out to execution. One of them asked once more to be allowed to sing Koshkinen's song. Permission was granted. Then they asked to die with uncovered faces - and with hands raised to heaven they sang with might and main: 'Safe in the arms of Jesus, Safe on His gentle breast.' When the last lines had died out, the lieutenant gave the word "Fire!" and the seven Red soldiers had fought their last fight. We inclined our heads in silent prayer.

"What had happened in the hearts of others I do not know; but so far as I was concerned I was a new man from that hour. I had met Christ in one of His lowliest and youngest disciples and I had seen enough to realize that I, too, could be His. *The Lord looketh from Heaven; He beholdeth all the sons of men.* "Psalm 33:13. Jesus said: *"I am the resurrection and the life; he that believeth in Me, though he were dead, yet shall he live."* -John 11:25.

Note: The above has been in this column twice before, on Jan. 18, 1964, and again on Christmas Day, Dec. 25, 1965. The experiences of these men would never have happened if the "death penalty" sentence had not rested upon their heads, nor if they had failed to believe the death penalty was **real.** They would have died, but not in peace and rejoicing in the Salvation of The Lord Jesus Christ!

Will any soul ever have the experience of peace and rejoicing that these men had if he does not believe that God Almighty's "Death Sentence" rests on his head because of sin? *"Seek ye the Lord while He may be found, call ye upon him while He is near; Let the wicked forsake his way, and let the unrighteous man his thoughts; and let him return unto the Lord, and he will have mercy upon him; and to our God, for He will abundantly pardon.* '' Isaiah 55:5-7.

December 30, 1967

† † †

Are you concerned and troubled about the great increase in lawlessness? Violent hold-ups, stealing, cheating, swindling, murder, rape, adultery, and other kinds of violence and anarchy! At times these things strike mighty close to our homes, loved ones, and friends! And they will get closer unless some change is made.

In the days of Noah, God destroyed the earth and everything wherein was the breath of life excepting the eight members of Noah's family, and the animals he kept alive in the Ark according to God's orders. The cause of this judgment was for causes similar to the ones that exist today: *"Man corrupted God's way on the earth, and the earth was filled with violence.* '' With good reasoning and logic, it has been estimated there might have been four hundred and eighty billion people that perished - over a hundred times as many as now living on the earth! (We digress to again suggest in this column man had better leave the matter of "birth control" in the hands of The Almighty, where it belongs, lest He say of us what He did of one man: *"It had been good for that man if he had not been born!"* Matthew 26:24. We remind you that God says in His Word *"If we fear God, and keep His Commandments, the whole duty of man,"* God has engaged Himself to bless the "fruit of the womb" and take away sickness; also to bless the fruit of the ground in order there might be plenty to eat. Hear the words of the Man after God's Heart: *"I have been young, and am now old; yet have I not seen the righteous forsaken, nor his seed begging bread.*'' Psalm 37:25. Of course, however, unbelief and disobedience makes null and void these precious promises. It appears there is very little confidence in them today, with most of us!

"My Spirit shall not always strive with man . . ." The Almighty announced in the days of Noah, and sent the flood. Gen. 6:3. It may be the time has about arrived when His Spirit will quit striving with you and me! Until that time comes we would do well to remember that Christ told us to do some striving: "Strive to enter in at the strait gate; for many, I say unto you, will seek to enter in, and shall not be able!" Luke 13:24. We can strive to be "faithful unto death" to the vows made to God in joining His Church - "When thou vowest a vow unto God, defer not to pay it; for He hath no pleasure in fools; pay that which thou hast vowed." Eccles. 5:4. We should strive to be faithful in our testimony that The Bible is the Word of God, and be careful not to get in the "broad way" of unbelief of those who both in and out of the Church attack the Bible. We should strive to be faithful in our testimony that the Ten Commandments reveal the morality, righteousness, and very character of God; and strive to be workers together with His Holy Spirit in writing these Commandments in our hearts to the end we may accomplish the whole duty of man, which is "To fear God, and keep His Commandments."

We call attention to another judgment and visitation of God upon corruption and violence. This was by means of a vision, probably foretelling things shortly to come about in the city of Jerusalem. In the 9th chapter of Ezekiel we read: "And the Lord said unto him, go through the midst of the city, through the midst of Jerusalem, and set a mark upon the foreheads of the men that sigh and cry for all the abominations that be done in the midst thereof. And to the others [those with destroying weapons], he said in mine hearing, go ye after him through the city, and smite; let not your eye spare, neither have ye pity; slay utterly old and young, both maids and little children, and women; but come not near any upon whom is the mark; and begin at my sanctuary. Then they began at the ancient men which were before the house." Pay day, some day, is coming.

Concerning God's judgments and slaughter of the wicked,

the writer has had Divines, or Dry Vines, say to him: "God is not like that!" Permit this comment on that: Consider the slaughter, death, and suffering going on all the time in all the world; surely as the Scripture says: *"The whole creation groaneth and travaileth in pain and death even until now."* Think of the death, suffering, and sorrow in our own city, in our own generation, and the wars of former generations, history, and antiquity. If your god don't control all these things, then surely your god must have lost control. Surely you need to seek and find the God who has not lost control, even the true Christian's God - not one sparrow falls to the ground without His permission. He explains why all this death, slaughter, suffering: The cause is sin: disobedience to His laws and commandments: *"For the wages of sin is death!"* But, But. . . *"But the gift of God is eternal life through our Lord Jesus Christ - for God so loved the world, that He gave His only begotten Son, that whosoever believeth in Him should not perish, but have everlasting life."* John 3:16.

In closing, we quote two passages of Scripture in which God tells us how we can get rid of evil:

First is from Isaiah 26:9, 10: *"When God's judgments are in the earth, the inhabitants of the world will learn righteousness. Let favor be showed to the wicked, yet will he not learn righteousness: In the land of uprightness will he deal unjustly."* This is meant especially for those who have God ordained authority to keep law and order, and put away evil. Of course, there is no hope here when such authorities are themselves in rebellion against the judgments of the Almighty!

The Second is from Jeremiah 23:21 where God says if the prophets, even though He did not call them to prophecy, would stand in His counsel and cause His people to hear My Words: *"Then they should have turned them from their evil way, and from the evil of their doings."* The application here is especially for the clergy, preachers, teachers, parents, and all who claim to be Christian. Who is to blame, when wickedness grows and abounds, becomes rampant and worldwide, and the stench of man's vileness mounts up to heaven!

March 13, 1965

† † †

The following is from a historian concerning conditions about the time of the fall of the Western portion of The Roman Empire:

"As for the west, it was left to the mercies of the Barbarians! For twelve generations, murder, war, arson, plundering were the order of the day. One thing - one thing alone - saved Europe from complete destruction, from a return to the days of the cave-man and the hyena! This was the Church - the flock of humble men and women who for many centuries had confessed themselves the followers of Jesus, the carpenter of Nzazreth, who had been killed that the mighty Roman Empire might be saved the trouble of a street-riot in a little city somewhere along the Syrian frontier." (There were other things concerning the killing and its aftermath of The Carpenter of Nazareth of which evidently the eminent Historian knows nothing, sad to say!)

Some light and insight into the character and faith of some of "the flock of humble men - who confessed themselves followers of Jesus," and who saved Europe from complete destruction and a return to the days of the cave-men and the hyena, can be had from the historical facts concerning "The Theban Band."

It was about the year 283 A.D. Diocletian was the Emperor. He had bestowed upon his general Maximian, the title of Caesar, and sent him into Gaul to put down a rebellion among the Bengali and other factious tribes. After having conquered his enemies the Caesar brought from the East a legion called "The Theban," composed entirely of Christians, who he wished to employ in the persecution of

98

Christians. On learning how they were to be used, this Legion refused to march and formed its camp at the foot of the mountain now called The Great St. Banard. Maximian irritated at their disobedience, demanded troops from the Emperor to conquer the rebels. Diocletian sent reinforcements to him, ordering him to decimate the soldiers - which meant kill every tenth man - and then reiterate his commands that they help in the persecution of the Christians. After every tenth man was killed, the Thebans declared that they persevered in the resolution! Then Maximian commanded them to be decimated a second time, and that the survivors should obey orders. This second execution did not quell their courage!

The Theban Legion was commanded by three principal officers - Maurice, Euxperus, and Candidus, who exhorted them to die for their faith; and recalled to their recollection the example of their comrades, whom martyrdom had already conducted to heaven. Still, they wished to avert the wrath of the tyrant, and addressed to him a remonstrance, full of nobleness and firmness:

''We are your soldiers, my lord, but we freely confess that we are the servants of God; we owe to our prince duty in war, to God our innocence; we receive from you pay. He has given us life; we cannot obey you and renounce God our Creator, our Master, and yours. If you ask of us nothing injurious we will obey your orders as we have to this time; otherwise we shall obey Him rather than you. We offer the services of our arms against your enemies, but we do not believe we are permitted to bathe them in the blood of the innocent. We took an oath to God, before we did to you, and you can have no confidence in the second, if we violate the first. You command us to seek out Christians, in order to punish them; you have no need to seek others, behold we are such! We confess God, The Father, author of all things, and Jesus Christ His Son. We have seen you put to death our companions without mourning, and we have rejoiced that they have been honored in suffering for their God. Despair has not driven us to revolt; we have arms in our hands, but we have not used them. We prefer to die innocent, rather than live culpable!"

Maximian, not being able to conquer a courage so heroic, ordered his officers to put them all to death: troops were marched to surround them, and cut them to pieces, but instead of offering the least resistance, these unfortunate soldiers laid down their arms and offered their necks to their persecutors! The earth was inundated with blood! Six thousand men, the usual number of a legion, were put to death by orders of the tyrant!

It is not the glare and glamour of uniforms, guns and other weapons of warfare of a marching host that really make a soldier, but rather that oath he took to defend and serve, and if need be die, for his country. How he fulfills that vow is what tells the true story!

"Am I a soldier of The Cross, a follower of The Lamb? -A charge to keep I have, a God to glorify - Help me to watch and pray and on Thyself rely, Assured, if I my trust betray, I shall forever die!"

March 30, 1963

We trust it will be an encouragement to all the true and sincere people of God to be reminded of several long periods of time in the earth when men dwelt without fear for their families, loved one, and property, due to kings, rulers, and governing authorities who would not countenance or put up with lawlessness. May I ask any or all in whatever category you may belong who claim to believe that the "death penalty" does not prevent crime: Did you ever see a dead man commit murder? Did you ever see a dead man rape a woman or girl? Do you reckon there was any rape, adultery, homosexuality, or other crimes in Sodom on that morning shortly after Lot went out of the City and God rained fire and brimstone from heaven upon it?

The following statement is made not for the purpose of offending any man, but rather for the purpose of the writer not offending God Almighty: From my knowledge of The Bible, if I take the position the "death penalty" does not restrain and prevent, I make God out to be a liar many times in His Word, and in fact reject the entire economy of The Almighty revealed in John 3:16: *"For God so loved the world that He gave His only begotten Son, that whosoever believeth in Him should not perish, but have everlasting life."* Maybe we need to meditate on these words of The Lord Jesus Christ: *"Ye do err, not knowing The Scriptures, nor The Power of God!"* Meditate on the, and repent!

Regardless of what others do, or profess, you continue to *"Fear God and keep his commandments; for this is the whole duty of man." "Be not weary in well-doing, for in due season we will reap, if we faint not."* Continue to pray, as Christ taught us:

"Thy kingdom come, thy will be done in earth, as it is in heaven. Deliver us from evil." Remember that a number of times, God has told us in His Word: *"The earth shall be full of the knowledge of the glory of the Lord, as the waters cover the sea."* "For nothing should the people of God more devoutly pray than that 'their great men might be good and God-fearing men!'"

"Democratic Institutions exist by reason of their virtue. If ever they perish it will be when you have forgotten the past, become indifferent to the present, and utterly reckless as to the future." "When you have forgotten the past!" The following is a reminder of a few incidents of the past:

Not forgetting the past: let's turn to Oliver Cromwell about the 1650's A.D., and remember that God used him in England, Scotland and Ireland to put down evil, rebellion and disorder.

Not forgetting the past: in the year 617 A.D. Edwin was crowned King of Northumbria, one of the seven divisions of England in the period of The Heptarchy. It was from this

King that Edinburgh got her name. It was said first of him that in his days "a woman with her babe might walk scathless from sea to sea." The people tilled their fields and gathered their harvests in quiet and safety. Men no longer feared the thief and robber; stakes were driven by the roadside spring, where the traveler found a brass cup hanging for his use, and no thief durst carry it off . . . "Thus the church as the great civilizer, had already begun its work in Teutonic Britain."

Again, **not forgetting the past:** in the year 1066 A.D. the grandson of a Norse pirate was recognized as King of England. His ways were masterful and his measures severe, but the results were beneficial. He was a hard drillmaster; but England needed a drillmaster, and the English were the first to recognize it. Life and property were protected as they had never been done and protected under native English kings. Even the *Chronicle* is forced to recognize "the good peace he made in the land, so that a man might go over the realm alone with his bosom full of gold unhurt. Nor durst any man slay another, how great so ever the evil he had done." "The good peace he made in the land!"

Don't forget again that the conqueror's son, Henry I, demanded respect and obedience to his laws, and won the title - "Lion of Justice." "And no man durst mido against another."

Not forgetting the past: around 1200 to 1230 A.D., Genghis Khan came out of the Gobi desert and conquered the cities of civilization. No other man except Alexander the Great, long before the time of Genghis Khan ever made such a change in the world during one lifetime. Southern China was conquered, he swept over Russian princes, and over the brave Poles and Hungarians. His general, Subotai, got as far as Vienna, where his forces turned back from Europe of their own accord - doubtless because France and Germany went to their knees in prayer to God Almighty! Genghis Khan demanded obedience to his Law: Mongol accounts say cart loads of gold and silver stood nearby without any guards to watch over them, so utterly was the Law of Genghis Khan, which forbade stealing, obeyed!

Somewhere, somehow, this Magnificent Barbarian, had gotten ahold of God Almighty's 8th Commandment: *"Thou shalt not steal."* He believed it! He enforced it! (Would God we would do the same!) Because of that Law peace prevailed for thousands of miles around him. At a "Council of his Conquerors," he said: "I have gained the mastery by carrying out our Law. Only severity keeps men obedient. An action is only good if you carry it out to the end." His commandments were obeyed even after his death. It was as if he sat on the raised throne of the council of the Mongol Khan. Everything written down in his Law was carried out by the generations that followed him. When his grandson, Batu Khan, ruled, there was a saying in Russia that "a dog cannot bark without permission of Batu Khan." And it was also said that a young girl alone could carry a sack of gold safely from the River Don to the City of The Khans. What is wrong with such power, when it is used to stop stealing and protect women?

Above records of five rulers testify to the ability of men to keep law and order, suggest we think on our ways.

What is the trouble? The answer is as plain as the nose on your face: We have forsaken the Commandments of our God!

March 8, 1976

† † †

Often, or generally speaking, when you begin to talk about the Puritans there be many that "tear their shirt, or skirt" and holler and squall "witch-craft, witch-hunters." And there is a cause for this. *"Come now, and let us reason together."*

Probably it was thirty years ago that the writer heard a

"theological professor" say in his sermon that we had learned today there was no such thing as a "Witch." It is my understanding that even today witches and witch-doctors are real folks and exert tremendous influence and power in certain parts of the world. And have read and heard of very Godly Missionaries telling of the depressing effect experienced even by themselves in lands that have long been without or never influenced by genuine Christianity. It could be that the reason we know or experience so little of such things is due to the good job the Puritans did in "witch-hunting," at which we mock today. However, all this must be wrong and out-moded, for surely such a man as this "learned professor" in such a prominent position would not have made such a statement in such a prominent place unless he knew what he was talking about.

A witch, or a supposed witch, seeing there is no such thing, is usually considered to be a woman endowed with supernatural and demoniac powers of a special and peculiar sort. Since this "wise man" announced there was no such thing, is it not reasonable to assume that he and his associates had examined every spirit that does now or has in the past, occupied every "house of clay" created from the time of Adam and Eve down to the latest baby born, appraised and assessed these spirits and found that none could be classified in the "witch category?" How in the world did they accomplish such a stupendous talk in a relatively short life time? Have often thought I would like to ask this "learned professor" if they had developed a "spiritual test tube" at the cemetery, or seminary, in which they can isolate spirits and determine their character, powers, limitations, etc.? Such a development in itself would be an astounding marvel, but that is a small matter in comparison with the feat of rounding up all the spirits of the past, present, and maybe the future, herd them singly or in great droves into the test tubes, and give them all a "clean bill of health" in so far as "demoniac power" is concerned!

Far be it from me to be guilty of heresy, but frankly, I am

skeptical! Why, the "rooster" that made this announcement in behalf of himself and his collaborators was at the time only about twenty-five years of age! But these are the days of marvels! Once heard of a colored preacher who made the charge that all women were possessed of seven devils. His official board "called him on the carpet" and demanded Scripture for such a statement. His reply was that Scripture recorded Mary Magdalene as the only woman who had seven devils cast out, and therefore, all the rest of them still had 'em! According to this reasoning, all men must be possessed of a "legion of devils!" Believe I could come nearer going along with the colored preacher than the "divinity professor."

Moses spent two different periods of forty days each up on Mount Sinai alone with God, talking and listening to Him; and no telling how much time he spent with God in The Holy Place in The Tabernacle where we are told: *"And The Lord spake unto Moses face to face, as a man speaketh unto his friend."* Exodus 33:11, and Numbers 12:6-8. More than once Moses addressed God as *"The God of the spirits of all flesh."* In Job 40:11, God says *"Whatsoever is under the whole heaven is mine."* In Ezekiel 18:4 God says *"Behold, all souls are mine - the soul that sinneth shall die."* God Almighty created all spirits, all souls! If you want to spend your time and occupy your mental factory with the problem of why He permitted some to get evil - He tells us it was man's own choice - you are at liberty to do so, but as for me, and I would advise you to do the same, I intend to spend the rest of my time and occupy my mental members with the job, and getting all the assistance I can from The Holy Spirit, in departing and fleeing from evil, in fighting evil spirits, even hunting for witches and witch-doctors - and I believe I have enough spiritual discernment to spot and detect a big bunch of the latter class - *"Ye suffer fools gladly, seeing ye yourselves are wise!"*

In Exodus the 20th Chapter, just after God finished speaking The Ten Commandments to Israel from Mount

Sinai, verse 22, begins: *"And the Lord spake unto Moses, Thus shalt thou say unto the children of Israel,"* and God Almighty Himself is still speaking when you get to chapter 22 and verse 18: *"Thou shalt not suffer a witch to live."* One of the clearest and most glorious prophecies of the coming of Christ, quoted in Acts 7:37 by Stephen - whose face shone like that of an angel - in his apology that ended in his martyrdom, appears in connection with the warning and condemnation of familiar and evil spirits in human form! Deut. 18:9-16. We better keep our mouths shut about the "unseen world of spirits" of which we know little or nothing lest we end up ourselves in the possession of a "witch" or devil.

Deut. 29:29 says: *"The secret things belong unto The Lord our God: but those things which are revealed belong unto us and our children for ever, that we may do all the words of this law."*

Get familiar with this Book of God, *The Bible.* *"Thy word have I hid in mine heart, that I might not sin against Thee."* Psalm 119:11. If you can't accept it as God's revelation of Himself, you will be safer and better off to get out of The Church: *"And whosoever shall fall on this stone shall be broken; but on whomsoever it shall fall, it will grind him to powder."* Matthew 21:44.

December 1, 1962

† † †

Coming Judgment

Division Six

Ding, Dong, Dell; There is fire in Hell! Who put it in? Jesus Christ, God, 'tis He!

Ding, Dong, Dell; The fire is out! Who put it out? The D.D.'s Doubt!

The writer found the above copied down in an old note book - don't know the author. Most of the following was written by way of comment:

"Thus saith the Lord: Cursed be the man that trusteth in man, and maketh flesh his arm, and whose heart departeth from the Lord . . . Blessed is the man that trusteth in the Lord, and whose hope the Lord is . . .Jeremiah 17:5, etc.

The late Sam Jones said: "The man who throws hell fire out of his creed, when he arrives in hell will have to revise it, and then there will be nothing in it but hell fire!"

About the year 1535 there was a terrible time in Munster, Germany. The Anabaptists took over, made a king, murdered, pillaged, raped, in the name of religion. In that period Martin Luther was living. Plurality of wives was permitted, and for several years this bunch held sway. Luther, in commenting on them said: "Such gross work and crime is the work of children or baby devils, the fruit of the work of Doctor of Divinity Devils - those who reject the Word of God and the infallibility of His Book, the Bible." Doubtless, their counterpart today are the smart, wise, brilliant men (brilliant and wise in the eyes and wisdom of men, fools in the eyes of God) who "cast away The Law of The Lord of Hosts" and reject the infallibility of and supernatural in the Holy Scriptures.

In the days of John Calvin a terrible death dealing plague broke out. It was very contagious and most of the preachers refused to minister to the afflicted and dying, saying they knew it was their duty, but they had rather go to the devil.

For the sake of argument, if you knew that in order to get right with God, you had to cut out Sunday sports, golf, baseball, fishing, etc., etc., and spend an hour a day, more or less, reading your Bible or on your knees before God, go to Church Sunday morning, Sunday night, yea, and prayer meeting Wednesday night, wonder how many would be like the preachers of Calvin's day who said they would rather go to the devil! That was a little over 400 years ago. Think of it! 400 years in the fires of hell, with eternity still to go! Lord, have mercy on us!

As stated, the above was found written down in an old note book of the writer's. It was his intention to try and dress it up the best he could with grammar, rhetoric, logic, and all that sorter stuff to make it presentable. However, in its present condition we believe it capable of being used of God to bless all such as *"Think on their way, and turn their feet unto God's testimonies, delay not, but make haste to obey God's Commandments,"* and can be very profitable for such a time as this. See Psalm 119:59, 60.

The D.D.'s doubt has not put out the fire of hell, but on

the contrary, has brought many of our great cities a realistic foretaste.

"I have not sent these prophets, yet they ran; I have not spoken unto them, yet they prophesied. But if they had stood in my counsel, and had caused my people to hear My words, then they should have turned them from their evil way, and from the evil of their doings." Jeremiah 23:21, 22.

Standing in the midst and beholding the horrors of the destruction of Jerusalem at the hands of the King of Babylon, Jeremiah said in Lamentations 2:14: *"Thy prophets have seen vain and foolish things for thee: and have not discovered thine iniquity, to turn away thy captivity; but have seen for thee false burdens and causes of banishment."*

"I have not troubled Israel; but thou, and thy father's house, in that ye have forsaken the commandments of the Lord . . ." 1st Kings 18:18.

"If My people, which are called by My name, shall humble themselves, and pray, and seek My face, and turn from their wicked ways; then will I hear from heaven, and will forgive their sin, and will heal their land." 2nd Chronicles 7:14.

August 12, 1967

† † †

The article in this column on July 30th commented on the sign "Forget Hell" seen on the front of an automobile. More than one correspondent wrote to correct us; One stated that hell as used was an "expletive" and not a "noun;" and another said it did not have Biblical significance of hell.

These explanations made me think of a story I once heard. A man got killed in an accident while at work on his job. His friends and co-workers were faced with the necessity of breaking the tragic news to his wife. One by one they begged to be excused. Finally, one man volunteered. He was asked if he thought he could do it in a diplomatic and sympathetic way in order to soften the shock as much as possible? Just leave it to me, he said. He knocked on the door and when a lady answered it he asked: "Is this the widow Brown." "I am Mrs. Brown, but I am not a widow." "Lady, you just THINK you ain't no widow. Am sorry to have to tell you your old man got killed about an hour ago in an accident on his job!"

Folks, you "just THINK you are not profane" when you use the word hell in such a careless way, taking it out of its Biblical context, setting and significance! You are playing with fire! You are playing with the "fire prepared for the devil and his angels" and unrepentant men and women! "Unquenchable Fire!" *Hear how the Lord Jesus Christ* spoke of it in Mark 9:43, etc. *". . . go into hell, into the fire that never shall be quenched: where the worm dieth not, and the fire is not quenched!"* (Very likely the word "worm" refers to the souls of men and women rejected and abandoned for all eternity by the God of Mercy and Grace because they refused to turn from their evil and devilish ways and accept the "so great salvation" He has provided in the sacrifice and atonement in the *"Blood of the Lamb that taketh away the sins of the world,"* The Lord Jesus Christ! God's Word tells man his whole duty is to *"Fear God and keep His Commandments."* And God has provided the means by which man can "do his duty." It was Cromwell who said: *"God will curse me, if I put personal interests above duty!"*]

Is not anyone, regardless of who it is, in great danger of being profane unless the object of his using the word hell is to warn men and urge them to "flee the wrath to come," as did John the Baptist, as did Jesus Christ, His Apostles, and faithful servants down through the ages, and as His faithful witnesses do today?

If I mistake not, I recall seeing recently that one of our candidates for Governor told some of his opponents to "go to hell!'' Is not a governor supposed to be sort of a shepherd of the sheep? Should not such a one strive to get their opponents, even their enemies, to stay away from hell and ''flee the wrath to come?'' ''Devoutly thankful ought we to be for the gift of great and good men. They are God's noblest work. - For nothing should the people of God more devoutly pray than that their great men may be good men. One honest statesman - one great, sanctified, devout, Christian man in the Senate or cabinet of a nation, or at its head - is worth more to a nation than all the riches of El Dorado, and is surer defense than all her armies and navies.''

We are certainly in bad need of the Biblical message of Hell when proclaimed in The Fear of The Lord, and applied faithfully to the evil conduct of men raging in rebellion and revolution against God's Commandments, God's Government, and God's King, the Lord Jesus Christ. The most terrible, the most horrible message that ever fell upon the human ear, it is this Scriptural message concerning hell, and hell fire!

If you wish to talk about hell without being profane, think of the text in Psalm 9:17: *''The wicked shall be turned into hell, and all the nations that forget God.''* Talk of the wickedness of man in Sabbath desecration, in murder, in sex vileness and immorality, stealing, lying, greediness of gain and coveteousness as indicated by the strikes. (I might beg a man for a job, I might beg a man for a higher wage, but to try to force him to grant my requests by injuring his business and causing him loss - I have not so learned Christianity and Christ. In Matthew 20:15, Christ said to some complaining laborers: ''Is it not lawful for me to do what I will with mine own? Is thine eye evil, because I am good?'' Do we not now have man-made laws that make it unlawful for a man to do what he will with that which is his own: *''Beware of making laws in the face of God - telling the Almighty you will meet all His Dispensations, and stay things, whether He will, or no.''*]

111

"All nations that forget God shall be turned into hell." Here, also, you can find good ground for talking about hell without being profane. Consider how our nation has forgotten God by banning His book, The Bible, and The Lord's Prayer from our schools!

There is almost no end to other Scriptures which furnish a good text for talking about hell profitably, and not profanely. Will mention one other, Proverbs 23:13, 14: *"Withhold not correction from the child; for if thou beatest him with the rod he shall not die. Thou shalt beat him with the rod, and shall deliver his soul from hell!"* That sounds like "Beat the hell out of him!" Faithful application of this message from God might be profitably exercised among many teen-agers, students, rioters, riot leaders and instigators.

The first recorded words spoken by Christ after His baptism were an approval of all the Scriptures: *"Man shall not live by bread alone, but by every word that proceedeth out of the mouth of God."* Matthew and Luke 4:4.

We repeat: Folks, you just "THINK" you are not profane when you use the word hell out of its Scriptural setting and significance!

August 27, 1966

✝ ✝ ✝

For a Labor Day Holiday Exercise, we suggest you get your Bible and turn to the 16th and 17th chapters of The Book of Numbers, read them over and over again - read them until you are familiar enough with their contents to be able to close The Book, meditate all the way through, observing and thinking about all the details.

You will find here the historical record of how God Almighty handles an unlawful "demonstration" and "strike" against Providential Authority. "History is our Heaven-appointed instructor. It is the guide for the future.

112

The sea of time we navigate is full of perils. But it is not an unknown sea. It has been traversed for ages, and there is not a sunken rock or a treacherous sand-bar which is not marked by the wreck of those who have proceeded us." There is no portion of history fraught with more valuable, faithful and truthful instruction than that found in God's Book, the Bible. "The majestic outgoings of the Almighty, as developed in the onward progress of our race, infinitely transcend, in all elements of profoundness, mystery, and grandeur everything that man's fancy can create. The cartoons of Raphael are beautiful, but what are they when compared with the heaving ocean, the clouds of sunset and the pinnacles of the Alps? The dome of St. Peter's is man's noblest architecture, but what is it when compared with the magnificent rotunda of the skies?

"There is not a sunken rock or a treacherous sandbar which is not marked by the wreck of those who have proceeded us!" Behold the wreck and terrible results of the "demonstrations" and "strike" recorded in God's History Book: There were four men especially that stirred up the trouble. Their names were Korah, Dathan, Abiram, and On. All of them were men of high position and well known in the nation. They claimed that Moses had exalted himself and usurped authority at the expense of the rest of the people who had the right to have a "say-so" in the operation of the government. Their propaganda was very popular with the masses, and just about everybody agreed with them. They won to their side 250 princes of the nation: "famous in the congregation, men of renown." All the governors of the tribes joined with them, the supreme court, the other judges, lawyers, sheriffs, big business tycoons, and all the soldiers and "brass" of the army - probably with the exception of Joshua and Caleb. This great mob - great in numbers, position and influence - "demonstrated against Moses and Aaron, accusing them of usurping and grabbing authority that really belonged to all the people!

Before this mob of "demonstrators," Moses fell upon his

face - not for "fear of them," but rather in "fear for them," for already God was talking with Moses, and he foresaw the clouds and heard the thunders of God's wrath that was about to descend. Moses told them that God would settle the matter on the morrow, and he told the 250 Princes to get censers and put fire and incense in them - a mode and manner of worship at that time - and on the morrow come before the Lord, and He would reveal whom He had chosen to run the business. On the morrow, the whole congregation gathered to "demonstrate" in favor of the Princes. Then the Glory of God appeared, and God said to Moses and Aaron: *"Separate yourselves from this congregation, that I may consume them in a moment."* Moses and Aaron interceeded and begged God not to destroy all the people because of one man's sin! (Note this significant fact, the "demonstrators" had been deluded and misled by one man, or their several leaders! *"They do the mob wrong, who seldom or never are guilty of atrocities till they are deluded and misled."*] God heard Moses plea for the people. He told him to tell the people to get away, segregate themselves, and separate from the strike leaders and demonstrators. We now quote from the 16th Chapter of Numbers: *"And Moses . . . spake unto the congregation, saying, Depart, I pray you from the tents of these wicked men, and touch nothing of theirs, lest ye be consumed in all their sins . . . and Dathan and Abiram came out, and stood in the door of their tents, and their wives, and their sons, and their little children: 'And Moses said, Hereby ye shall know that the Lord hath sent me to do all these works: for I have not done them of mine own mind. If these men die the common death of all men: then the Lord hath not sent me. But if the Lord make a new thing, and the earth open her mouth, and swallow them up, with all that appertain unto them, and they go down quick into the pit, then shall ye understand that these men have provoked the Lord! And it came to pass as he had made an end of all these words, that the ground clave asunder that was under them; and the earth opened her mouth, and swallowed them up, and their houses, and all the men that appertained to them, went down alive into the pit, and the earth closed upon them, and they perished from among the congregation, and all Israel that were round about them fled at the cry of them; for they said, lest the earth swallow us up also.''* John the Baptist preached in preparing for the coming of Christ. *"Flee the wrath to come!"*

Doubtless above the cry of those fleeing the earthquake was heard the terrible and horrifying screams of the 250 Princes as they burned to death, fire from the presence of The Almighty having kindled among them. These men stood there prepared for worship with their censers, fire and incense. During their lifetime two of Aaron's sons had burned to death in the act of unacceptable worship; they knew it, and it had been a warning to them.

We need to take heed to what we are doing in our acts of worship: concerning the one day in seven God has set aside as Holy; concerning the House of God dedicated and set aside as sacred for worship; and concerning His Holy Word: *"For thou hast magnified thy Word above all thy name."* Psalm 138:2. God said to Moses one time, and to Joshua at another: *"Take off your shoes, you are on holy ground."*

"God will curse me, if I put self interest above duty!" Instead of repenting and seeking forgiveness, next day the congregation accused Moses and Aaron of murder, killing the people of God!" There are still those about who accuse God of murder, and also his servants who seek to proclaim and carry out His severe judgments. They were still not cured of their "demonstrating and striking spirit." And again the Glory of God appeared:" . . . sin, evil and rebellion cannot stand and abide the glory of God! God said to Moses: *"Get you up from this congregation, that I may consume them in a moment!"* Immediately the consuming began by means of a plague! Moses told Aaron to run quickly into the midst of the congregation, to make an atonement for the people, and stand between the living and the dead. Probably it did not take Aaron but a few minutes to perform this service, but before the job was done and the plague stayed,

14,700 were dead! *"Who is able to stand before this holy Lord God?"* 1st Samuel 6:20. *"Forbear thee from meddling with God!"* 2nd Chronicles 35:21.

"There is not a sunken rock or a treacherous sand-bar which is not marked by the wreck of those who have preceeded us!" Behold, consider the results of this wreck God tells us about in His History Book: Probably about 50 people swallowed up by the earth opening her mouth, and alive they went down into "the pit!" (God's Word records two men going alive from this life into Heaven, but here it appears that two or three entire families went alive from this life into the "pit of hell!") Also, casualties in this wreck included 250 Princes suffering the horrible death by fire! Then, the death toll by plague was 14,700! A total of about 15,000! As terrible as this was, it is but a "drop in the bucket" compared to what would have happened had not Moses "stood in the breach" and made intercession with God to spare the several million "demonstrators" and "strikers" seeking to remove him from his Providential and God-ordained position and authority!

If you are one of those who "mock, and sit in the seat of the scornful" concerning the judgments of God revealed in the Bible, in God's Name, why don't you get out of The Church of the Lord Jesus Christ, if you have taken the vows to join? Have you not sense enough to recognize that terrible judgments upon man are revealed in every news media of every day, and *"that not one sparrow falls to the ground without the permission of The Almighty?"* And that similar calamities and judgments have been the portion of every generation that ever lived! The cause is sin, rebellion against the Creator, even as recorded in the third chapter of Genesis, which chapter blind fools call "myths."

"Christ is the answer!" But it is not only the Christ, the Sacrifice, who said "forgive" and "turn the other cheek, etc.," but also the Christ, the King of Kings, the Lord of Lords, whose first recorded words after His baptism were:

"Man shall not live by bread alone, but by every Word that proceedeth out of the mouth of God!" Matthew and Luke 4:4.

September 3, 1966

† † †

Back in the days when execution of criminals was by public hanging, it is said that they were very popular attractions. One writer says that often twelve or fifteen thousand attended. On one occasion when the weather was stormy and threatening, he reported that only eight thousand came to see the sight. Another story tells of a wife and children attending the hanging of the husband and father: The man was brought to the gallows sitting on his coffin which was in a one-horse wagon, and there right in front of the mob near the gibbet stood his wife with a baby in her arms and several children holding to her skirt. "Go home, Mary," he said, "this is no place for you and the children." "Yeah," she replied, "That is the way you have always been, never willing for me and the kids to have a little pleasure!"

In the 21st chapter of 2nd Samuel there is the account of a multiple hanging, seven men at one time. The Jewish law required that the bodies should be taken down before sundown, but these seven men, though Jews, were hung by the Gibeonites, non Jews, and their bodies were left hanging indefinitely. All these men were cousins, descendants of King Saul. The mother of two of them camped near the horrible scene and kept the birds off their bodies by day, and beasts by night. After she had kept this up for quite a while King David heard about it, and sent and had them taken down and buried.

This and other terrible judgments found in the Bible, God Almighty's Book revealing Himself to man, if traced back to their source, will reveal the caue of the calamity. They are written for our instruction and example that we may avoid the curse of God falling on us for similar sin, or sins! In this case we will have to go back about 500 years to the time of Joshua. In the 9th chapter of the Book of Joshua is the record of how Joshua and the princes of Israel were tricked and deceived by the pagan Gibeonites whom God had ordered should be destroyed. They accepted and acted on lying speech, circumstances, and appearances, instead of asking and waiting upon God who had already told them what to do, and swore to let them live, making the oath "In the Name of The Lord." (We might well ask ourselves if our nation and its leaders have been tricked and deceived in the past two decades by peoples who are the open and avowed enemies of The God we profess!) Under such circumstances most men would probably consider such a vow void. However, the Almighty did not consider it void since it was made "In His Name," and when it was violated, about 500 years later, judgment fell! The vow was made by the proper government authorities of the nation, and was broken many centuries later by the supreme governing authority, King Saul. He killed some of the Gibeonites, a people who were their servants according to the ancient treaty, and which protected them, and a people whom so far as we know had lived up to their part of the treaty and therefore were in no position to defend themselves. We are told that Saul's purpose was the fame and exaltation of his own reputation and name among his people.

The real important thing for us to note in this account, as well as in all Biblical records, is to "watch God work," and observe His ways, actions, and attitudes in order that we might "learn of Him" whom to know is Eternal Life. He is "The Judge of all the earth," and we are on our way to appear before His judgment seat! God's judgment for this "breach of promise" did not fall in the days of King Saul, but later when David was King. The judgment was a famine of three years duration. How many starved and perished we are not told. *"And David inquired of The Lord, and The Lord*

118

answered, It is for Saul and his bloody house, because he slew the Gibeonites." David consulted with the Gibeonites that were left, and an agreement was made that seven of Saul's sons were to be turned over to them to be hung to make atonement. This account for the hangings recorded in 2nd Samuel, 21st chapter, *"And after that God was intreated for the land"* -verse 14. And the famine came to an end.

God's terrible judgments we find in The Old Testament of the Bible might well be likened to "child's play" in comparison with those declared in The New Testament: *"outer darkness, everlasting fire prepared for the devil and his angels; the worm dieth not and the fire is not quenched; weeping, and wailing, and gnashing of teeth, and no rest day and night forever and ever;"* and other such statements, practically all of which were spoken by Christ Himself and the beloved Apostle John in the Book of Revelation. It appears that probably the judgments in the Old Testament, or most of them, might be temporal only, and the sufferings and agony relieved by death. In the punishment foretold in the New Testament, death flees from some who long for it.

The reaction of the present day "top brass" in the ecclesiastical world regarding the judgments foretold in the New Testament is one of dismissal with a "sneer," and a "smear" upon those who warn men that this is the Word of God, and urge them to *"flee the wrath to come."* The reaction of this same class towards those in the Old Testament is usually to attack the character of the Holy Lord God Almighty; one who is *"highly esteemed among men"* and in the church has called Him a "Dirty Bully," and another has said He is Hitler-like, and another has said "He is my devil," and one so-called Christian minister remarked he would not walk across the street to speak to the God of the Old Testament! These men could be borne with a little better if they were outside of the Protestant Christian Church, but probably all of them at their ordination took solemn vows accepting the Authority of the Scriptures of the

Old and New Testaments as the infallible Word of God, the only rule of faith and practice.

But for the time being "Let them alone" - that is what Christ told His disciples regarding the Church leaders when He was upon earth in the flesh. *"Look to yourselves!"* In Psalm 138:2, the Psalmist says of God: *"For Thou has magnified our word, our vows made in His Name, maybe in* His House, maybe with one hand raised towards heaven and the other placed on His Book, the Bible? How have you magnified your word, church member, preacher, citizen, lawyer, policeman, sheriff, judge, legislators, senators, governors, presidents, all men! Has lapse of time, change of customs, change in your beliefs, justified a "breach of promise," or voiding a vow made to God, or to man! To know God is Eternal Life. Visit this public hanging scene recorded in His Word, and meditate on the cause of it in connection with your own vows to God, and man. *"Be sure your sin will find you out,"* was spoken to those who made a vow in case they failed to fulfill it. Here we have the record in God's Book of a vow made and after 500 years had rolled by it was broken, and judgment fell! Don't think I would like to attend a public hanging, but think it is very profitable to me that I have stopped and looked a while at the multiple hanging in the 21st chapter of 2nd Samuel. Thank God that we can get forgiveness for broken vows, even if it means some judgment in this life. But if we ask and accept that forgiveness, let us beware of further neglect and carelessness concerning them!

February 2, 1963

Practical Christianity

Division Seven

"For such a time as this!" To how many who claim to be Protestant Christians does this quote mean anything? Maybe we are unduly critical and pessimistic but doubt if one in ten know its Scriptural setting and context. Jews ought to know. Could hardly expect Catholics to know since their spiritual food is not only rationed, but also predigested. If you want to eat that way, it is your privilege in this land of freedom, and in some other countries, but think it is "command food" in parts of the world today.

In the centuries past we are told that great numbers of martyrs perished for refusing to eat "command food!" *"Daniel purposed in his heart that he would not defile himself with the portion of the king's meat, and with the wine which he drank."* Daniel ate that which God told him to eat, and it surely "paid off." The great world dictator King fell on his face before Daniel and worshipped him, and at another time he made a decree that if any people, nation, language spoke anything amiss against The God of The

Hebrew children they should be cut in pieces, and their houses made a dunghill.

Another King clothed Daniel in scarlett, put a chain of gold about his neck, and proclaimed him third ruler in the kingdom. Daniel spent the night in a lion's den in company with an angel of God who made the lions as harmless as kittens! During his life time great world rulers rose and fell, one went crazy and lived the life of a beast for a time - we got a lot of folks like that about now - others were slain, but *"Daniel continued even until the first year of King Cyrus."* Daniel's influence and faith continue still to bless all generations of mankind who have learned of him and to trust his God.

It is not too big a job to get to know him today, just get familiar with the first six chapters of The Book of Daniel. Get the facts in your mind so you can think on them after you close the book. For the present maybe you better not spend too much time on the last six chapters or you might get in water over your head and drown! Read them, but be careful about interpreting until you grow a little more. Martin Luther, speaking of Predestination, advised not to "fly too high" into the Celestial mysteries of God lest you fall and break you neck, for it is better to abide by the "swaddling clothes" of the manger until you grow a little more strong in faith and knowledge. The "Diet of Daniel" together with his steadfastness of purpose was the secret of his great success, aside from the fact that *"The Lord had laid His hands on him"* and he was a chosen vessel.

Martin Luther chose the "Diet of Daniel." He tells of how some years after he became a monk he found a Bible. He devoured it, reading it over and over again. His fellow monks told him he would be worth more to their order if he would quit reading that Book so much, get a sack and go out in the city and beg food and other gifts for the monastery. Thank God they were not able to pull him away from "The Book," for his life and testimony changed the course of history, and has done more to bring liberty to the individual and nations than probably any other one thing since the days of the Apostles.

Some historian has truly said that we are all a different people and living in a different world because of his teaching and testimony. The noted French historian, Michelet, though a Catholic was a great admirer of Luther, and he acknowledges in the preface of his *Life of Luther* that he was indebted to him for the liberty he enjoyed of writing as he wanted to. 445 years ago next Wednesday, Oct. 31st, Luther nailed some papers to The Church door challenging the religious "status quo" of his day. He was judged a heretic by The Church and tried. The unusual punishment for the condemned unless they recanted was death by fire at the stake. At the Diet of Worms - this does not mean the eating of worms, but here diet means a great deliberative Assembly, and Worms was the name of the city where it was held - at this Diet Luther was tried and condemned. "There were present at the Diet, besides the Emperor, six electors (governors), one arch-duke, two landgraves, five margraves, 27 dukes, and numbers of counts, archbishops, bishops, etc., in all, 206 persons. (Surely the Supreme Court were all there, just called by some other name at that time. You boys who "tear your shirt" these days when one questions or resists its judgments should take note of this.)

Expecting to have to go to the stake and burn alive, Luther stood his ground against the whole bunch - he had some friends in the crowd. He said to The Emperor and the rest of the crowd: "It is not safe to go against the Word of God and conscience. Here I stand. I can do no other. God help me." God did help him, and delivered him, and they failed to get him to the fiery stake! He has spoken to all generations since in his great song *A Mighty Fortress:* "Let goods and kindred go, this mortal life also; the body they may kill; God's truth abideth still; His Kingdom is forever." We who call ourselves Protestants are supposed to "follow in his train!"

The first recorded words of Christ after His baptism were: *"Man shall not live by bread alone, but by every word that proceedeth out of the mouth of God.*" Matthew and Luke 4:4. The Creator of Life, The Preserver of Life, The Redeemer of Life, ought to know that which is essential for man to live, is it not so? Towards the close of His Ministry, Jesus said to The Church and national leaders: *"Ye do err, but not knowing the Scriptures, nor The Power of God."* There are 1440 minutes in every 24 hours. If we were to spend 40 minutes a day reading our Bible consecutively we could look at *"every word that proceedeth out of the mouth of God"* two or three times every year, and still have 1400 minutes of every twenty-four hours to do other things. There is no good excuse for the Christian not to know what is in The Bible. Forty minutes a day spent in reading God's Word is a season definitely spent in the presence of God Almighty, if we are sincere.

You will doubtless soon have trouble in this exercise for the devil will fight to break it up, and he may get you in the "lion's den," but it will be well worth it to have a visit from the angel of God: *"The angel of God encampeth round about them that fear Him, and delivereth them."* Psalm 34:7. The Apostle Paul told Governor Felix: *"And herein do I exercise myself, to have always a conscience void of offence toward God, and toward men."* (It is the writer's conviction that this New Bible has the poison of unbelief in it, and would advise you to hold on to the King James version. A few obsolete words and phrases here and there are not going to poison you, but passages produced by unbelief are dangerous, for *"Faith cometh by hearing, and hearing by The Word of God."*]

Did not get to comment on "Such a Time as This" in particular. You can find it in its setting and context in the 4th chapter of The Book of Esther.

October 27, 1962

† † †

One day many years ago a man was riding his mule down the road on a trip to visit a King. This was one of the modes of travel in those days for even great men, and this traveler was indeed a great man, internationally known and famous as a wise man and a prophet. Recently, the peoples of the world watched and followed with great interest the journeys of the astronaut around the earth in outer space, earth watching a man's journey in the heavens. Those who read this are invited to watch a short trip of a man going along one of earth's roads. *"He that sitteth in the heavens"* was watching this trip, and was so interested and concerned that He sent down an Angel to be a "roadblock" - and there is good Scriptural ground for thinking this Angel might have been none other than Christ Himself. See 1st. Cor. 10:4. - Am of the opinion that it will do our world much greater good and benefit to watch this man and his mule on their trip, and so let us go along with them in our mind's eyes.

Man and beast appear to be contented and happy and each occupied with their own thoughts. The great man was probably thinking with much pleasure and anticipation of the great honors, riches and rewards promised him by the King who had invited him to come and do a job, a job that would not tax his physical energies too much, for all that would be required of him would be that should do some "cussing" - curse Moses and his people whom God had delivered from the bondage of Egypt and Pharoah, probably the most powerful king of that day and generation.

Have heard a story about the devil going fishing - imagine it was on The Sabbath, or The Lord's Day - he baited his hook with a bottle of liquor and soon caught a drunkard; next with a deck of cards, or dice, and shortly had a batch of gamblers; he caught the biggest fish of all when the bait was money, silver or gold; the coveteous, avaricious, the greedy of gain, etc. - Did you know the Bible says *"the greedy of gain"* trouble their own house? Often those who are "greedy of gain" excuse or justify themselves on the ground they are seeking to benefit and better provide for their house, home, wife, children, and their future welfare, but God says you are making trouble for your own house. The devil's fishing was just fine until he ran out of bait. He decided to try his luck with no bait on the hook, quickly got a strike, and pulled up a fellow "cussing!" God's Third Commandment says: *"Thou shalt not take the Name of The Lord thy God in vain, for the Lord will not hold him guiltless that taketh His Name in vain."*

Why do the heathen rage? "A heathen is one who does not believe in The Lord of the Bible," and he rages against The Bands and The Cords of restraint of God's Moral Law and Ten Commandments! Do you ever hear any rage these days against God's Third Commandment? Are you guilty? The devil gets you without bait!

As to the mule, probably his thoughts and anticipation also were very pleasant as he looked forward to visiting royal stables, keeping company with ass royalty and nobility, and with them eating the King's fodder and other fancy feed. Suddenly, however, these happy and contented travelers became upset and greatly disturbed; For no apparent reason the mule became frightened and turned out of the road into the fields. For a long time the master had owned this mule and ridden her on many trips, but she had never acted like this before. He whipped her, and as he was an expert at "cussing" probably used some harsh and bitter words that made the mule's long ears burn to their nethermost tips! He got her back in the road and things went along o.k. for a time, until they came to a place where the road was narrow and a wall or fence on each side. Here the mule became frightened again, and in trying to get out of the road, mashed the rider's foot or leg against the fence! She had to take another beating with the whip, and another lashing from her master's tongue.

They resumed their trip again, but doubtless both man and beast were troubled and their happiness and contentment had departed. They came to a place of one way traffic where the road was so narrow there was no room to turn to the right or left. Here the mule laid down with the rider on her! A third awful flogging with the whip followed, together with more sharp, cutting and choice "cussing," which continued until the ass began to talk with man's voice! -If I had been the rider I think I would have gone away from that place, changed my mind about which way to go, and even though I had plenty of time on my hands, would have gone away in a hurry, that is, if I could have without being cut down by the unseen visitor! - Suddenly the rider quit his beating and cussing the ass and joined him on the ground, falling flat on his face, for he saw what was causing the ass to bank: there standing blocking the road was The Angel of God with His sword drawn: *"The Lord opened the eyes of Balaam, and he saw the Angel of The Lord standing in the way, and His sword drawn in His hand; and he bowed his head, and fell flat on his face. And The Angel of The Lord said unto him, Wherefore hast thou smitten thine ass three times? Behold, I went out to withstand thee, because thy way is perverse before Me; and the ass saw Me, and turned from Me these three times: unless she had turned from Me, surely also I had slain thee, and saved her alive."* Numbers 22: 31-33.

The Book of Numbers, chapter 22 through 24 give the record concerning Balaam. It was Mark Twain, I think, who said it was not the things in The Bible that he did not understand that troubled him, but it was those he did understand. The New Testament tells us in 2nd Peter 2:15, 16 that Balaam *"loved the wages of unrighteousness; but he was rebuked for his iniquity; the dumb ass speaking with man's voice forbade the madness of the prophet."* And in the Book of Jude, verse 11: *"Woe unto them! For they have gone in the way of Cain, and ran greedily after the error of Balaam for reward."* Is it not very clean and easy to understand from this passage of God's Word, His revelation of Himself to man, God's attitude and action against avarice, the coveteous and greedy of gain?

The Tenth Commandment: *"Thou shalt not covet thy*

neighbor's house, thou shalt not covet thy neighbor's wife, nor his man servant, nor his maid servant, nor his ox, nor his ass, nor anything that is thy neighbor's." Obedience to this commandment would bring blessing and peace to our land in quick order. A genuine Christian is one who has had this Commandment written in his heart by The Spirit of God! Genuine Christianity will do away with stealing, cheating, swindling, graft, race troubles, strikes, and various and sundry assortments of evil and devilment, for at the bottom of them all is "coveting" that which God in His Providence has given to someone else. "Is your life a channel of blessing?" Or is it a curse on account of being "greedy of gain" and thereby troubling your own house, your own community, your state, your country, your world? Here we have the account of Heaven watching the journey of a man on earth, and opening the mouth of a dumb ass to resist and rebuke him! Remember the words of The Angel: *"I went out to withstand you, because thy way is perverse before Me; and the ass saw Me, and turned Me these three times; less she had turned from Me, surely also now I had slain thee, and saved her alive."* *"Beware of coveteousness,"* warned Christ in Luke 12:15, etc.

How will it be with you, with me, when our eyes are opened and we see an Angel of God? Surely that experience is just ahead for us when we have to move out of this "house of clay," this body! *"The Angel of the Lord encampeth round about them that fear Him, and delivereth them."* Psalm 34:7. Contrast this verse, however, with that of Psalm 78:49: *"He cast upon them the fierceness of His anger, wrath, and indignation, and trouble, by sending evil angels among them."* It appears that the way our day and generation rage against 'The Laws of God that we have qualified ourselves for "evil angels!"

June 15, 1963

Jacob had four wives. In his day and time it was neither against the law or customs. However, it is very likely that he did not want but one, for a man in love as much as he was, is not interested in other women. It appears that the others were rather "pushed on him" by circumstances. He was in love with a beautiful girl named Rachel, the daughter of his Uncle Laban, who was also his boss. When the time came for a labor contract, Jacob did not call on his union bosses and their lawyers to represent him in the bargaining. He knew what he wanted and did not "beat around the bush" in stating his terms: "I will give you seven years of time and labor, and you give me Rachel for my wife." Nothing was said about vacations with or without pay, retirement, old age pensions, fringe benefits, etc. - he was raring to close the trade and get to work earning his pay.

"And Jacob loved Rachel - and Jacob served seven years for Rachel; and they seemed to him but a few days, for the love he had to her." Genesis 29:18-20. In the Song of Solomon, 2:2, the bridegroom likens his girl to the Lilly, and by comparison, all other women are Thorns, and the bride likens her man to the Apple Tree, and by comparison other men are just woods. This appears to be the kind of love that Jacob had for Rachel, and is the grounds for the suggestion that Jacob would have had only one wife if let alone. We suggest that the marvelous purity and integrity of Joseph's character was the first-fruits of this great love that enabled Jacob to stand and endure hardships and mistreatment for seven years, and look on it as passing in a few days!

Jacob had twelve sons and one daughter, the two youngest sons being the sons of his beloved, Rachel, Joseph being the firstborn. So Jacob loved Joseph above all the others, and either could not help showing it, or did not mind doing so. At the age of 17 years he began helping his brothers tend the flocks which sometimes kept them away from home. Joseph's conduct won for him the envy and hatred of his brothers; he reported to his father the wickedness and sin of some of the boys; again he wore a "coat of many colors," given him by his father, which doubtless was much better than anything they had; and probably the worst offense of all was the telling of several dreams he had indicating that in time he would rule over them. This was more than they could take, decided they would not put up with it, and began to make plans to get rid of him.

If a hen keeps sitting on eggs, they are either going to hatch, or rot. It has been truly said that if one has the eggs of hatred and ill-will in his heart, don't try to get rid of them but continues to nurse and keep them warm, in time they will hatch out in murder, or rot his very soul. The opportunity came before long for the brother to get rid of Joseph. They were a long way from home attending their flocks, but Joseph was back home with his father. In time Jacob sent Joseph to check up on them, seeing if they were well and getting along all right, and taking them some good things to eat from home. When they saw him coming at a distance, their hatred and envy choked out all other feeling, and they decided to kill him and take his bloody "coat of many colors" to his father and tell him they found it, and if it was Joseph's, surely some wild beast had eaten him up: *"And we shall see what will become of his dreams!"* - They did live to see! So you and I can see today, if we have eyes to see, and don't let the devil blind us.

When Joseph's oldest brother, Reuben, heard of the plan he persuaded them not to murder the boy, but throw him into an old pit or well in the wilderness and leave him there to die. However, his plan was to save him and take him back to his father. While the boy was down in the well begging and pleading with them to take him out, the brothers were outside eating the good stuff he had brought them from home, maybe pies, cakes, etc. As they were so engaged there came into view a band of Ishmaelites, traveling and trading people like we call gypsies. They agreed, all but Reuben who seems to have been absent, that they could not only avoid murder but make some money by selling Joseph.

So they pulled him out and sold him to the gypsies, who carried him down into Egypt and sold him again to an army officer, Potiphar, Captain of the Kings Guard. The brothers pocketed their money, killed a sheep, dipped the "coat of many colors" in the blood, and carried it back to their father with their "big lie."

Did Joseph's brothers get rid of his witness and testimony against their evil deeds? Punishment and judgment overtook them, and it would have been much better if they had taken heed to his warning. Did they help matters by getting envious about his "coat of many colors," or jealous because of his dreams? They lived to see him in Royal Robes, riding royal chariots, and the cry of "bow the knee" as he passed along. The secret of this great life was: *"God was with him!"* However, is it not true that the things he said and did as a result of God's Presence in his life, were the very things that caused hatred, envy and jealousy?

The story of Joseph begins in Genesis chapter 37. Chapter 38 digresses, takes up Joseph again in chapter 39, and then to the end of this Book.

November 19, 1966

† † †

We are undertaking to make John Wesley our guest columnist today. When Wesley considered the prodigous increase of the Methodist Society, "from two or three poor people, to hundreds, to thousands, to myriads," he affirmed that such an event, considered in all its circumstances, had not been seen upon the earth since the time that St. John went to Abraham's bosom. But he perceived where the principle of decay was to be found:

"Methodism is only a plain, Scriptural religion guarded by a few prudential regulations. The essence of it is holiness of heart and life: the circumstances all point to this; and, as long as they are joined together in the people called

131

Methodists, no weapon formed against them shall prosper. But if ever circumstantial parts are despised, the essential will soon be lost, and if ever essential parts should evaporate, what remains will be dung and dross.

"I fear, wherever riches have increased, the essence of religion has decreased in the same proportion. Therefore I do not see how it is possible, in the nature of things, for any revival of true religion to continue long. For religion must necessarily produce industry and frugality, and these cannot but produce riches. But as riches increase, so will pride, anger, and love of all the world in all of its branches. How then is it possible that Methodism, that is, a religion of the heart, though it flourishes now like the green-bay tree, should continue in this state? For Methodists in every place grow frugal and diligent; consequently they increase in goods. Hence they proportionally increase in pride, in anger, in desire of the flesh, the desire of the eyes, and the pride of life. So, although the form of religion remains, the spirit is swiftly vanishing away. Is there no way to prevent this - this continued decay of pure religion? We ought not to prevent people from being frugal and diligent; we must exhort all Christians to gain all they can, to save all they can; that is, in effect, to grow rich. What way, then, can we take, that our money may not sink us to the nethermost hell? There is one way, and there is no other under heaven. If those who gain all they can, and save all they can, will likewise give all they can, and save all they can, then the more they gain the more will they grow in grace, and the more treasure they will lay up in heaven.

"Every man ought to provide the plain necessities of life for his wife and children, and to put them into a capacity of providing those things for themselves when he is gone, I say, 'these,' - the plain necessities of life, not delicacies, not superfluities; for it is no man's duty to furnish them with the means either of luxury or idleness. The designedly procuring more of this world's goods than will answer the foregoing purposes; the laboring after a larger measure of worldly substance; a larger increase of gold and silver; the laying up of more than these ends require, is expressly and absolutely forbidden." And Wesley maintained, that whoever did this practically denied the faith, was worse than an African infidel, became an abomination in the sight of God, and purchased for himself hellfire! (How many of us need to pray the prayer of the Publican found in the 18th chapter of Luke, with similar humility: *"God be merciful unto me, a sinner!"* Alas, how many of us are praying and thinking of ourselves as the other man told about: *"God, I thank Thee that I am not as other men are . . ."*) Said Wesley: "I call God to record upon my soul, that I advise no more than I practise. I do, blessed be God, gain, and save, and give all I can: and, I trust in God, I shall do, while the breath of life is in my nostrils!"

Wesley had at heart the advice which he gave and dwelt upon it with great earnestness, and in one of his last sermons before his death, he said: "After you have gained all you can, and saved all you can, wanting for nothing, spend not one pound, one shilling, one penny, to gratify either the desire of the flesh, the desire of the eyes, or the pride of life, or for any other end than to please and glorify god. Having avoided this rock on the right hand, beware of that on the left. Hoard nothing. Lay up no treasure on earth, but give all you can, that is, all you have. I defy all the men upon the earth, yea, all the angels in heaven, to find any other way of extracting the poison from riches. After having served you between sixty and seventy years, with dim eyes, shaking hands, and tottering feet, I give you this advice, before I sink into the dust. I am pained for you that are rich in this world. You who receive 500 pounds a year, and spend only 200, do you give 300 back to God? If not, you certainly rob God of that 300! You who receive 200 and spend but one, do you give God the other hundred? If not, you rob Him of just so much. 'Nay, may I not do what I will with my own?' Herein lies the ground of your mistake. It is not your own! It cannot be, unless you are lord of heaven and earth.

'However, I must provide for my children.' Certainly: but how? By making them rich? Then you will probably make them heathen, as some of you have done already! (Why do the heathen rage? God tells us why in the Second Psalm.) Secure them enough to live on; not in idleness and luxury, but by honest industry. And if you have not children, upon what Scriptural or rational principles can you leave a groat behind you more than will bury you? Oh! leave nothing behind you! Send all you have before you into a better world! Lend it, lend it all unto the Lord, and it shall be paid you again. Haste, haste, my brethren, lest you be called away before you have settled what you have on this security. When this is done, you may boldly say, 'Now I have nothing to do but to die! Father, into Thy hand I commend my spirit! Come, Lord Jesus! Come quickly!''

Do you consider the above testimony "too extreme?" We may consider it "too conservative" when we appear before the judgment seat of the Almighty to give account of the deeds done in the flesh! *"That which is highly esteemed among men is abomination in the sight of God."* So spoke the Lord Jesus Christ just before telling us of the rich man in hell fire - Luke chapter 16.

September 24, 1966

† † †

Commenting on the last, first - crime creeping on the Church. A few months back as the writer came out of a Sunday morning worship service he shook hands at the door with one of the Church Officers, and noted he had a big bad place on his head. Said I: "Why, you have the same name as a man I noted the papers said got knocked in the head by a bank robber!" Said he, "I am the man!" Thank God he was not brought to Church for funeral!

About a month ago two Sunday School boys sat and talked together waiting for the service to start - one of the boys is

134

over three score years and ten and the other is not so far behind. The younger boy told this story: Departed a few days ago for a vacation time in Florida with a lot of clothes and equipment in the car. Spent the first night in City Hotel along my route. Next morning found the car windows had been broken and all my stuff stolen - crime surely mistreated that Sunday School boy!

Crime is also creeping in homes - too often we read of where a parent or other member of the family kill one or more of the others! A man told me he took a walk after supper for exercise; As he passed one home overheard an angry male voice: "I am going to kill you!" Reply of a female voice: "Better dead than live with you!"

Now get your Bible and turn to Jeremiah chapter 6 and begin reading, starting at verse 16: *"Thus saith the Lord, Stand ye in the ways, and see, and ask for the old paths. Where is the good way, and walk therein, and ye shall find rest for your souls . . . also I set watchmen over you, saying, Harken to the sound of the trumpet, but they said, we will not harken!"* "We will not walk therein . . . we will not harken!" *"Therefore, hear ye nations, and know, O congregation . . . Hear O earth; behold, I will bring evil upon this people, even the fruit of their thoughts, Because they have not harkened unto my words, nor to my law, but rejected it!"*

Ask for the Old Paths, where is the good way, and walk therein! One Old Path and Good Way is the Mid-Week Prayer meeting. Am of the opinion that for the most part this Old Path and Good Way has been supplanted with "eatin' Meetin's" and of the conviction that generally such meetings "grieve the Spirit of God" unless their object is to feed those in real need and hungry for the necessities of life.

Have read quite a bit in the newspapers recently regarding the First Baptist Church of Atlanta, and have been much pleased and inspired for the past year, more or less, as have noticed how in their Sunday Church advertisement they call attention to that Old Path, that Good Way, The Mid Week Prayer Service.

Creeping Crime Cursing our Citizens and Counties and Churches! Calling Consecrated Christians to Cry to Christ to Cleanse His Church Jesus said to Peter: *"If I wash thee not, thou has no part with me!"*

February 12, 1972

Second Psalm & Acts 4:25

WHY DO THE HEATHEN RAGE?

Vol. 3

A compilation of newspaper columns which appeared in leading newspapers across the nation from 1962 to 1981.

Morality

Division One

An article in *The Atlanta Constitution* of Oct. 21st had a headline spread across six columns of the page reading: "Teen-Age Sex Activity Here is Alarming, Judge Holt Warns." Some of the activity reported is so vile we would rather avoid mentioning it even by a sort of respectable name by which the devilment has gained entrance into nearly all of society everywhere -- sex vileness for which God ordered the utter destruction of the Canaanites, men, women, and children, saying they were so vile "... *the land itself vomited out her inhabitants*"; and activity for which there fell a rain of fire and brimstone upon Sodom and Gomorrah that utterly consumed them and left the land cursed!

In the article, there were suggestions for remedies such as a "study committee," -- some things get so vile they don't deserve study for cleansing but only the consuming fire, and that is one of the reasons The Almighty built hell and the lake of fire, and His Word tells us that those guilty of adultery, fornication, sex abnormalities, and fail to repent and turn from their evil and get forgiveness "*shall have their part eternally in the lake that burneth with fire!*" Other suggestions for remedy in the paper article were education, more money, etc. However, the Honorable Judge made a suggestion that "*savors of the things of God,*" rather than man: "Children also need to be answered with a strong no at times, as well as a stiff application of force to the seat of the pants so as to instill in them a healthy understanding of authority!" Amen, and Amen!

We quote from an editorial in the Nov. 5th *Atlanta Constitution:* "DeKalb Juvenile Judge Curtis Tillman said the

5

snowballing rate of juvenile delinquency will turn the county into an 'asphalt jungle' within five years unless --!'' The Judge was further quoted as saying: ''We will never do the job you expect of us until you give us the tools to work with.'' We would call attention to the ''tool,'' or ''tools'' God Almighty speaks of in Proverbs 23:13, 14: *Withhold not correction from the child: For if thou beatest him with the rod, he shall not die, thou shalt beat him with the rod, and deliver his soul from hell!''* That sounds like ''beat the hell out of him!'' I thank God that some of the hell in me in the days of my youth was gotten rid of in that manner, ''The tools we need!''

Think of the trouble, the crime, murder, violence, not to speak of the money saved, we could be rid of for the small price of a rod or strap, or a switch without price or money, if used in accord with God's Word!

Again, on the front page of the morning paper, Nov. 10, we read: ''Council to Combat Crime Among Youth, Urged Here!'' Combat Crime! Much of it can be ''batted'' out of the heart, out of the community, and out of society with a rod or strap in the hands of those who fear God and believe in obeying His Commandments, which is the whole duty of all men. So says The Lord God Almighty, The Lord God Omnipotent, Everlasting! Surely He must feel bad that so many of the great of the earth disapprove. Verily, they are now having their reward! The greatest power, force and influence in the establishment of this great nation was ''Faith in the God of The Bible,'' which caused them to ''Follow after such strict obedience'' to God's revealed will and ways that they were called Puritans, a name at which many now mock! We now enjoy ''walking on the high places of the earth'' because God is faithful to His promises to bless men and their children who *''obey and keep His Commandments.''* Now while we see this inheritance slipping away, we are trying to maintain it without that faith in The God of The Bible that produced it!

''Heathen'' are those who do not believe in The God of The Bible. God names them as kings and rulers, or such as governors, judges, and those who have authority over us, and

6

the people who imagine a vain thing and support those over them in their effort to get rid of God's Commandments, Law and Rule. The reaction of The Almighty to this rebellion is described in the Second Psalm as follows: *"He that sitteth in the heavens shall laugh: The Lord shall have them in derision. Then shall He speak unto them in His wrath, and vex them in His sore displeasure."*

The laughter of God, the derision of God, the voice of God speaking in His wrath and sore displeasure vexes, perplexes, plagues, scourges, and confuses men, deceives and causes men to believe a lie. Here we find the causes of the problems of young and old, of sex, of crime, murder, death and violence, etc. vexing and perplexing the nations. Elijah was the Prophet taken to Heaven, by-passing death and the grave. In his days God withheld the rain for three and a half years and a terrible famine cursed the land. King Ahab blamed Elijah for the trouble. Elijah replied: *"I have not troubled Israel: But thou, and thy father's house, in that ye have forsaken the commandments of the Lord, and hast served Balaam."* Or the devil! 1st Kings 18:18.

November 13, 1965

† † †

Concerning heathenish raging against morality and God's Seventh Commandment: *"Thou shalt not commit adultery."* In the first few verses of the eighth chapter of The Gospel of John, we are told that Jesus early in the morning came into The Temple, sat down, began teaching the people when the scribes and Pharisees brought before Him a woman taken in the act of adultery, saying that Moses in The Law said such should be stoned, what did He say? Jesus did not answer them, but stooped down and began writing on the ground, but when they continued asking, He stood up and answered them and then stooped down again to write while the scribes and Pharisees left for a "cooler climate," their own consciences having made "that spot too hot!"

7

We are not told what the writing was, and, naturally, there has been much speculation about it, which probably is all right if done in reverence and for profit, for the Scriptures say, *"It is the glory of God to conceal a matter, but the honor of kings to search it out."* A good guess as to what was written might be: "Where is the man? Did you not say she was taken in the act?" Their saying that Moses said she should be stoned was only half of the story, for The Law said: *". . . they shall both of them die, both the man that lay with the woman, and the woman; so shalt thou put away evil from Israel"* (Deut. 22:22 and Levitucus 20:10).

If we prefer the evil to the remedy, it is because of ignorance, blindness, and unbelief of the eternal judgment and justice of The Almighty! Of course, Jesus, being God as well as man, knew where and who the man was: *"Thou God, seest me! . . . The eyes of God are in every place, beholding the evil, and the good."* So, Mr. Adulterer, Mrs. and Miss Adulteress, God knows who you are and where you are -- whether the scribes and Pharisees find you, or not; every one of us must give account of ourselves unto God! Beware, lest you "wrest" this Scripture passage and think Jesus is indifferent to immorality and adultery! He did not abrogate God's Law of severity by saying to the woman *"Neither do I condemn thee, go and sin no more,"* but, on the contrary, He "magnified" The Law and made it honorable by taking upon Himself the woman's death penalty, and, shortly afterwards, died a much more horrible death than stoning -- crucifixion! It surely cost Him to say *"Neither do I condemn thee, go, and sin no more!"*

"Where is the man?" might have been what Jesus wrote on the ground. Last week this column told a story about three men, A., B., and C., and how Mr. B. had an illegitimate child in an Orphans Home -- which he failed to support. Mr. C. said the Orphans' Home Superintendent was a friend of his and told him about this, not in gossip, but it came out as he was telling of some of his operational problems, and the information was kept confidential and not made the subject of gossip. However, after it was too late, Mr. C. said that there was one party he should

8

have told about his knowledge of this affair, and that was the guilty party; he should have gone to him as a friend to try to persuade him to correct his wrong, repent, and make restitution as far as possible and support or help support the child, for God's Word says, *"If any provide not for his own, and especially those of his own house, he hath denied the faith and is worse than an infidel!"*

With The Almighty, it is restitution, if possible, or retribution! If you don't know the meaning of these words, it would be well for you to learn and meditate upon them! *"The Word of the Lord came unto me, saying, Son of man, hear the word at My mouth, and give warning from Me. When I say unto the wicked, Thou shalt surely die; and thou givest him not warning, nor speakest to warn the wicked from his wicked way, he shall die in his iniquity, but his blood will I require at thine hand. Yet, if thou warn the wicked, and he return not from his wicked way, he shall die in his iniquity; but thou hast delivered thy soul!"* (Ezekiel 3:16-19).

Mr. Paul Smith had several fine cows and sold his preacher neighbor milk and butter. The preacher told his son to go over between Sunday School and Church time and get some butter for dinner. The boy loafed and killed time and his father was already preaching when he got back to Church, and the preacher, being warmed up to his subject, happened to cry out in his exhortation just as his son entered: "What did Paul say?" "He said you were not going to eat any more of his butter until you paid for what you done got!"

Preachers, pay your debts, especially the debt due all the people due to your solemn Ordination Vows to proclaim The Word of God, and keep on telling us more of "what Paul said," such as "He that don't provide for his own has denied the faith and is worse than an infidel." We need to hear a lot more of that kind that affects our every day conduct; but also, don't forget to tell us what Ezekiel and the other prophets declared in "Thus saith the Lord." The first recorded words Christ spoke after His baptism were: *"Man shall not live by bread alone, but by every word that proceedeth out of the mouth of God"* (Matthew and Luke 4:4). It appears that we and our nation are in danger of losing our life! In Jeremiah 23:21, 22, we read: *"I have not sent these prophets, yet they ran: I have not spoken to them, yet they prophesied. But if they had stood in My counsel, and had caused My people to hear My Words, then they should have turned them from their evil way, and from the evil of their doings."* First Timothy 5:8: *"But if any provide not for his own, and especially those of his own house, he hath denied the faith, and is worse than an infidel."*

What about failing to "provide for those of your own body?" Mr. C. says he warned his friend, B., indirectly of his evil and profane ways, but he didn't feel comfortable about it since he may have failed to do his whole duty because he did not tell him he knew of this particular and awful sin in his life, and strive to get him to repent and make what restitution he could -- at least, to help in the support of the child. If he failed, he might make amends somewhat by warning you, if guilty.

We hear a great deal about our government supporting, and probably thereby encouraging illegitimacy! Where are the men? If you are responsible for one or more of such children, you better hear "What Paul said," speaking for God Almighty. Look them up and make as much restitution as possible! The Law of God says *"both the man and the woman shall die!"* Mr. Adulterer, Mrs. and Ms. Adulteress, have you "Come to Jesus" for forgiveness, cleansing, and grace to "go and sin no more!"? Christians, if the woman brought to Jesus by His and her enemies got saved, how much more might some of the multitudes of guilty all about get saved and cleansed if brought to Jesus by the testimony and prayers of His and the sinners friends -- *"Ye are my friends, if you do whatsoever I have commanded you."*

September 14, 1963

† † †

10

Concerning conditions about the time of the fall of the Western portion of the Roman Empire, a certain historian says: "As for the West, it was left to the mercies of the Barbarians! For twelve generations, murder, war, arson, plundering were the order of the day. One thing -- one thing alone -- saved Europe from complete destruction, from a return to the days of the cave-man and the hyena! This was The Church -- the flock of humble men and women who for many centuries had confessed themselves the followers of Jesus, the carpenter of Nazareth, who had been killed that the mighty Roman Empire might be saved the trouble of a street riot in a little city somewhere along the Syrian frontier."

Is not murder, robbery, rape, immorality, rebellion, and lawlessness the order of our day just about all over the world? Are we not returning to the days of the cave-man and hyena as many go about in near nakedness, and acting as the beasts that perish in sex relations, rejecting and discarding God Almighty's Laws concerning the family, marriage, and sex relations? Would it not be wise for us to give more thought to the Church, and the character it had that saved Europe from a return to the cave-man and the hyena? For the most part, The Church today is not composed of a flock of humble men and women who confess themselves followers of Jesus, but rather, a flock of proud, vain, presumptious, and lawless wretches that take the Name of God in vain!

Another historian looking across the centuries of experiences of the English people says: "The lapse of Church discipline was a certain symptom of political and social anarchy." Is there not social and political anarchy rampant just about all over The Globe? We suggest, we urge, that you think about The Church -- The Church of The Lord Jesus Christ. And make it personal. Your own relations. Have you taken her vows upon you, and how are you fulfilling them? What knowledge, what experience have you in spiritual matters?

In Mark Twain's Christian Science, Book 1, Chapter 9, he makes an appraisal of a Church of 500 members. He divides

11

them into an upper crust of about 25, and a lower crust of 475. In the top crust, there will be a man or two whose training and ability makes him capable of sizing up some great manufacturing scheme and recognize promptly its value, or lack of value. And there will be another man or two who can do the same with a great and complicated educational project; and a man or two who can do likewise with some engineering or scientific proposition; and so on and on. But none of these batches of experts will be able to understand and pass upon and give valuable information concerning the project out of his line. And probably, not one man in the entire lot will be competent to examine capably, a religious scheme, new or old, and deliver a judgment upon it which anyone need regard as precious. There you have the top crust.

In the lower, 'There will be 475 men and women present who can draw upon their training and deliver incontrovertible judgment concerning cheese, and leather, and cattle, and hardware, and soap, and tar, and candles, and patent medicines, and dreams, and apparitions, and garden truck, and eats, and baby food, and warts, and hymns, and time-tables, and freight-rates, and summer resorts, and whiskey, and law, and surgery, and dentistry, and black-smithing, and shoe-making, and dancing, and Hyler's candy, and mathematics, and dog fights, and obstetrics, and music, and sausages, and dry goods, and molasses, and railroad stocks, and horses, and literature, and labor unions, and vegetables, and morals, and lamb's fries, and etiquette, and agriculture. And not ten among the 500 -- let their minds be ever so bright -- will be competent, by grace of the requisite specialized mental training, to take hold of a complex abstraction of any kind and make head or tails of it!''

Doubtless, this appraisal comes near to telling the truth, the whole truth, and nothing but the truth. We Church folks know just about everything except The God and His Word we profess to believe, and yet just about all are proud and presumptuous regarding their religious knowledge and likely to get offended and angry if told our offering of worship and service is not acceptable to God. Many has been the time the writer has heard people told "nothing can separate you from the love of Christ," many of whom he knew to be living like the devil, and for the devil!

(While speaking of Mark Twain, we will pass it on as sort of a public service if it can be of any value to any Christian Scientist. He had a brilliant and giant intellect, and he gave a great deal of thought and study to Mrs. Eddy and her religion, and he came up with this explanation of The Scientist Unpardonable Sin. Quote: "The former Unpardonable Sin has gone out of service: We may frame the new Christian Science one thus: 'Whatsoever member shall think, and without our Mother's permission act on his own think, the same shall be cut off from the Church forever.'")

The late Sam Jones tells this incident that happened in Georgia concerning a man of whom he says: "The biggest case of religion broke out on him of any man in all that part of the country." He said it was told of one of our best men. He was a married man; he was young and came to church one day, and his wife was not with him on that occasion. When the brother had preached the Word, he stood up, for that preacher had said in that sermon: "If a man will do before he gets religion like he thinks he will do after he gets it, he will get it." When he was through preaching, the preacher opened the door of the Church and this man walked right up and joined the Church. He went home, and his wife said: "What sort of meeting did you have?" He said, "We had a splendid meeting and I joined the Church." "You joined the Church?" "Yes." "Have you got religion?" "No." "well, what in the world did you join the Church for before you got religion?" "Well," he said, "the preacher said if I'd do before I got religion like I thought I ought to do after I got religion, to come up and join the Church, and I joined it." "Well," she said, "that is a mighty strange way to me." That night before going to bed, he said, "Wife, get the Bible: I'm going to read a chapter and have family prayer." "What are you going to do that for and you ain't got religion?" "Well, the preacher said if I wanted to get religion, to do before

13

I got religion as I thought I would do after I got religion, and you know if I was a Christian I'd have family prayers in my house every night.''

And the next morning before breakfast he told his wife to get the Bible, and that he was going to pray again, and she said: "You are the strangest man I ever saw, to pray in your family when you have not got any religion.' And he went on and on; and on the next Wednesday night she went to prayer meeting with him, and at the prayer meeting the preacher called on him to pray, and he knelt down and prayed the best he could; and after he got out of the Church his wife took his arm, and she said: "Ain't you a nice man to pray in public and got no religion. What in the world did you do that for, husband?'' 'Well,'' he said, "the preacher told me if I would do before I got religion, as I thought I ought to do after I got religion, I would get religion, and I know that Christians pray in public.'' And he just kept right on along that line for three weeks, and the biggest case of religion broke out on him of any man in that part of the country!

The explanation is found in John 7:17: *"If any man will do His Will, he shall know of the doctrine, whether it be of God, or whether I speak of myself."*

"It is no secret what God can do! What He has done for others, He will do for you!''

April 13, 1963

† † †

The first article appearing in this column a little over a year ago made this statement: "Our trouble, the world's trouble, is that we have a corrupt form of Christianity! A Christianity that has been shoved off its base, off its foundation: The Law of God! The first recorded words of Christ after His baptism were: *'Man shall not live by bread alone, but by every word that proceedeth out of the mouth of God'''* (Mat. and Luke 4:4).

14

"If we would judge ourselves, we should not be judged" (I Cor. 11:31). In the same article, the writer judged himself, saying, that if he were a professed Christian and member of an Evangelical Protestant Church, and found he was unwilling to sincerely strive to perform the vows taken, or did not now believe as he did when they were taken; if science and modern knowledge and research with their wonderful accomplishments had so influenced him that he could no longer believe and accept the great fundamentals and foundations of Historic Christianity such as the Supreme Authority and Infallibility of The Scriptures of The Old and New Testaments for faith and practice, then it was his duty and obligation to resign and get out of The Church. To deliberately remain in such unbelief and false pretenses was to join the devil and his hosts in their effort to usurp The Kingdom of God, and he deserved to be classed with the most miserable wretches who have ever disgraced God Almighty's earth; and it would be better to have a millstone hanged about his neck and drowned in the sea, as it would be likely that he is in the class of that man of whom Christ said: *"Good were it for that man if he had never been born." "Forbear thee from meddling with God"* (II Chron. 35:21).

A corrupt form of Christianity that has been shoved off its base, off its foundation: The Law of God! The devil got into the Garden of Eden and corrupted the faith of Adam and Eve! *"Yea, hath God said,"* the serpent asked, casting doubt on the Commandment of God? The result of their corrupted faith was death and the curse for themselves and all the human race! If I don't believe and accept this, I have that liberty and privilege, but I don't have the moral right to remain in a truly Christian Church. To do so indicates my integrity has got "cancer," and in the end it will do for my soul what an unchecked cancer will do for my body!

In Genesis 6:12, we read: *"And God looked upon the earth, and, behold, it was corrupt: for all flesh has corrupted His way upon the earth."* The results of this corruption of God's way, or God's Commandments, found grace in the eyes of The Lord." This meant that Noah was told the flood was coming, and also

15

how to prepare for it. *"By faith Noah, being warned of God of things not seen as yet, moved with fear, prepared an ark to the saving of his house . . ."* He believed what God said, accepted the plans and specifications for The Ark, went to work -- Faith without works is dead -- built the Ark and sailed above the terrible destruction and desolation!

In that day Noah was the only man who *"found grace in the eyes of The Lord.'* But listen to what God now says to men and women of our day:

"For the grace of God that bringeth salvation hath appeared to all men, teaching us that, denying ungodliness, and worldly lusts, we should live soberly, righteously, and godly, in this present world; looking for that blessed hope, and the glorious appearing of the great God and our Saviour Jesus Christ; who gave himself for us, that he might redeem us from all iniquity, and purify unto himself a peculiar people, zealous of good works!" (Titus 2:11-14).

To you and me, the grace of God appearing to us, means that God has told us another flood is on its way, a flood of fire, to consume the world and its wickedness. It also means that He has given us plans and specifications for another kind of "Ark" that fire cannot hurt: Witness the three Hebrew children walking in the fire with The Son of God -- Daniel 3rd Chapter. It is put mighty plainly above ". . . teaching us that," etc. Consider carefully and prayerfully everything the grace of God makes known to us concerning the building of your "Ark," my "Ark." The Hebrew children refused to be shoved off the "firm foundation" of God's Commandments, even resisting and bucking the power of the greatest King of that day!

"For the eyes of The Lord run to and fro throughout the whole earth, to show Himself strong in behalf of them whose heart is perfect toward Him" (II Chron. 16:9). We suggest that we may have a "perfect heart towards the Lord," even though our feeble and week efforts miss the perfect mark a long ways.

April 20, 2963

† † †

16

Hear the Word of The Lord" concerning a little boy who died very young, and God's reasons for taking him away from his parents and loved ones. His name was Abijah, he was a prince, his father was the King, Jereboam the first King of Israel after the division of the nation into two kingdoms, Israel and Judah. Jeroboam was an outstanding young man and a natural leader; very industrious and a hard worker who did not loaf or kill time nor look for a "feather-bed" job. King Solomon noticed these characteristics in him and was so much impressed that he advanced him to be ruler over all the house of Joseph. Not only was King Solomon pleased with him, but also The King of Kings, God Almighty, and when the time of division came, God chose him to be King over the Ten Tribes of Israel.

But Jeroboam made a mighty bad record as King. From the time he became King until the destruction of Israel and the scattering of the people was about 300 years; the Kingdom of Judah lasted about 100 years longer until the Babylonian Captivity. During these 400 years, the following quotation appears about 25 times in appraisal of some of the other rulers, most of them Kings of Israel: *"He walked in the sins of Jeroboam, the son of Nebat, who made Israel to sin."* What a record to leave! And that record written in God's Book! "My record is on high," said Job. So is mine, and so is yours, and God will in time or eternity, turn the light on them! *"What I have written, I have written,"* said Pilate! Surely, we should be greatly concerned about our records not only for our own good, but also in view of the serious consequences to children and those who come after! *"Visiting the iniquities of the fathers upon the children until the third and fourth generation of them that hate Me,"* says The Almighty in His Second Commandment! Believe it or not, this accounts for a lot of the terrible things told about in the newspapers every day. God calls on His people to bear witness for Him, whether "any hear, or any forbear."

Would it not be wise to try and pin-point the "sin" of Jeroboam and get a clear understanding and picture in our minds as to what it was -- in order to guard against "walking in

17

it''? God sent a Prophet to Jeroboam while he was still working for Solomon and told him that He was going to divide the nation into two kingdoms because of Solomon's idolatry and disobedience, and that God would make him the King over Ten of The Tribes -- note he was told plainly why Solomon's son would lose them -- but Rehoboam, the son of Solomon, would remain King over the other two tribes **Because, Because** on account of David's obedience and faithfulness. God had promised David that his son should reign forever -- and David's great Son, The Lord Jesus Christ, now in 1963, sits at the right hand of God and reigns. He has not lost control! Beware, lest you be found with a corrupt and spurious form of christianity that conforms to the world, the flesh, and the devil, one that draws near to God with the mouth but keeps the heart far away!

The Prophet told Jeroboam, God offered him the same promises as David, an everlasting kingdom, if he would walk in obedience and faithfulness, as David did. However, after Jeroboam got to be King, he forgot -- or paid no attention to -- this promie of God. He faced what he in his natural and carnal reasoning considered to be a very serious and dangerous situation, for the Law of God required that he and his people go up to Jerusalem to the Temple to worship certain times every year. Now Jerusalem was the capital city of the rival Kingdom of Judah, and he figured if the people kept going there in time they would want to return to the house of David, and kill him. God said, obey Me and walk in My ways like David and your kingdom will last forever, but Jeroboam ''said in his heart'' I will lose my people, my kingdom, and my life if we keep going up to Jerusalem to worship. So, believing God who had promoted him to be King did not know what was best under the circumstances, he set up two other places of worship in his own land and told the people it was ''too much'' for them to have to go way up to The Temple at Jerusalem and he was making it easy and more convenient and attractive, and further, he was streamlining and modernizing and bringing the worship up to date to conform to the new ideas of The New Day, The New Deal, and The New Frontier, or what have you, and making all

18

more realistic and less mystical by adding a couple of Golden Calves, yet still they were worshipping *"the God who brought them out of Egypt."* If this is not the spirit that dominates and permeates much of our so-called worship in this day and generation, then this scribe is badly fooled. What makes it so terrible is that the judgment of God is more sure to fall than the sun is to rise tomorrow, unless we repent and turn again to the ways of God set forth in The Bible.

The above is a little word picture of *"Jeroboam, the son of Nebat, who made israel to sin"* whose little son became dangerously ill. No doubt the King loved his little boy as much as any who may read this, and in his grief and sorrow, he remembered the "man of God" who told him God would promote him to be King. He told his wife to disguise herself so she would not be recognized as The Queen and go to the Prophet in behalf of the little boy -- it may be that the disguise was due to shame for the way he had dishonored God. By this time, the old Prophet was blind, but God told him who the coming visitor was, what she wanted, and what answer to make. So, let us hear the reason God gave for taking this child away from his parents and loved ones: *"Go, tell Jeroboam. Thus saith The Lord God of Israel, forasmuch as I exalted thee from among the people, and made thee prince over my people Israel, and rent the Kingdom away from the house of David, and gave it thee; and yet thou hast not been as my servant David, who kept my Commandments, and who followed Me with all his heart, to do that only which was right in mine eyes; but hast done evil above all that were before thee . . . Therefore, behold, I will bring evil upon the house of Jeroboam . . . and will take away the remnant of the house of Jeroboam, as a man taketh away dung, till it be all gone. Him that dieth of Jeroboam in the city shall the dogs eat; and him that dieth in the field shall the fowls of the air eat; for The Lord hath spoken it . . . and the child shall die. And all Israel shall mourn him; and bury him: for he only of Jeroboam shall come to the grave, because in him is found some good toward the Lord God of Israel in the House of Jeroboam."*

Since the little boy had some good in him, God was not willing to leave him in the "mess of that family," probably lest he also get corrupt like the others, and end up like them, physically at least, in the belly of dogs or buzzards! In this instance, God revealed why He took the soul of the little child back to Himself. Jesus said: *"Suffer the little children to come unto Me, and forbid them not: for of such is the kingdom of God."*

The account of the sickness and death of little Abijah is found in the 14th chapter of I Kings.

It is interesting and striking to note that Rehoboam's son who succeeded him as King of Judah had the same name as the boy who died, Abijah. King Abijah and King Jeroboam went to war against each other. Jeroboam was defeated and lost 500,000 killed, and so far as we know, it is the largest number slain in one battle in all history where there is an authentic record, half a million! (II Chronicles 13:17). Unless you are one of those *"Who sit in the seat of the scornful"* regarding God's Book, The Bible, we suggest you learn of avoid, and beware *". . . walking in the ways of Jeroboam, the son of Nebat, who made Israel to sin!"*

September 28, 1963

† † †

"Keep thy foot when thou goest to the house of God, and be more ready to hear, than to give the sacrifice of fools: for they consider not that they do evil" (Ecclesiastes 5:1).

"And they shall teach my people the difference between the holy and profane, and cause them to discern between the unclean and the clean" (Ezekiel 44:23).

Last week this column pointed out a number of instances where instant death and judgment came from the hand of God upon certain Bible characters who came into His presence in worship and made offerings unacceptable: To Cain came the curse and banishment from the presence of God; to Nadab and

20

Abihu, death by fire from the presence of God; to King David's servant, Uzza, death by the stroke of The Almighty; the great King Uzziah was also struck by God, while in the act of worship, with leprosy, and a slow and horrible death followed; and Ananias and his wife, Sapphira, were struck dead by God in the act of trying to enter The Church for ulterior motives, and lying to God and The Holy Spirit -- the effect of this judgment upon this man and his wife upon the Church had quite a reaction as revealed in Acts 5:11-13: *"And great fear came upon all the Church, and upon as many as heard these things -- And of the rest durst no man join himself to them -- And believers were the more added to the Lord, multitudes, both men and women!"*

"Now all these things happened unto them for ensamples; and they are written for our admonition -- wherefore let him that thinketh he standeth take heed lest he fall" (I Cor. 10:11, 12). What were the great sins of these people? Since they were written for our admonition, should we not consider them for our safety in time and in eternity? We suggest that the sin of Cain and the great King Uzziah was that of pride and presumption -- in Psalm 19:13, it appears that presumption is called "the great transgression," and some thing this "great transgression" is the "unpardonable sin," and if not, it produces it! King David prays God to keep him back from it. Regarding Nadab and Abihu who died such a horrible death after previously having had a marvelous supernatural experience and revelation and fellowship with The Almighty, it may be that Leviticus 10, verses 8 and 9, indicate they oferred "strange fire," while more or less drunk, but certainly, it was due to indifference and carelessness, if not pride and presumption also! In the case of Ananias and his wife, their great sin was trying to get into the church for selfish self-interest and coveteousness and lying to God and The Holy Spirit and man in their effort to do so.

A popular slogan these days is "Go to Church." Good, but consider what you are doing, and why, and *"Keep thy foot when thou goest to the House of God,"* learn the "difference between the holy and profane," lest you offer the sacrifices of

21

fools! *"And this is life eternal, that they might know Thee the only true God, and Jesus Christ, whom Thou hast sent"* (John 17:3). Get knowledge of God from the above Scriptures concerning His attitude towards those who offer worship carelessly, profanely, ignorantly, and with ulterior motives.

There are certainly good Spiritual grounds for refusing some entrance into the House of God, and even throwing them out for their own good and safety! Jesus used a whip of cords in driving some out of God's house, and later, His disciples remembered it was written of Him: *"The zeal of Thine House hath eaten Me up."* In Matthew 18:15-17, Jesus gave instructions and grounds for the excommunication of an individual, and considering him a heathen. In the first few verses of I Corinthians 5, the Spirit of God speaking through the Apostle Paul, urges The Church *"In The Name of The Lord Jesus Christ"* to throw out a certain offensive individual, and *"To deliver such a one unto Satan for the destruction of the flesh, that the spirit may be saved in the day of The Lord Jesus Christ."* The object of The Spirit in ordering him thrown out was that he might be saved!

Today, we fear to throw out the evil ones lest they be lost -- no doubt they are already lost and are taught to "believe a lie" by the churches' refusal to use discipline! If you come to the Church in repentance towards God, and faith towards The Lord Jesus Christ, seeking to *"flee the wrath to come,"* God will receive you. But if you come seeking to satisfy the lusts of the flesh, social, political, or some other self-seeking coveteous ends, beware lest you offer "strange fire" and meet the wrath and curse of God! Isaiah 9:16: *"For the leaders of this people cause them to err; and they that are led of them are destroyed."*

A great English historian standing on the high ground of his knowledge of these peoples and their experience across the centuries sasid: "The lapse of Church discipline was a certain symptom of social and political anarchy." Christians, pray that God will cleanse His Church, beginning with you and me.

† † †   May 11, 1963

The greatest oak tree you ever saw, the largest that ever grew, once upon a time was condensed and compacted in the shell of a little acorn. The power of life that the Almighty put within it enabled it to draw food from the earth, water, sunshine, etc., and develop itself to its greatness and enormity and serve man, bird, and beast. We suggest that the First Psalm of The Bible, God Almighty's Book revealing Himself to man, might be likened to the Acorn in which is condensed and compacted the great Truths of God revealed by the great and mighty Tree - The One Hundred and Fifty Psalms. Every message of every Psalm can be easily related or connected to one or the other messages of the First Psalm: the blessing, the fruitfulness, and the happiness of those who delight to meditate and walk in The Law of The Lord, or the curse upon the ungodly who do not so. Consider the Second Psalm, the opening words of which are "Why do the heathen rage?" The "heathen ragers" are named as "people who imagine a vain thing, kings, and rulers, who set themselves in opposition to God's Laws and His Anointed, His King" - a king's duty is to rule, reign, proclaim and enforce laws and put down the rebellious. The heathen are warned to submit to God's King, make peace with Him, or perish when His wrath is kindled but a little!

"Clouds arise, and winds blow, by orders from God's Throne," says the hymn by Isaac Watts. Was much impressed with the words of the Cardinal in the funeral service of the late President Kennedy, about as follows as he addressed The Almighty: "Thou hast commanded the soul of the departed to leave the earth and return unto God who gave it." Think that was about the first thought that occurred when the news came of the President's assassination: *"Not one sparrow falls to the ground without your Heavenly Father's permission,"* and therefore, it must be "commanded by God on orders from His Throne." Probably more than once this statement was heard in the funeral service: God has commanded his soul from time to eterniuty. Therefore, is it not the part of wisdom to give primary thought and consideration to Him that hath the power to command life and death, and secondary thought and

23

consideration to the manner and means by which the commands are executed, lest an overdue attention to the manner or means offend The Commander? Daniel, in interpreting the "Handwriting on the Wall" (Daniel 5), said to the King: *"The God in whose hand thy breath is, and whose are all thy ways, hast thou not glorified!"* What about you, me?

We understand the Communists are "passing the buck" of responsibility for The President's death to the "extreme rightists," and if we read the news correctly, many great men, or rather men occupying great positions, agree with them. If they be right, then we will have to plead guilty to being guilty of part of the responsibility for the tragedy, and unless the liberals and leftists convert us, we want to move further and further to the "right." Our interpretation of a "genuine rightest" is a fundamentalist who accepts the Scriptures of The Old and New Testaments as the Divine Inspired Word of God, and therefore, of complete Authority. *"When the Son of Man comes in His glory, and all the holy angels with Him, then shall He sit upon the Throne of His glory; And before Him shall be gathered all nations; and He shall separate them one from another."* -- there is some "segregation" for you to consider -- as a shepherd divideth his sheep from the goats; And He shall set the sheep on His right hand. Let me be a "genuine rightist" in spite of the fact that they probably have a "mixed multitude of camp followers" trailing along behind.

Whenever terrible and shocking calamities befall, naturally men begin to cry:why? why? O why? And doubtless, we do well if sincere, for The Word of God says, *"It is the glory of God to conceal a matter, but the honor of kings to search it out."* If you believe The Bible, and will read The Bible and note the context of such words as **Because, Wherefore, Therefore**, etc., in time you can find just about all the answers to the "whys." And you won't have to read far until you begin to find God making explanation with "because". In the third chapter of Genesis: *"And the Lord God saith unto the serpent. Because . . ."* And the next word "because" is inferred in what was said to the

24

woman: *"And unto Adam He said, Because. . ."* Unto Cain God said: *"If thou doest well, shalt thou not be accepted? and if thou doest not well, sin lieth at the door."* Abraham "did well," and note the place of "because" in what God said: *"By myself have I sworn, saith The Lord, for Because thou hast done this thing, and hast not withheld thy son, thine only son; That in blessing I will bless thee, and in multiplying I will multiply thy seed . . . and in thy seed shall all the nations of the earth be blessed: Because thou hast obeyed my voice."* "The curse shall not causeless come," the Scriptures say. Certainly they infer also "blessings shall not causeless come!"

November 30, 1963

† † †

The answer to this question which is the opening words of the 2nd Psalm of the Bible, God Almighty's Revelation of Himself to man, is found in the words immediately after the question: They rage to get rid of God's Commandments and orders given to the creatures of the Creator for their own good, profit, protection, benefit and blessing: *"Blessed is the man that walketh not in the counsel of the ungodly, nor standeth in the way of sinners, nor sitteth in the seat of the scornful, but his delight is in the law of the Lord, and in His law doth he meditate day and night. And he shall be like a tree planted by the rivers of water. . ."* (1st Psalm). There are places in the Bible where God says of some of His people they were worse than the heathen. Maybe that time is here now! Whose fault is it that we are not "that blessed people whose God is the Lord"?

What is your personal attitude and actions regarding God's Commandments and orders to man? God has condensed His orders and Commandments into what at times is called "The Ten Words". They were written "with the finger of God" on two tables of stones. God made Himself to be His own messenger to deliver them to mankind. Nearly four thousand years ago, He came down from Heaven upon Mount Sinai, where several million men, women, and children were gathered

25

before the Mount. They beheld, and they heard as the mountain trembled and rocked with earthquake, cyclones, furious storms, all being enveloped in a great and terrible fire. When the noise and fury of the scene quieted, they heard the voice of God speaking out of the midst of the fire His Ten Words which He had written with His finger on two tables of stones, later given to Moses. God wrote, God spoke, these words audibly to several million men, women and children, and afterwards, delivered the tables of stone to Moses.

Mother, father, preacher, teacher, priest, or whoever takes upon himself the Name of God and calls himself a Christian: what is your attitude and actions towards the Commandments of the Almighty, the Ten Words? Do you respect them, observe them, teach them, and trust with all your heart the God who gave them? But, if you look upon these revealed truths, as well as the previously revealed truths in the Book of Genesis as "myths," in God's Name, may I ask you why are you in a truly Protestant Christian Church? Why don't you get out? You were not forced or compelled to join, as was the case in days gone by some non-protestant churches when they had great political and ecclesiastical power -- and doubtless, they will do so again if the time ever comes when they can get by with it! If you do not believe and cannot accept the great fundamental doctrines that produced true Protestantism and the blessing of liberty, freedom, etc., that have flowed therefrom; have you not got the honesty, the integrity, to resign, get out, and go join some church or organization that does not object to unbelief, heresy, apostacy, hypocrisy, and what not! *"Forebear thee with meddling with God!"* (II Chronicles 35:21).

Nearly 2,000 years after Sinai, God came again to the earth in Christ Jesus, who was born of a virgin without human father. In fulfilling His ministry, in the 16th chapter of Luke's Gospel, Christ revealed the flight of a human soul after death into hell fire! When this soul found there was no way out he entreated Heaven to send to the earth and warn his five brothers least they also come in his abode in torment. The answer came back: *"They have Moses and the prophets; let them hear them . . . If*

26

they hear not Moses and the prophets, neither will they be persuaded, though one rose from the dead!'' Christ arose from the dead on the third day for the salvation of His people -- Praise God! Moses and the prophets are the schoolmaster to bring us to Christ. The right use and faith concerning the Ten Words will bring the soul to Christ and His Salvation. You folks, and even denominations, who neglect or reject God's Ten Words, but talk much about the resurrection and New Testament would do well to meditate day and night on these words of Christ: *''If they believe not Moses and the prophets, neither will they be persuaded, though one rose from the dead.''* When in the Temptation Scene the devil quoted a Scripture to destroy another one, the implication is that such "tempts God." The Apostle Paul speaks of and warns of "believing in vain!" (I Corinthians 15:2). And Jesus in John 5:44 asks: *''How can ye believe . . . and seek not the honor that comes from God only?''* Can one find the honor that comes from God only and cast away "The Law of the Lord," the Ten Words that reveal the very character, righteousness, holiness of the Lord God Omnipotent?''

Ecclesiastes 12:12-14, sums up and puts in a nutshell, the above truth: *''Of making many books there is no end; and much study is a weariness of the flesh. Let us hear the conclusion of the whole matter: Fear God and keep His commandments; for this is the whole duty of man. For God shall bring every work into judgment, with every secret thing, whether it be good, or whether it be evil.''*

Christ said: *''To him that hath shall be given but from him that hath not shall be taken away that which he seemeth to have.''* No doubt the true meaning of this is that if we fail to use our God-given gifts, they will be taken away.

Consider how generally it is true that God's gift to man of the Ten Words have been taken away. Are they in His Church being taught and lifted up, or being used for discipline? Have they been taken out of the home and family by neglect? The Government by law has taken them out of the public schools!

27

Have they not been taken away so far as our sports and recreation life is concerned? What place has *"Remember the Sabbath Day to keep it holy"* therein? Has *"Thou shalt not covet anything that is thy neighbor's"* been lost and taken out of the labor unions' conduct? Surely, the Seventh Commandment, *"Thou shalt not commit adultery"* has been lost and rejected largely in our sex life! We might go on and on! It may be that the fruit of Sodom and Gomorrah is again ripe for harvesting for the fire of hell!

"Friends of God" need to go into action, stand up before God and plead! Ten righteous souls in Sodom would have turned aside the fire and brimstone rained from Heaven!

February 26, 1966

† † †

Historical

Division Two

On three different occasions, at least, Christ spoke these words. Also, recorded at least three times are these words of Christ: *"Heaven and earth shall pass away, but My Words shall not pass away."* Our present Supreme Court, our present Government, and you and I will soon pass away. The life and testimony faithfully based on Christ's Words will not pass away even when the *"heavens roll together like a scroll"* and the earth vanishes away like smoke!

The following is the "tale of two women," a historical tale, showing the fulfillment of Christ's Words concerning abasement and exaltation about 1700 years after they were spoken. One of the women was Princess Sophia of Russia, born highly exalted, but died in awful abasement; the other was The Empress Catherine who was born in humility, but died in great honor and exaltation.

Princess Sophia was the daughter of a Czar of Russia. Her father was married twice and had six children by his first wife, two sons the oldest, Theodore and John, and four daughters of whom Sophia was the oldest. By his second wife there were two children, Peter The Great, and a daughter. One the death of the father, Theodore was made Czar. Both Theodore and his brother were very sickly. This Czar died after six years, and as his brother was an epileptic, he was passed over and Peter was proclaimed Emperor in 1682, when only ten years old.

By the ancient law and usages of the Muscovite monarchy, the daughters were excluded from the succession altogether. Indeed, not only were the daughters excluded themselves from

29

the throne, but special precautions were taken to prevent their ever having sons to lay claim to it. They were forbidden to marry, and in order to make it impossible that they should ever violate this rule, they were all placed in convents before they arrived at marriageable age and were compelled to pass their lives in seclusion! (Praise and thank God and the Lord Jesus Christ for "Genuine Protestantism," and the liberty it has to women and men!) So, Princess Sophia and her sisters were placed in convents.

In spite of the ancient law and usages of the Muscovite monarchy, and in spite of the rules and laws of the monasteries, Sister Sophia was much discontented and by cunning and scheming she got her release from the convent for the supposed purpose of nursing and taking care of her sick brother, the Czar. How well she took care of his sick body we do not know, but it appears that it was not long, through her ambition for self-advancement and exaltation, she was taking good care of her brother's job, in reality "ruling the roost" with great power and influence in the court and especially with the commanding officer of the Czar's Guard. However, she failed in her effort to get her epileptic brother John proclaimed Emperor, yet on account of her great desire to save and serve her country -- or her own self-advancement -- she stirred up revolt and came near getting Peter and his mother killed. They escaped almost by "the skin of their teeth," but great numbers of the nobles and others were slaughtered before the rebellion was put down.

When Peter The Great began exercising the power, Sister Sophia was sent back to the convent. While Peter was absent from his country on a tour of some other nations, another rebellion was hatched for his overthrow. Three of the prominent leaders drafted an address to Sophia, inviting her to take the crown on the success and overthrow of Peter. Peter returned home and in a terrible manner, crushed the revolt. He had the three men who drafted the address hanged just outside of Sophia's convent window. "And then, by his orders, the arm of the principal man among them was cut off, the address (asking her to assume the crown) was put into his hand, and, when the fingers had stiffened arround it, the limb was fixed to the wall in Sophia's chamber, as if in the act of offering her the address, and ordered to remain so until the address should drop, of itself, upon the floor!'' -- Princess Sophia, worn out with the agitations and dangers through which she had passed, and crushed in spirit by the dreadful scenes to which her brother had exposed her, all her ambitions and aspirations forever extinguished, and the last gleam of earthly hope faded away from her mind; for six years longer she pined away under the influences of disappointment, hopeless vexations, and bitter grief, and then the nuns of the convent followed the body to the tomb. Born highly exalted, placed by God in a palace, but not satisfied and content with these blessings, made the effort to ''go higher'' at the expense of others, and she experienced terrible abasement in fulfillment of Christ's Words 1700 years before!

Probably about the time Sophia was born in the palace, a girl was born in a little village of Livonia. Her parents were in very humble circumstances, and they both died when she was a little child, leaving her in a very destitute and friendless condition. The parish clerk, teacher of a little school, took her into his home. One account says the clerk and all his family died of a plague about the same time, and a minister of a nearby town found the little girl, Catherine, alone in the home with the dead bodies of the family. She begged him for a piece of bread. He took the child in his home and raised her. When grown, with the minister's permission, she married a Swedish Army officer who had befriended her when taken captive after one battle. Shortly after her marriage her husband was either killed or captured, and she never heard of him again. The wars were almost continuous in those days, and she was captured again later by the Russians and in danger of being sold as a slave to the Turks. A Russian General saved her from this calamity and put her under the protection of the women who served his own quarters. While Catherine was growing up in the minister's home her ambition and desire appeared to be worthily to fulfill a woman's job in the Russian General's headquarters, by her humility, industry, and desire to serve, she not only won the esteem of the General, but also the other women and servants, and in time, found herself overseer of all the work done by the women. The General said he had never been served better.

One of the high Russian Princes on a visit to the General noticed Catherine. The result was that she was advanced to the same position in The Prince's Headquarters. Later, Peter the Great, The Emperor and Czar, on a visit to the Prince, noticed Catherine, and decided he needed her in the palace. She served so well and faithfully, Peter "fell for her" and decided he needed her for his Queen. They were secretly married in 1707. The marriage was supposed to be a secret for a time, but several years later, Peter highly honored his Queen with a great public celebration confirming the marriage. High officials of other nations were invited and attended the grand festivities. She was a great help and comfort to Peter, and often traveled with him in his war duties. It is said, at one time, by her wisdom and self-denial, she saved Peter and his army when they appeared to be hopelessly entrapped by the Turks.

At the death of Peter the Great in 1725, Catherine was proclaimed Empress and ruler of that great and powerful Empire. Sophia undertook to break the ancient Moscovite rule, forbidding the crown to a woman by self-exaltation and ambition. She failed and the end was terrible abasement. Catherine, by humility and ambition to fulfill her God ordained mission as a woman, did break the old Muscovite rule, and was highly exalted to be The Empress of that great Empire!

"Whosoever exalteth himself shall be abased, and he that humbleth himself shall be exalted."

On three separate occasions, at least, Christ spoke the above words. One time in Matthew 23:12. This is the chapter in which He so terribly denounced the Scribes, Pharisees, and Hypocrites -- the Church and secular leaders of that day -- calling them snakes, vipers, and asking *"How can ye escape the damnation of hell?"* Another time He spoke the same words in Luke 14:11. Here they were used to rebuke those who "exalted themselves" by seeking the best and highest seats for "self" when invited to a feast! (Consider what He might have to say to those who without invitation -- unless it is to stay away -- seek choice seats in another man's house or place of business!) A third time when Christ spoke these words is in Luke 18:14. In this passage He tells of the two men who went up to the Temple to pray: The Pharisee and the Publican. On account of self-exaltation, the Pharisee's prayer was not heard, but the Publican went home justified in the sight of God on account of his penitence and humility.

Deuteronomy 32:29: *"O that they were wise, that they understood this, that they would consider their latter end."* Have you been at the business of "exalting self" all your life? It may not be too late for you to repent, or turn, and the rest of your days seek to exalt and honor your God! In John 5:55, Christ asked: *"How can ye believe, which receive honor one of another, and seek not the honor that cometh from God only?"* A good question for you to try and answer!

January 1, 1966

† † †

In the year 1625, Charles the First ascended the throne of England. The political creed of Charles was a short one; he believed in "the divine right of kings" and also the "divine right of his bishop." There was no place for a Parliament in his system, except as a cumbersome and annoying method of securing money for the purpose of government.

From the first, Charles was at war with his Parliament, and soon there was an era of arbitrary government -- 1639-1640. It has been estimated that at the outbreak of the American Revolution seventy-five percent of the people of English blood of the northern colonies were descendants of men and women who had been driven out of England by the tyranny of Charles and his little archbishop -- by the way, these are the two

33

responsible for the "Declaration of Sports" promulgated in those days that made it legal for the profanation of the Sabbath -- both of these boys ended up by losing their heads on the chop block, however, to their worldly credit, it might be said they were not "chicken" about doing as they pleased on God's Day!

During this period of arbitrary government "The Star Chamber Court" made history by passing out judgments and sentences for "flogging, for one or more ears to be cut off, or slitting noses, or for face branding." In spite of these severe judgments, and censoring of the press, many hardy souls fought on "underground," some enduring more than once the atrocities of the court! With such conditions, is it any wonder that Civil War broke out in 1641, and all of the nation was in uproar? Scotland was hostile. One of the worst massacres of history occurred in Ireland in 1641 and all that nation was in an uproar. The great mass of the English people were disloyal and ready to take advantage of the first sign of weakness on the part of the government.

Civil War! Take a glance at the opposing forces: The king's forces and supporters were thorough courtiers, many of them soldiers of fortune, princes of royal and noble blood such as two nephews of the King, Prince Rupert and Prince Maurice, gay worldlings who hated Puritanism and despised Puritans -- doubtless, there are multitudes of their descendants in our land today. On the other side, supporting Parliament, were the great mass of "God Fearing" yeomanry, tradesmen of the towns, etc.

For ten years, the Great Civil War desolated England. The economic life of the nation suffered terribly. Thousands of individuals had been ruined, and public works abandoned and in cases, destroyed altogether. Thousands of acres had been thrown out of cultivation. Little respect was shown for civil law, crime and violence had increased steadily; murder, arson and highway robbery were common events of daily life -- sounds about like our day, is it not so? These were only symptoms of a deeper malady, the general decay of civilization.

God, in His mercy, gave Parliament the victory. Twenty-four years after Charles was crowned, on the 30th of January, 1649, after a trial by the High Court of Justice, King Charles was condemned to die. Three days before the Court had given its decision, declaring Charles Stewart to be "a tyrant, traitor, murderer and public enemy to the good people of this nation," and fixed the death penalty. On the 30th, he was led out to Whitehall to die: "And when the tragedy was over, and the masked executioner held up the gory trophy of his art, he shouted to the horror stricken crowd, "Behold the head of a traitor!"

A few years after the king's death, England, Ireland, and Scotland were at peace and prospering. When Charles ascended the throne, England's government and power were looked down upon, if not scorned, by other nations. At the time of the death of The Protector, Cromwell, England was respected and feared both as a land and sea power -- someone said of the Prime Minister of France: "He was more afraid of Cromwell than the devil!"

"Watch God Work!" Consider the change God wrought in England, Ireland, and Scotland between 1641 and 1659: from chaos and confusion to order, peace, and prosperity. Consider the human instruments with which He worked. We quote Ezekiel 22:29,30: *"The people of the land have used oppression, and exercised robbery, and have vexed the poor and needy; yea, they have oppressed the stranger wrongfully. And I sought for a man among them, that should make up the hedge, and stand in the gap before me for the land, that I should not destroy it: But I found none!"*

We suggest that in Oliver Cromwell, God "found His man to stand in the gap." During the first few years of the Great Civil War, Prince Rupert's horsemen and cavaliers swept the cavalry of Parliament off the field of battle. However, the sturdy Puritan infantry and foot soldiers of Parliament forces victoriously withstood the king's infantry. There was a country squire by the name of Oliver Cromwell. He had a cousin among the nobility by the name of Hampden by whose influence he might have obtained military preference. However, he asked no special favors for himself, but appeared to be content with the office of captain in the cavalry. When Prince Rupert's cavaliers played havoc with Parliament's horsemen, Cromwell managed to keep his men together and from being routed and scattered. Cromwell analyzed the success of Prince Rupert's cavaliers, and said to his cousin, Hampden: "Your troops are most of them decayed serving men and tapsters, and such kind of fellows, and their troops are gentlemen's sons and persons of quality. Do you think that the spirits of such base and mean fellows will ever be able to encounter gentlemen that have honor, courage and resolution in them?" Cromwell then went to work to raise a cavalry regiment of a very different mettle. As he himself expressed it, he proposed to match "men of religion" against the "king's gentlemen of honor." The result was the organization of the famous "Ironsides," a body of men who possessed the loftiest religious enthusiasm, tempered and hardened by the severest discipline.

Cromwell's Ironsides were men that had the true "fear of God" in their hearts; and gradually, lost all other fear: "Truly, they were never beaten at all," he says. They swept Prince Rupert and his cavaliers off the face of the earth. The Prince then took a job of Admiral in the king's navy, but it was only a question of time until Cromwell's Ironside Navy swept Prince Rupert and his ships off the ocean, or to its bottom -- have forgotten just what did happen to the Great Prince in the end, but the last I recall he was wandering about.

Do not forget the "past." The above recalls to remembrance some very significant history of our past. It is the first step in the downfall of our "democratic institutions" ; forgetting. The second downward step is indifference, and the third "utter recklessness." Are not our "democratic institutions" now fast failing in favor of institutions of socialism and communism? Lord God of Hosts, be with us yet, lest we forget! Lest we forget! **August 16, 1969**

† † †

Many years ago there was only one drug store in Decatur. The orders phoned in were delivered by bicycle. At the time of this story and incident, a colored boy had the job. Most of the time there was nothing much for him to do but wait around. Often he was found taking a nap. One day he was seen in front of the store just out of the door fast asleep, head reared back, and mouth wide open. The doctor diagnosed and got a big spoon full of quinine and dumped it in his mouth and hurried back in the store. The boy jumped up and ran to the curb spewing and spitting, and then rushed in the store and cried, "Doctor, do something for me quick, maybe I'se dying, I'se foaming at the mouth: think my 'bile' done busted!"

A letter the writer has just gotten reminded me of this story. It appears my recent comments complimentary to Oliver Cromwell acted like "quinine" in the author's religious or political system and "His bile done busted!" As this man seems to take the position of being a Christian, I thought of writing him and asking his permission to reprint his letter in this column, as I like to give my opponent's view when feasible, but alas, alas! There is too much "bile" in it!

"Blessed are ye when men shall revile you, and persecute you falsely for My sake, and say all manner of evil against you: Rejoice, and be exceedingly glad for great is your reward in Heaven." The author closed his letter: "Sorrowfully Yours!" If my appraisal of Cromwell reviles you and speaks evil for your views of him for Christ's sake, you should not be "Sorrowful," but rather rejoice, for great is your reward in heaven! Why, in Luke 6:23, Christ said: *"Rejoice ye in that day, and leap for joy . . ."* Man, ought you not to be "dancing" instead of "sorrowful"?

One of the worst massacres in history occurred in Ireland in 1641. If not mistaken, the root of the trouble back there was the difference between the Protestants and the Catholic. Is it not the same bitter root the cause of the trouble we are reading about every day now? At the risk of throwing "quinine" and "busting bile" again, it appears to this writer they are badly in need of Oliver Cromwell in Ireland right in this hour!

"At 42 years of age, Cromwell was a plain country squire. Yet at 43, he took up the study of war and soon secured a place among the world's greatest captains. At 50, he turned to politics and soon won for himself a place among 'the most vigorous and resourceful of statesmen.'" Guided by the sure instincts of a great man, strong nature, enthusiastic, yet always practical, he advanced step by step to that position from which for him there was no escape save death. It is true that he won his place by the sword; and yet only the sword could save England from anarchy and secure the fruit of that liberty for which a generation of Englishmen had struggled. He won his place by the sword, and he ruled by the sword. It has been said of him: "In an age of fanaticism he was the only fanatic who remained sane." It has also been said of him: "Here is a man whom the world is just beginning to understand!"

After Parliament won victory in the great Civil Wars against Charles the First during the 1640s, due largely to the genuis and military mastery of Cromwell, he was sent to Ireland with his Ironsides to put down revolt, anarchy, and lawlessness. He arrived there in 1649. Ormond was in charge of the English and Irish forces resisting Parliament. Ormond's forces were weak, having recently suffered reverses. On this account, as well as fear to come out in the open and fight with a man of Cromwell's record of victorious battles, instead of meeting him in the open field they retired behind high walls of such fortresses as Drogheda and Wexford in hope of tiring him out by a series of vexatious sieges lasting months, or maybe years, and many of them (for there may have been a dozen), a score or more such walled fortresses all over the land. But they did not know the man with whom they were dealing. On the 3rd of September, Cromwell appeared before Drogheda, and on the 10th, summoned its garrison of 2,800 men, the flower of Ormond's English soldiery to surrender. The garrison refused, and the next day Cromwell took the place by assault. No quarter was given and every man in arms was put to death, save a few who were shipped off as slaves to the sugar planations of the

Barbadoes.

The next month Cromwell appeared before the fortress of Wexford, summoned them to surrender or suffer the fate of Drogheda. They refused, thinking they could withstand any assault. As I recall the details, the first assault did fail. On the second assault, Cromwell placed himself at the head of his troops and made them a speech about as follows: "My pretty men, failure will not do, we must take this place, we cannot afford to sit down here and starve them out, and maybe starve ourselves out of food and finances." He led the assault in person, took the fortress, and the garrison suffered the same fate as the defender of Drogheda. It was not necessary to repeat the bloody lesson a third time. To most of the garrisons, the summons to surrender was sufficient. Cromwell's reasons given for this severity was that it would deter others from resistance, shorten the war and "tend to prevent the effusion of blood in the future!"

The writer is somewhat familiar with Cromwell, as a result of the History Book he had in College; also, reading somewhat of the great English Historian, David Hume; also, reading quite a bit of what that great character and English Historian, Thomas Carlyle, had to say about Cromwell; but most of all, he thinks he has learned most about Cromwell by reading The Almighty's Book: The Holy Bible.

August 29, 1969

† † †

In Jeremiah 6:16, we read: *"Thus saith the Lord, stand in the ways, and see, and ask for the old paths, where is the good way, and walk therein, and ye shall find rest for therein."* Is not the answer the "run-of-the-mine" church members and so called Christians given to the Lord today?

We think it will help you to "Remember all the way the Lord hath led our nation," and be obedient to the above commands: *"Stand in the ways, and see, and ask for the old paths, where is the good way, and walk therein,*" to the end we might find rest for our souls.

Concerning the Pilgrims -- Lest We Forget!

"Democratic Institutions exist by reason of their virtue. If ever they perish, it will be when you have forgotten the past, become indifferent to the present, and utterly reckless as to the future." This quotation was copied from the monument of Thos. E. Watson on the Capital ground in Atlanta. Are our Democratic Institutions now headed for wreck and ruins on the rocks of socialism and communism? *"Lord God of hosts, be with us yet, lest we forget, lest we forget!"*

[Note: Most of the following facts of history, etc., are taken from the book "The Hand of God in History", written about one hundred years ago by Rev. Hollis Read, A.M.]

"The Mohammedans," says M. Oelsner, "would have discovered America even centuries before Columbus, had not their fleet been wrecked in a tempest, after clearing the straits of Gibralter." Is not this something for us to still remember, and for which to thank God?

The great navigator, Columbus, is said to have been a diligent and devout student of prophecy, and he was actuated in no small degree in his venture westward, "by the hope he cherished of extending the Kingdom of Christ." And in the mind of his royal patroness (Isabella of Aragon), the conversion of the heathen to Christianity was an object "paramount to all the rest."

The first discoverers of this continent were Roman Catholics and America was taken possession of and made subject to Catholic governments. Nothing seemed more probable at one time than that France would be the owner of New England -- and these hills and valleys would have languished under the crucifix and the mitered priests, and groaned beneath the heavy rod of the Roman Pontiff -- even as has Mexico, Central and South America, for hundreds of years! (It appears today as if we might be on our way back to superstitious and spiritual slavery!) "Eternal vigilance is the price of liberty!" New England was early an object of desire of the French. As early as the year 1606, De Mont explored and claimed for France, the rivers, the coasts, and the bays of New England. The hostile savages first prevented their settlement. They did not yield their purpose. Three times in the following year, the attempt was renewed. Twice they were driven back by adverse winds, and the third time, wrecked at sea. Again, did Pourtrincourt attempt the same enterprise, but was, in like manner, compelled to abandon the project. At a still later period, a French armament of forty ships of war, under the Duke D'Anville, was destined for destruction in New England. It sailed from Chebucto, in Nova Scotia, for the purpose. In the meantime, the pious people, apprised of their danger, had appointed a day of fasting and prayer, to be observed in all the Churches. While Mr. Prince was officiating in Old South Church, Boston, on this fast day, and praying most fervently that the dread calamity might be averted, a sudden gust of wind arose so violently as to cause the clattering of the windows (till then, the day had been perfectly clear). The Reverend gentleman paused in his prayer, and looking around on his congregation with a countenance of hope, he again commenced, and with great devotional ardor, supplicated The Almighty to cause that wind to frustrate the object of their enemies. A great tempest ensued, in which the greater part of the French fleet was wrecked. The Duke and his principal General committed suicide, thousands were drowned, and many died of disease, and a small amount returned to France, without health, and spiritless, and the enterprise was abandoned forever!

"The first colony in North America, save Mexico, was a Protestant colony, planted by Casper de Coligni, as a City of Refuge for Protestants. It was destroyed expressly as Protestant! Thus was North America baptized by Jesuit priests with Protestant blood; yet despite all the machinations of Rome, God has confirmed the covenant and made this land the asylum and hope of the Protestants."   -Bancroft.

There were many varieties and sects of the Protestants, but it was the Puritans that were chosen by God as the materials with which to rear the superstructure of religion and government in the New World. Before the arrival of the Pilgrims, a grant had been given and a colony had been established in New England, called Plymouth, but this did not prosper. A new and modified patent was then granted to Lord Lenox and The Marquis of Buckingham. But no permanent settlement was made. It was reserved to the Puritans! Here should be nurtured, in the cradle of hardships, and perils from the savages, and from the wilderness, and sufferings manifold and grievous, a spirit which should nerve the moral muscle of the soul, and rear a soldiery of The Cross made of of steadier stuff, and animated by a purer spirit than the world had before known. The Pilgrims were the best men, selected from the best portion of the best nation on the face of the earth.

"The institutions of this country, both ciuvil and religious, were cast in the mold of Puritanism. Had any other of the colonies been allowed to stand in this relation to the whole, how different would have been the cast of American liberty and religion! As it was, men of the most unbending integrity and untiring industry; men humble and unobtrusive, yet courageous and immovable at the post of duty: yielding when wrong, yet inflexible when right; plain and frugal, yet intelligent and liberal; men who had been nurtured in the school of persecution, and suffered the loss of all things, that they might breathe the uncontaminated air of freedom; men who hated oppression, abhorred ignorance and vice -- who were in their very souls, republicans and Christians -- these were the men, chosen out by sovreign Wisdom, to control the destinies of the New World. And they have done it. The enterprise and intelligence, the undying love of liberty, the religious spirit -- I may say, the population of our Puritan colonies, have spread themselves over the whole continent. And what is worthy of special remark, these only prosper in our country. You look in vain over the wide expanse of our territory to find thrift and prosperity, temporal and spiritual, except under the auspices of

42

our Puritan influence. Who people our wide western domains, and plant there the institutions of learning and religion? Who found our colleges and seminaries, publish our books, teach our youths, sustain our benevolent enterprises, and go on pagan lands to make wretchedness smile, and ignorance to speak wisdom? By whose skill and industry rolls the railroad cars over the length and breadth of our great land, and whiten the ocean with canvass? Who, if not the sons of the Pilgrims, nerved with the spirit of the Pilgrims? Tell me, in what proportion, in any section of our country, the people are leavened with the leaven imported in the Mayflower, and I can tell you in what proportion they are enterprising, prosperous, moral and religious people.

"Compare Massachusetts and Mexico. Mexico was colonized just one hundred years before Massachusetts. Her first settlers were the noblest spirits of Spain in her Augustan Age; the epoch of Cervantes, Cortes, Pizarro, Columbus, Gonzalvo de Cordova, Cardinal Ximines, and the great and good Isabella. Massachusetts was settled by the poor Pilgrims of Plymouth, who carried with them nothing but their own hardy virtues and indomitable energy. Mexico, with a rich soil, and adapted to the production of every metal used by man -- Massachusetts, with a sterile soil and uncongenial climate, and no single article of transportation but ice and rock! How have these blessings, profusely given by Providence, been improved on the one hand, and obstacles overcome on the other? What is now the respective condition of the two countries? In productive industry, widespread diffusion of knowledge, public institutions of every kind, general happiness and continually increasing prosperity; in letters, arts, morals, religion -- in everything which makes a people great, there is not in the world, and there was never in the world, such a commonwealth as Massachusetts. And Mexico -- what is she?

The object of the brother who wrote the above about a hundred years ago was not to disparage our neighbors to the South, but rather, to remind North America "Lest we forget,"

43

as well as to bear witness to all men that it is *"The fear of the Lord, and obedience to His Commandments"* that makes individuals and nations strong, virile, and blessed of The Almighty. *"And thou shalt remember all the way which The Lord thy God led thee . . ."* (Deuteronomy 8:2). *"Lord God of hosts, be with us yet, lest we forget, lest we forget!"* Lord God of hosts, we have forgotten, have mercy upon us, that we may repent and bring forth fruit meet for repentance! *"He that hath eyes to see, let him see."*

July 11, 1968

† † †

"Thus saith the Lord: Cursed be the man that trusteth in man, and maketh flesh his arm, and whose heart departeth from the Lord . . . Blessed is the man that trusteth in the Lord, and whose hope the Lord is . . ." (Jeremiah 17:5).

The late Sam Jones said: "The man who throws hell fire out of his creed, when he arrives in hell will have to revise it, and then there will be nothing in it but 'hell fire'!"

About the year 1535, there was a terrible time in Munster, Germany. The Anabaptists took over, made a king, murdered, pillaged, raped, in the name of religion. In that period Martin Luther was living. Plurality of wives was permitted, and for several years this bunch held sway. Luther, in commenting on them said: "Such gross work and crimes is the work of children or baby devils, the fruit of the work of Doctor of Divinity Devils -- those who reject the Word of God and the infallibility of His Book, the Bible." Doubtless, their counterpart today are the smart, wise, brilliant men (brilliant and wise in the eyes and wisdom of men, fools in the eyes of God) who "cast away The Law of The Lord of Hosts" and reject the infallibility of and supernatural in the Holy Scriptures.

In the days of John Calvin a terrible death dealing plague broke out. It was very contagious and most of the preachers refused to minister to the afflicted and dying, saying they knew

44

it was their duty, but they had rather go to the devil.

For the sake of argument, if you knew that in order to get right with God you had to cut out Sunday sports, golf, baseball, fishing, etc., etc. and spend an hour a day, more or less, reading your Bible or on your knees before God, go to Church Sunday morning, Sunday night, yea, and prayer meeting Wednesday night, wonder how many would be like the preachers of Calvin's day who said they would rather go to the devil! That was a little over 400 years ago. Think of it! 400 years in the fires of hell, with eternity still to go! Lord, have mercy on us!

As stated, the above was found written down in an old note book of the writer's. It was his intention to try and dress it up the best he could with grammar, rhetoric, logic, and all that "sort of stuff" to make it presentable. However, in its present condition, we believe it capable of being used of God to bless all such as ". . . *THINK ON THEIR WAY, AND TURN THEIR FEET UNTO God's Testimonies, delay not, but make haste to obey God's Commandments,*" and can be very profitable for such a time as this. See Psalm 119:59, 60.

The D.D.'s doubt has not put out the fire of hell, but, on the contrary, has brought many of our great cities a realistic foretaste.

"I have not sent these prophets, yet they ran; I have not spoken unto them, yet they prophesied. But if they had stood in my counsel, and had caused my people to hear My Words, then they should have turned them from their evil way, and from the evil of their doings" (Jeremiah 23:21, 22).

Standing in the midst and beholding the horrors of the destruction of Jerusalem at the hands of the King of Babylon, Jeremiah said in Lamentations 2:14: *"Thy prophets have seen vain and foolish things for thee: and have not discovered thine iniquity, to turn away thy captivity; but have seen for thee false burdens and causes of banishment."*

"I have not troubled Israel; but thou, and thy father's house,

in that ye have forsaken the commandments of The Lord . . ." (I Kings 18:18).

"*If My people, which are called by My name, shall humble themselves, and pray, and seek My face, and turn from their wicked ways; then will I hear from Heaven, and will forgive their sin, and will heal their land*" (II Cronicles 7:14).

August 18, 1967

† † †

"*Righteousness exalteth a nation; but sin is a reproach to any people*" (Proverbs 14:34). Am I uplifting my nation? Let us examine and judge ourselves: "*For if we would judge ourselves, we should not be judged!*" (I Corinthians 11:31).

Quoting a letter received this morning, and our reply: "Sir, when in the Bible did it say, 'Take a stick and beat the hell out of him'? It talks about disciplining a child? Thank you." -Signed with address. The reply: "*Withhold not correction from the child; for if thou beatest him with the rod, he shall not die. Thou shalt beat him with the rod, and shalt deliver his soul from hell!*" (Proverbs 23:13, 14).

The first recorded words spoken by Jesus Christ after His baptism by John the Baptist were: "*Man shall not live by bread alone, but by every word that proceedeth out of the mouth of God*" (Matthew 4:4, and Luke 4:4).

Also quoting the last two verses of the Book of Ecclesiastes: "*Let us hear the conclusion of the whole matter; fear God and keep His Commandments; for this is the whole duty of man, for God shall bring every work into judgment, with every secret thing, whether it be good, or whether it be evil!*" Friend: Give your heart to the God that created you. "*And be thou faithful unto death, and I will give you a crown of life*" (Revelation 2:10).

This is the writer's witness and testimony: Ye are my witnesses says God many times in the Old Testament, and

46

Christ many times in the New Testament. What follows concerns some significant history about the date September 4th.

In the writer's judgment, God Almighty, who sure is a "Man of War," as we are told in Exodus 15:3, and *Whose eyes run to and fro throughout the whole earth, to show himself strong in the behalf of them whose heart is perfect towards Him*" (II Chronicles 16:9). This Holy God found a Man into whose hands He put a rod, strengthened, and stirred up to "Beat the Hell out of three Nations within a period of about 15 years, about 1640-55. If I mistake not, during this period there were 3 or 4 great, terrible, and very decisive battles fought in England, Scotland, and Ireland, in different years, but all on and around the 4th of September.

Consider this about "the man" God's eyes found to do the job: He became so disgusted with Sabbath Desecration, Immorality, Crime, all sorts of Lawlessness, that He decided to move across the ocean to the American Colonies, made arrangements, and was on the boat to sail. But King Charles, the First of England knew him, refused to let him leave, and had him taken off!

It appears God needed him to lead the movement that cut off the King's head in 1649. He also led the movement that was victorious in Scotland in bringing law and order and blessing, in spite of the fact he was opposed by many of the Great and High Scotch Divines, or Dry Vines, as some called them. In a quick and terrible way, he put away the horrible lawlessness, crime, and et cetera in Ireland! (For months, if not years, see in today's news of crime, etc. nearly every day in Ireland. It always reminds me of the record of God's Man cleaning up Ireland in the year 1650). The record says that the French King was so afraid of Oliver Cromwell that he behaved himself!

It is the writer's understanding that all the great decisive battles in these wars in England, Scotland, and Ireland were fought on, or just about, the Fourth Day (4th) of September! Also, that if in any one of them he had been defeated, his power

47

would have been at an end.

Let all Christians think on these things around September Fourth Period, and in view of our crime and lawless condition, "Pray God to fight for us!" "He Changes Not!"

"Righteous exalteth a nation; but sin is a reproach to any people!"

September 2, 1973

† † †

On May 8th the writer began preparing an article for this column, but did not get it finished in time for that week. If not mistaken, May 8th is the great Joan of Arc Day in France -- the great day of celebration of the victory and entrance into Paris.

"Consider this unique and imposing distinction. Since the writing of history began, Joan of Arc is the only person, of either sex, who has ever held supreme command of the military forces of a nation at the age of seventeen!" *-Louis Coussuth*

Now quote extracts from Mark Twain: "Judged by the standards of one century, the noblest characters of an earlier one lose much of their luster, judged by the standards of today, there is probably no illustrious man of four or five centuries ago, whose character could meet this test at all points. But the character of Joan of Arc is unique. It can be measured by the standards of all times without misgiving as to the result. Judged by any of them, judged by all of them, it is still flawless, it is perfect; it still occupies the loftiest place possible to human attainment, a loftier one than has been reached by any other mere mortal.

"When we reflect that her century was the brutalist, the wickedest, the rottenest in history since the middle ages, we are lost in wonder at the miracle of such a product from such a soil. The contrast between her and her century is the contrast between day and night. She was truthful when lying was the common speech of men; she was honest when honesty had become a lost virtue; she was a keeper of promises when the keeping of a promise was expected of no one; she gave her great mind to great thoughts when other great minds wasted themselves upon pretty fancies or upon poor ambitions; she was modest, and fine, and delicate when to be loud and coarse might be said to be universal; she was full of pity when a merciless cruelty was the rule; she was steadfast when stability was unknown, and honorable in an age that had forgotten what honor was; she was a rock of convictions in a time when men believed in nothing and scoffed at all things; she was unfailingly true in an age that was false to the core; she maintained her personal dignity unimpaired in an age of fawnings and servilities; she was of a dauntless courage when hope and courage had perished in the hearts of her nation; she was spotlessly pure in mind and body when society in the highest places was foul in both -- she was all these things in an age when crime was the common business of lords and princes and when the highest personages in Christendom were able to astonish even that infamous era and make it stand with an aghast attitude at the spectacle of the atrocious lives black with an unimaginable treacheries, butcheries, and beastialities.''

Comment: Genuine Christianity, sincere and true faith made Joan of Arc what she was!

''The work wrought by Joan of Arc may fairly be regarded as ranking any in history, when one considers the conditions under which it was undertaken, the obstacles in the way and the means at her disposal. Caesar carried conquest far, but he did it with trained and confident veterans of Rome, and was a trained soldier himself; and Napoleon swept away the disciplined armies of Europe, but he also was a trained soldier, and he began his work with a patriot battalion inflamed and inspired by

49

the miracle working new breath of Liberty breathed upon them by the Revolution-eager young apprentices to the splendid trade of war, not old and broken men at arms, despairing survivors of an agelong accumulation of monotonous defeats; but Joan of Arc, a mere child in years, ignorant, unlettered, a poor village girl unknown and without influence, found a great nation lying in chains, helpless and hopeless under an alien dominion, its treasury bankrupt, its soldiers disheartened and dispersed, all spirit, torpid, all courage dead in the hearts of the people through long years of foreign and domestic outrage and oppression.

"Their King cowed, resigned to its fate, and preparing to fly the country; and she laid her hand on this nation, this corpse, and it rose and followed her. She led it from victory to victory. She turned back the tide of the Hundred Years War. She fatally crippled the English power, and died with the title of "Deliverere of France", which she bears to this day. Sincere and true faith, faithfully worked at and endured will bring about the will of God in your life, in mine! At least three times in the Gospels, Christ said: *"He that endureth to the end shall be saved!"* And in Revelation 2:10, He said: *"Be thou faithful unto death, and I will give thee a crown of life!"*

June 16, 1973

† † †

Before breakfast, Sunday morning, March 25th, in the year of our Lord nineteen hundred and seventy three, the writer spent about half an hour reading the Bible, part of his daily Scripture reading time. It covered several chapters in the book of Daniel. Most of the following are excerpts from the sixth chapter of Daniel.

Darius the Median took over the kingdom the night Belshazzar the Chaldean Ruler was slain. He was killed the same night of the great profane feast given by King Belshazzar and his Court at which time a handwriting appeared on the wall telling him "He had been weighed; he had been found wanting; his end was at hand!"

It pleased Darius to set over the Kingdom an hundred and twenty princes, which should be over the whole kingdom; and over these three presidents; of whom Daniel was first; that the princes might give accounts unto them, and the king should have no damage. Then this Daniel was preferred above the presidents and princes, because an excellent spirit was in him; and the king thought to set him over the whole realm.

Then the presidents and princes sought to find occasion against Daniel concerning the kingdom; but they could find none occasion nor fault; forasmuch as he was faithful, neither was there any error or fault found in him. Then said these men, we shall not find any occasion against this Daniel, except we find it against him concerning the law of his God. Then these presidents and princes assembled together to the king, and said unto him, King Darius live forever. All the presidents of the kingdom, the governors and princes, the counsellors and captains, have consulted together to establish a royal statute, and make a firm decree, that whosoever shall ask a petition of any God or man for thirty days, save of thee, O king, shall be cast into the den of lions. Now, O king, establish the decree, and sign the writing, that it be not changed, according to the law of the Medes and Persians, which altereth not. Therefore King Darius signed the writing and the decree.

Now when Daniel knew the writing was signed, he went into his house; and his windows being open in his chamber toward Jerusalem, he kneeled upon his knees three times a day, and prayed, and gave thanks before his God, as he did aforetime. Then these men assembled, and found Daniel praying and making supplication before his God. Then they came near, and spake before the king concerning the king's decree; has thou not signed a decree, that every man that shalt ask a petition of any God or man within thirty days, save of thee, O king, shall be cast into the den of lions? The King answered and said, the thing is true, according to the law of the Medes and Persians, which altereth not. Then answered they and said before the king. That Daniel, which is of the children of the captivity of Judah, regardeth not thee, O king, nor the decree thou hast signed but maketh his petition three times a day. Then the king when he heard these words, was sore displeased with himself, and set his heart on Daniel to deliver him; and he labored until the going down of the sun to deliver him. Then these men assembled unto the king, and said unto the king, know O king, that the law of the Medes and Persians is, That no decree nor statute which the king established may be changed. Then the king commanded. And they brought Daniel, and cast him into the den of lions. Now the king spake and said unto Daniel. Thy God whom thou servest continually, he will deliver thee. And a stone was brought, and laid upon the mouth of the den; and the king sealed it with his signet, and with the signets of his lords; that the purpose might not be changed concerning Daniel. Then the king went to his palace, and passed the night in fasting, no music, and no sleep . . . Then the king arose very early in the morning and went in haste unto the den of the lions. Then said Daniel unto the king . . . *"My God hath sent his angel, and hath shut the lions mouths, that they have not hurt me, forasmuch as before him innocency was found in me . . . and the King commanded, and they brought those men which had accused Daniel, and they cast them into the den of lions, them, their children, and their wives, and the lions had mastery of them, and brake all their bones in pieces or ever they came to the bottom of the den."*

On more than one occasion during its lifetime this column has borne witness it believed our late FBI Director Hoover *"Loved righteousness and hated evil [Ye that love the Lord, hate evil]"* (Psalm 97:10), and it wishes to bear similar witness to Chief

52

John Inman, Atlanta Police, and I surely wish to bear witness to all men. God Almighty's witness. Ninth Commandment: *"Thou shalt not bear false witness against thy neighbor"* (Daniel, Chapter 9:4): *"And I prayed unto the Lord my God, and made my confession, and said, O Lord, the great and dreadful God . . ."* Daniel, himself, was able to get to the bottom of the den and spend the night without hurt, however, the men, their children, and wives were broken to pieces by the lions before getting to the bottom!

April 7, 1973

Law and Order

Division Three

"Withhold not correction from the child: for if thou beatest him with the rod, he shall not die. Thou shalt beat him with the rod and deliver his soul from hell!"

"Again, hear the words of the Lord, being the first recorded spoken by Jesus Christ after His baptism by John the Baptist" (Matthew and Luke 4:4).

"Man shall not live by bread alone, but by every word that proceedeth out of the mouth of God."

And another again, hear the word of the Lord in Hebrews, chapter 12 (12, 5, etc.): *"Have ye forgotten the exhortation which speaketh unto you as children, my son, despise not the chastening of the Lord, nor faint when thou art rebuked of him; for whom the Lord loveth He chasteneth, and scourgeth every son whom He receiveth, if ye endure chastening, God dealeth with you as with sons; for what son is he whom the father chasteneth not? But if ye be without chastisement, whereof all are partakers, then are ye bastards, and not sons!"*

Is not the implication above very clear and plain that neglect of punishment of evil will result in death and hell? Humanly speaking of recent years and today, are we not experiencing "Death and Hell"?

Here is a story and incident observed and experienced by the writer many years ago: There was anarchy and lawlessness in a boys' school of about middle age teens. For the most part, it showed up in only one manner: the shooting of rubbers. For the most part, the ammunition was spit-balls, but the zeal of some

55

of the law breakers and anarchists caused them to begin shooting little wire staples which would have knocked out an eye or done other serious body injury. One boy fixed up for his rubber-gun a large wad of paper, soaked it a long time in his spit, aimed at another boy's cheek and fired. Alas! Alas! Poor marksmanship! The target was missed and instead of the cheek a hit was made on a big canvas picture hanging on the wall -- the picture cried out like a pistol shot! The teacher seemed to know the guilty party. Asked him if he did it and on admitting guilt, was ordered up front. Another boy was sent out to the "bushes" to get some "rods" or sticks. The bad boy was "Beaten with the Rod" while the whole school looked on -- God's orders were carried out; all saw it, one boy felt it!

Can you guess the result? This anarchy and lawlessness was broken up. Not only the boy that was whipped publicly stopped shooting rubbers, but all the others. Spitballs quit flying about and wire staples that might have knocked out eyes or given a life injury ceased flying. We consider that in plain and unvarnished language, God Almighty said in Proverbs 23:13, 14: "Beat the hell out of him with a stick!" Physically and humanly speaking, the "hell" in this instance as a result of the disobedience and anarchy was the danger of loss of eyes or other serious injury. Thank God the teacher obeyed the Word of God found in Proverbs 23:13, 14: *"Withhold not correction from the child; for if thou beatest him with the rod, he shall not die, and deliver his soul from hell!"*

Hear the Word of the Lord to the first created man: *"Obey or die! Perish!"* Or, to break His command down in more detail, the Almighty said to His creatures: Beat him with the rod and deliver his soul from hell; you can give him forty stripes at one whipping; if a boy or older one gets uncontrollable, stone him to death (that is the way we kill bad snakes) or put him to death and send his soul back to the God who gave it by the sword, the spear, hanging, fire, or otherwise!

Would like to make a request of you if your name is on some genuine Protestant Christian Church: Get familiar with every word that proceedeth out of the mouth of God in a King James Version of Holy Scriptures, and if you cannot submit and accept, resign and get out!

"Forbear thee from meddling with God" (II Chronicles 35:21).

December 16, 1972

† † †

Creeping crime cursing our citizens and cities and churches!

Calling consecrated Christians to cry to Christ to cleanse His Church! Said Jesus to Peter: *"If I wash thee not, thou has no part with me!"* (John 13:8).

Commenting on the last, first -- crime creeping on the Church. A few months back, as the writer came out of a Sunday morning worship service, he shook hands at the door with one of the Church Officers, and noted he had a big bad place on his head. Said I, "Why, you have the same name as a man I noted the papers said got knocked in the head by a bank robber!" Said he, "I am the man!" Thank God, he was not brought to Church for funeral!

About a month ago two Sunday School boys sat and talked together waiting for the service to start -- one of the boys is over three score years and ten and the other not so far behind. The younger boy told this story: Departed a few days ago for a vacation time in Florida with a lot of clothes and equipment in the car. Spent the first night in City Hotel along my route. Next morning, found the car windows had been broken and all my stuff stolen -- crime surely mistreated that Sunday School boy!

Crime is also creeping in homes -- too often we read of where a parent or other member of the family kill one or more of the others! A man told me he took a walk after supper for exercise: As he passed one home, overheard an angry male voice: "I am going to kill you!" Reply of a female voice: "Better dead than live with you!"

57

Now get your Bible and turn to Jeremiah, chapter 6, and begin reading at verse 16: *"Thus saith the Lord, stand ye in the ways and see, and ask for the old paths, where is the good way, and walk therein, and ye shall find rest for your souls . . . also I set watchmen over you, saying, harken to the sound of the trumpet, but they said we will not harken. We will not harken!"* We will not walk therein . . . We will not harken! *"Therefore, hear, ye nations, and know, O congregation . . . Hear O earth: behold, I will bring evil upon this people, even the fruit of their thoughts, because they have not harkened unto my words, not to my law, but rejected it!"*

Ask for the Old Paths, where is the good way, and walk therein! One Old Path and Good Way is the Mid-week Prayer Meeting. Am of the opinion that for the most part this Old Path and Good Way has been supplanted with "eatin' meetin's" and of the conviction that, generally, such meetings "grieve the Spirit of God" -- unless their object is to feed those in real need and hungry for the necessities of life.

Have read quite a bit in the newspapers recently regarding The First Baptist Church of Atlanta, and have been much pleased and inspired for the past year, more or less, as have noticed how in their Saturday Church advertisement they call attention to that Old Path, that Good Way, The Mid Week Prayer Service.

Creeping Crime Cursing our Citizens and Cities and Churches! Calling Consecrated Christians to Cry to Christ to Cleanse His Church! Jesus said to Peter: *"If I wash thee not, thou hast no part with me!"*

February 12, 1972

† † †

Several hours ago big headlines in the Newspaper: **J. Edgar Hoover Dead!** Within the past year this column bore witness to the fact it considered Mr. Hoover a "God send" to our nation, and asked all who could join in giving thanks to God for his

58

ministry. And Amen! Soon came to mind a verse or two from the Bible: Exodus 15:2-4: *"The Lord is my strength and song, and he is become my salvation; he is my God, and I will prepare him an habitation; my father's God, and I will exalt him. The Lord is a man of war! The Lord is his name."* The Lord is a man of war! The Lord is a man of war! The Lord is a man of war! Friend! If your God is not a "Man of War", suggest you better investigate and see "what you got!"

"For the eyes of the Lord run to and fro throughout the whole earth to show himself strong in the behalf of them whose heart is perfect towards him!" (II Chronicales 16:9). Several times, the Bible calls Abraham, the Friend of God. Consider how God at one time, made him a "man of war" and he whipped in war several kings and their armies -- Genesis 14:14-24. Also, consider how God made Moses a "Man of War", and Samson and other Judges, "Men of War," King David and other Kings, mighty "Men of War," and down through history to our day! This witness testifies that God has greatly blessed our nation during the past forty or fifty years by making J. Edgar Hoover "a mighty man of war" against evil, crime, and lawlessness! Again, Thank God.

It appears to this writer that about fifty years ago as "the eyes of God went to and fro throughout our land, He observed a poor boy down in Texas shooting jack rabbits to help feed his parents and family, and God decided to show Himself strong in the boy's behalf in making him a 'mighty man of war!' The boy's name was Audie Murphy." War came on with Germany and Audie went to war. Audie departed this life about August, 1971. We are quoting part of his war record as reported by a fellow soldier and observer:

"The kraut tanks rumbled past Lt. Murphy's position, passing him by as close as 50 yards, and firing at him as they passed. The kraut infantry line, consisting of two full companies of 125 lmen, surged up across the open meadow in a wide arc. Then I saw Lt. Murphy do the bravest thing that I have ever seen any man do in combat," wrote Lt. Walter

Weispfenning in his official report of the engagement. "With the Germans only 100 yards away and still moving up on him, he climbed onto the slowly burning tank destroyer and began firing the 50-caliber machine gun. There he was, completely exposed and silhouetted against the background of bare trees and snow, with a fire under him that threatened to blow the destroyer to bits if it reached the gasoline and ammunition. Standing on the top of the TD, Lt. Murphy raked the approaching enemy forces with machine gun fire. Twelve krauts, stealing up a ditch to flank him from his right were killed in the gully at 50 yards range. His clothing was torn and riddled by flying shell fragments and bits of rock. Bullets ricocheted and careened off the tank destroyer as the enemy concentrated their full fury on this one man stronghold. He was wounded in the leg by fragmentation from an 88-mm shell but he kept on fighting. With blood spreading over his torn trouser leg, he continued to hold off the entire German force of about 250 men, aided only by our artillery fire. After an hour long fight, exhausted, bleeding profusely and his ammunition spent, Lt. Murphy limpted back to his company. He reorganized his men and led them in a violent attack on the enemy, driving the Germans from the area. Lt. Murphy then had his wound treated on the field. He consistently refused to be evacuated. Lt. Murphy's intreped stand, fighting alone against overwhelming odds, enabled his regiment to hold ground that was won at a heavy cost in blood."

"God is a man of war!" Quoting from Revelation 12:7, etc.: *"And there was war in heaven; Michael and his angels fought against the dragon . . . and the great dregon was cast out, that old serpent, called the devil and Satan . . . and they overcame him by the blood of the Lamb and by the word of their testimony, and they loved not their lives unto the death!"*

May 13, 1972

† † †

For a long, long time the writer has proposed to make an

apology to many friends who have written -- and maybe some other kind of folks -- for failing to reply. There have been stamped envelopes received for reply that through procrastination were never honored -- in fact, I fear that in one or two instances, a one dollar contribution to help with the expense received and no note of thanks -- inexcusable! The writer has no office force. Have never been able to dictate satisfactorily. If I feel I can be of any help to you, do not bother about writing again and again, until you get some action, if it does not worry you too much.

On Friday, July 31st, the writer did not read the morning paper until supper time, in a cafe. There appeared in it a picture of several men -- all of whom appeared to be very happy and applauding victoriously. Am quoting the statement under the picture: "DELANO, Calif. -- Caesar Chaves (left, seated), leader of a five-year boycott against California grape owners, applauds as John Glumarra, Jr., whose family owns the biggest table grape vineyard in the world, holds up the union label of the AFL-CIO United Farm Workers Organizing Committee. Chaves and 17 Growers Wednesday shook hands over a contract giving workers a pay raise, and freeing 75 percent of California table grapes from the world-wide boycott. (Associated Press Wirephoto)."

As stated, the writer saw this in the morning paper while eating supper in a cafe. More than once this scribe has stated in this column he aims at spending one hour every day reading the Bible consecutively -- but that leaves him only 23 hours each day for sleeping, eating, playing, and obeying God Almighty's Fourth Commandment: *"Six days shalt thou labor."* When I got home from supper, one of the first things I did was to get my Bible and complete or begin my daily assignment. With my mind somewhat on the story of the Great Labor Grape Victory, was rather impressed with about the first passage I read, and here it is:

"For the Kingdom of Heaven is like unto a man that is an householder, which went out early to hire laborers into his

vineyard. And when he had agreed with the laborers for a penny a day, he sent them into his vineyard. And he went out about the third hour, and saw others standing idle in the market place, and said unto them: Go ye into the vineyard, and whatsoever is right I will give you. And they went their way. Again, he went out about the sixth and ninth hour, and did likewise. And about the eleventh hour, he went out, and found others standing idle, and saith unto them, why stand ye here all day idle? They say unto him, because no man hath hired us. He saith unto them, go ye also into the vineyard; and whatsoever is right, that shall ye receive. So when even was come, the lord of the vineyard saith unto his steward. Call the laborers and give them their hire, beginning from the last unto the first. And when they came that were hired about the elventh hour, they received every man a penny. But when the first came, they supposed that they should receive more; and they likewise received every man a penny. But when the first came, they supposed that they should receive more; and they likewise received every man a penny. And when they had received it, they murmured against the good man of the house, saying, these last have wrought but one hour, and thou hast made them equal unto us, which have borne the burden and heat of the day. But he answered one of them, and said, Friend, I do thee no wrong; didst thou not agree with me for a penny? Take that thine is, and go thy way; I will give unto this last, even as unto thee. Is it not lawful for me to do what I will with mine own? Is thine evil, because I am good? So the last shall be first, and the first last: For many be called, but few chosen!" (Matthew 20:1-16).

"A penny for your thoughts." None have offered me a penny, but will give several, hoping I can afford the loss of the penny: *"Righteousness exalteth a nation, but sin is a reproach to any people!"* *"He that is greedy of gain troubleth his own house!"* *"Coveteousness is idolatry!"* *"What shall it profit a man if he gain the whole world, and lose his soul!"* *"Is it not lawful for me to do what I will with mine own!"* **"Is it not lawful for me to do what I will with mine own?"**

The third time I ask: "Is it not lawful for me to do what I will with what God gives me?"

August 13, 1970

† † †

The following quote is from a Municipal Court Judge of another city: "A girl in her third year of college, twenty-one years of age, was picked up for shop-lifting. She stole a seventy-nine dollar coat." It appears that "education" may not be the cure for her crime! God says His Word will cure it. In Jeremiah 23:21, etc., God says of His witnesses, His prophets: *"But if they had stood in My counsel, and had caused My people to hear My words, then they should have turned from their evil way, and from the evil of their doings."* The following was in this column March 16, 1963. It tells of God's terrible judgment upon an unrepentent thief, his family and possessions, his nation and country! Have you stolen something? And never repented; never made any restitution? Note especially the last paragraph of this article!

The heathen rage to get rid of God's Commandments and their restraint. Consider God's 8th Commandment: *"Thou shalt not steal." "Let us hear the conclusion of the whole matter: Fear God and keep His Commandments: for this is the whole duty of man. For God shall bring every work into judgment, with every secret thing, whether it be good, or whether it be evil"* (Ecclesiastes 12:13, 14). *"The heart in your bosom is a 'muffled drum' beating a march for you to the cemetery,"* and the judgment of God: *"It is appointed unto men once to die, but after this the judgment"* (Hebrews 9:27).

Wherefore, Attention: Calling all thieves and robbers of various and sundry assortments: The bank robber, newspaper-rack robber, shop-lifters, the con-man, those who steal blankets, towels, napkins, forks, knives, spoons, salt-shakers, etc., automobiles, and the much lower down thieves who steal their neighbor's wife or husband, or the virtue of their sister or daughter; come one, come all, and all other kinds and hear, and behold, the judgment of God Almighty on a certain thief by name, his family, his wife and children, his sons, his daughters, and his oxen, and his asses, and all that he had. Consider this example of God bringing the secrets of this thief to light and terrible judgment.

Read about it in God Almighty's own Book, the Bible, His revelation of Himself, and His ways, and His acts to purge out and get rid of a thief! You can read about it in the 7th chapter of the book of Joshua. Joshua had just led the people across the River of Jordan on dry ground into the Promised Land. The first city to be taken and destroyed was Jericho. As Joshua stood near the city, the Angel of God appeared to him -- chapter 5:13-15. He was told how to capture the city, and given instructions what to do with it, and contents: *"And in the city shall be accused, even it, and all that are therein, to the Lord . . . and ye, in any wise, keep yourselves from the accursed thing, lest ye make yourselves accursed, when ye take of the accursed thing, and make the camp of Israel a curse, and trouble it. But all the silver, and gold, and vessels of brass and iron, are consecrated unto the Lord; they shall come into the treasury of the Lord"* (Joshua 6:17-19).

It is likely that some of the people had had no new suits or shoes in forty years, and were wearing the toggery of slaves with which they had left Egypt, although there had been some spoils from enemies destroyed along the way. There were some mighty fine clothes and other stuff being burned up in the destruction of the city of Jericho, fine suits from Babylon of the latest styles and finest texture. In spite of God's Commandment, it did not make sense to one man to destroy; here is the explanation he made later. *"When I saw among the spoils a goodly Babylonish garment and two hundred shekels of silver, and a wedge of gold of fifty shekels weight, then I coveted them, and took them; and, behold, they are hid in the earth in the midst of my tent, and the silver under it"* (Joshua 7:21).

"For God shall bring every work into judgment, with every secret thing. . . " The way God brought this secret thing to light and judgment was as follows: Israel lost the next battle! *"The curse causeless shall not come."* Even Joshua was discouraged and frightened! God had told him someone had stolen that which He told them to let alone, and He would not help them any more until the sin and sinners were purged and put away. There were above 500,000 men able to bear arms in the nation, and no one knew who was guilty except the thief, and the Almighty. God pointed him out to the whole nation by means of drawing lots; *"God shall bring every work into judgment, with every secret thing!"*

The terrible, horrible and devastating judgment upon this man and family and everything he possessed is liable to tempt one to be offended with the Almighty! If so, rebuke that spirit within you immediately, and remember that the Almighty is High and Holy, and we by nature are low and vile; and pray that our offense, anger, rage, or what have you, may be directed at the awful evil of stealing, rebellion, and anarchy against the Holiness, Justice, Goodness and Truth of the Holy, Holy, Holy, Lord God Almighty. The account of this terrible judgment upon stealing is given by quoting Joshua 7:24-26: *"And Joshua, and all Israel with him, took Aachan the son of Zerah, and the silver, and the garment, and the wedge of gold, and his sons, and his daughters, and his oxen, and his asses, and his sheep, and his tent, and all that he had; and they brought them unto the valley of Achor. And they stoned them with stones. And they raised over him a great heap of stones unto this day. So the Lord turned from the fierceness of his anger."*

"A heathen is one who does not believe in the God of the Bible." If a man really believes in "The God of the Bible", he will not only quit stealing, but turn back and make restitution of what he has stolen to the uttermost of his ability! And he will be jealous and zealous to stop everyone else from stealing that he possibly can! Achan and family's judgment, so far as we know, was temporal. They were stoned to death, and it was their lifeless bodies that were burned. The New Testament tells of thieves who failed to take advantage of the offer of forgiveness in Christ Jesus being "cast alive" into fire where *"The worm dieth not, and the fire is not quenched."* Mock, if you so desire, but as for me and my house, let us: *"Fear the Lord and depart from evil!"*

Someone has suggested that if Aachan had rushed out before the congregation and confessed before God's finger, the lot, pointed him out, things might have turned out different. Thieves and robbers. don't wait for "The Finger of God" to point you out before the "assembled universe!"

December 18, 1965

† † †

They rage to get rid of God's Law, His Ten Commandments, and His King, The Lord Jesus Christ. God has said in His Word that sometimes His own people act worse than the heathen in accomplishing these ends; What about our generation today in view of this recent statement of our F.B.I. Director J. Edgar Hoover: "We have on the loose in our country today a predatory monster called crime. It is growing in size and violence. Its far reaching forages threaten every city and hamlet in the nation, and it strikes fear in the heart and mind of the law-abiding public. It is ripping the very fiber of our society and our system of government." It appears that our rage and anarchy against God Almighty's Law, Ten Commandments, and His King is highly successful at the moment! Are you "passing the buck" to another and others? Do you examine yourself?

The following is a reprint of the article in this column on September 19, 1964: "The Great Reformer, Martin Luther, had a friend and associate whom the historian called 'Master Jobst.' One day he was dining with Luther and showed him some propositions according to which The Law ought not to be preached, since we are not justified by it. Luther got angry, and exclaimed, 'What! will my brethren propose such innovations

66

while I live!. . . Indeed, he who pulls down the Law, pulls down at the same time, the whole framework of human policy and society. If The Law be thrust out of the Church, there will be no longer anything recognized as sin in the world, since the Gospel defines and punishes sin only by recurring to The Law . . . If, I at the first inveighed against The Law, both from the pulpit and my writings, the reason was, that the Christian was at that time overladen with superstition, under which Christ was altogether buried and hidden, and I yearned to save and liberate pious God-fearing souls from this tyranny over the conscience. But I have never rejected The Law.''

Multitudes of those whom he set free from superstition and tyranny came to use their liberty for license and got to be corrupt in manners, customs, dress and morals. A few years before the end of Luther's life on earth, he left Wittenberg in disgust, saying he would never return. It was with great difficulty he was persuaded to return after a year or more absence.

While his motives were good, and profitable at first in inveighing against The Law, yet it appears the effects and results in some ways were bad. No man can trifle with God's Law and get by for long! Adam and Eve tried it, and died! Great individuals, great nations, great empires, and great civilizations have found it so from experience! They dashed themselves to pieces against "The Rock of Ages! The Word of God! And perished!" *"For all flesh is grass, and all the glory of man as the flower of the grass. The grass withereth, the flower thereof falleth away; but the Word of the Lord endureth forever. And this is The Word which by The Gospel is preached unto you"* (I Peter 1:24, 25 and Isaiah 40:6-8).

In our day and generation there are great multitudes calling themselves Christian who have accepted the propositions Master Jobst showed Luther. They have pulled down, they have quit preaching The Law on the grounds they are not justified by it. The Law is to a large extent cast out of the Church, and being pulled down with it and undermined is the whole framework of politics and society; and we have about come to the place where nothing is recognized as sin in the world by man. However, God Almighty still recognizes sin as disobedience to His Commandments: *"Sin is the transgression of the Law, God's Ten Commandments."* *"God is angry with the wicked every day -- the wicked shall be turned into hell, and all the nations that forget God!"* (Psalm 7:11 and Psalm 9:17).

In the Sermon on the Mount -- Mathew 5:13, etc. -- Christ said to His disciples: *"Ye are the salt of the earth -- Ye are the light of the world -- A city set on a hill -- Let your light so shine before men. . ."* Did you ever note and consider the very next thing He said to them: *"Think not that I am come to destroy the Law and the prophets. . . Till heaven and earth pass, one jot or one tittle shall in no wise pass from the Law, till all be fulfilled."* Is not the implication as plain as the nose on your face, the way to "salt the earth, shine the light," and be "as a city set on a hill" is to: *"Fear God and keep His commandments, which is the whole duty of man"* (Ecclesiastes 12:13).

What use have you for a servant or an employee that don't carry out orders? In pride and presumption, many testify that they are not under the Law and do not have to keep God's Commandments! John Wesley said, "All enemies of the Gospel are mere triflers by comparison with those who give you exemption from obeying God's Commandments!" Doubtless, no professed Christian will defend idolatry, profanity, dishonoring of parents, murder, adultery, stealing, false witness, and coveting, though they may practice one or more of them, but it appears that most of them will attack the Fourth Commandment: *"Remember the Sattath Day to keep it holy"* -- quit work and working your hired help, and seek to honor God. Jesus Christ said: *"Learn of Me,"* and also, *"To know God and Jesus Christ whom He sent is eternal life."* Hostility to the Fourth Commandment on the part of so-called Christians is probably back of the failure to preach The Law, discipline, and it explains the lawlessness, crime, immorality, and above all, the horrible apostacy, that prevails in high ecclesiastical circles! "The lapse of Church discipline was a certain symptom of social and political anarchy," said an English Historian as he looked across the centuries of English History.

In verses 13 and 14 or the 58th chapter of Isaiah God explains what it means "To Keep the Sabbath Day Holy," and makes wonderful promises to the obedient. They will come to delight themselves in the Lord, or enjoy and have a good time in God Almighty's company, association and service, and, *"be fed with the heritage of Jacob";* which means they will receive all the blessings of God's so Great Salvation for time and eternity! *"Eye hath not seen, ear hath not heard, neither hath it entered into the heart of man the things God hath prepared for them that wait for Him."* Disregard the Sabbath Day results in disregard and disobedience to all nine of the other Commandments: The Scripture says you break one and all are broken, for The Law is violated. Respect and obedience to the Fourth Commandment will result in respect and obedience to all other nine Commandments: *"For the mouth of the Lord hath spoken it."*

February 1, 1969

† † †

69

Judgment

Division Four

"An almighty justice does verily rule this world, it is good to fight on God's side, and bad to fight on the devil's side!"

Are you a fighter? If so, on whose side? Are you neutral? Some time ago, we were told of a promising young preacher who said he was not going to "fight". He had gotten his degree from the seminary and ready to go out in the world to do something or other. He testified he was a fundamentalist that believed in the Scriptures of the Old and New Testaments to be The Infallible Word of God, that he intended to so preach and teach, but he would not be contentious and "fight unbelievers, modernists, apostates, etc." -- Doesn't that sound and look sweet and lovely? We are of the opinion that such an attitude is not only wrong, but mighty dangerous.

In Revelation 3:15, Christ said of those *"neither cold nor hot, lukewarm, I will spue thee out of My mouth!"* Consider the picture Dante gives us of those down in hell who had been "spued out." There were sighs, lamentations, and loud cries of woe resounding through the starless air. Diverse tongues, horrible dialects, words of anguish, accents of wrath, voices high and hoarse, and clapping and wringing of hands make there a tumult which goes on forever like the sand when the whirlwind blows. This is the abode of the "lukewarm" who lived on earth "without infamy and without praise." They are mingled with the band of angels who, when Lucifer rebelled were neither rebels, nor faithful to God. Heaven drove them out because its beauty would have been dimmed by their presence; nor would the depth of hell receive them, because the damned below would have some glory on their account! Here were men who did not act a manly part during life, who did not know how to make up their minds and take a decisive step, but preferred to await events and reserve to themselves freedom to join the successful side. -- Justice and mercy hold them in equal contempt! They are displeasing to God and His enemies!

We trust our motive is not just to rail on the "lukewarm and non-fighters" but rather, to so get them "hot under the collar" to the end they may be stirred up "to fight the good fight of faith, and lay hold on eternal life!" We are persuaded, unless one "believes in vain", that the fundamental faith of the infallibility of the Scripture of the Old and New Testaments will so stir up and quicken a man not only to fight, but also to run -- *"Flee the wrath to come!"*

"The Lord is a man of war" (Exodus 15:3). Abraham, the Friend of God, fought several kings and whipped them -- Genesis 14:14, etc. Judge Deborah was a "woman of war" -- Judges 5:7. King David, the man after God's own heart, was a "man of war." The Apostle Paul was a fighter: *"I have fought a good fight, I have kept the faith"*; and he called upon all the true Christians to *"Put on the whole armor of God, that ye may be able to stand against the wiles of the devil. For we wrestle not against flesh and blood, but against principalities, against powers, against the rulers of the darkness of this world, against spiritual wickedness in high places. Wherefore, take unto you the whole armor of God, that ye may be able to stand in the evil day, and having done all, to stand"* (Ephesians 6:11). Thank God for the fighting of Luther, Calvin, Knox, Cromwell, Bunyan, Wesley, and the millions of martyrs from Stephen on down to those who today fight and suffer for the testimony of Christ and His righteousness! *"And there was war in heaven"* (Revelation 12:7, etc.)

September 13, 1975

† † †

"God is angry with the wicked every day. If he turn not, He [God] will whet His sword . . . " (Reckon maybe the Almighty is now whetting His sword for use on our nation this summer!) *"The wicked shall be turned into hell, and all the nations that forget God!" "Neither their silver nor their gold shall be able to deliver them in the day of the Lord's wrath;. . ." "Righteousness exalteth a nation; but sin is a reproach to any people." "Say ye to the righteous, that it shall be well with him . . . woe unto the wicked! It shall be ill with him;. . ." "And I will give children to be their princes, and babes shall rule over them . . . as for my people, children are their oppressors, and women rule over them!"* (Psalm 7:11 -- Psalm 9:17 -- Zephaniah 1:18 -- Proverbs 14:34 -- Isaiah 3:10, 11, 4, 12.)

The following is a reprint of the article that was in this column July 21, 1962:

"And in controversy they shall stand in my judgment; and they shall judge it according to my judgments; and they shall keep my laws and my statutes in all mine assemblies; and they shall hallow my sabbaths" (Ezekiel 44:24).

Are we interested in God's judgments in view of the way we learn and consider them? We ought to be inasmuch as we are hastening to the Judgment Seat of The Almighty! No telling how many may read this article and shortly thereafter, depart this life for that Appointment God has made for us. That is one appointment we will all keep and be on time! Are we interested in God's Laws and Statutes judging from the way we have learned what they are and what consideration we have given them? We ought to be interested, for they will be the basis of His judgment of us! Do we say we have accepted Christ, joined the Church, been baptized, and there is nothing for us to worry about, for:

"Who shall separate us from the love of Christ? -- For I am persuaded, that neither death, nor life, nor angels, nor principalities, nor powers, nor things present, nor things to come, nor height, nor depth, nor any other creature, shall be

able to separate us from the love of God which is in Christ Jesus our Lord" (Romans 8:35-39).

Wonderful, fine, that is, if those pronouns, "I, We, Us," fit and mean you and me! However, they refer to men and women who for Christ's sake "were killed all the day long, and accounted as sheep for the slaughter," and who were *"more than conquerors in tribulation, distress, famine, nakedness, peril, and sword!"* Many of us have not conquered the "love of lucre" enough to invest ten cents on the dollar in the business of God Almighty! And many have not conquered their love of ease, pleasure, sports, etc., enough to give God one day in seven, as He commands. But prefer golf to God, fishing to Faith, football-baseball and boating and bathing and booze to the Beatitudes of the Lord Jesus Christ in The Sermon on the Mount, and then there are those who prefer cash to Christ and so run their business on the Lord's Day for the sake of profit: *"What profit a man if he gain the whole world and lose his soul?"* Maybe the pronouns "Thee, Thou," a little further on in the 11th chapter of Romans, verses 19-22, come close to fitting us and getting our measure:

"Be not highminded, but fear, for if God spared not the natural branches, take heed lest He also spare not thee. Behold therefore the goodness and severity of God: On them which fell, severity, but towards thee, goodness, if thou continue in His goodness; otherwise thou also shalt be cut off."

The writer once heard the late great Bible teacher, Dr. Campbell Morgan, say that the Scripture that frightened him most was Judges 16:20.

"And he wist not that the Lord was departed from him!"

That was spoken of Sampson, the strong man, when he broke his vow! What sort of shape are our vows in? *"Be sure your sin will find you out!"* was spoken to those who made a vow and they failed to keep it!

Surely, we should be concerned about settling the controversy of Segregation and Integration in accordance with the judgments, statutes, and laws of God. It was God's judgment at the Tower of Babel that brought about the breaking up of the "one people" into peoples of many languages, races, colors, characteristics, etc. After much pruning, separation, and segregation in the family of Abraham, God produced the nation of Israel and told them: *"If ye will obey my voice indeed, and keep my covenant, then ye shall be a peculiar treasure unto me above all people: for all the earth is mine!"* The voice, the covenant, called for separation, for segregation! Many years before Abraham had made his servant swear that he would not take a wife for his son Isaac from among the heathen women of the land, but go back to the land from which he had migrated and get a wife for his son from among his own people. The 24th chapter of Genesis tells of the wonderful way in which the Angel of God guided the servant. By the way, consider in chapter 24, the Hand of God in guiding for separation and segregation, and then in chapter 34 the Hand of God blasting the effort of a tribe to integrate!

The nation of Israel was developed in and among another people, the Egyptians, but were kept separate and segregated in a section of the land called Goshen. By the Angel of God -- 1st Corinthians, 10th chapter, tells us that this Angel was Christ Himself -- they were miraculously saved and delivered from Egypt, and at Mount Sinai given the Ten Commandments and Laws of God, and then 40 years later brought into the land God promised Abraham, ordered to destroy the seven nations utterly that were in the land, and not to mingle and mix with the neighboring peoples. However, in spite of all God's provision and commands for separation, they rebelled and *". . . raged against the Lord and His Annointed, broke the bands and cast away the cords of restraint until the wrath of the Lord arose until there was no remedy, He vexed them in His displeasure, poured contempt upon kings and princes, made the judges and wise men fools, and in time part of the curse was the integration of a large part of the nation with the pagans, which produced a half or mixed breed of people called Samaritans."* Read 2nd Kings, chapter 17. † † † **April 4, 1968**

75

"The devil and evil men can be controlled and handled where you lean hard on the authority of God Almighty."

Fifty or more years ago a news item told of a man who ran afoul of law in Canada. At that time, Canada had a "whipping post" and a certain fellow due on that post escaped to the U.S.A. It was reported that he stated he would rather remain in this country and be tried for murder than go back home and take their medicine.

God Almighty's Word says whip an evil man -- not more than forty stripes -- and if still uncontrollable put them to death.

The first recorded words of the Lord Jesus Christ after His baptism by John the Baptist were: *"Man shall not live by bread alone, but by every word that proceedeth out of the mouth of God"* (Matthew and Luke 4:4). If you are not striving to learn and live by "every word that proceedeth out of the mouth of God Almighty", then you ought to have integrity enough to resign and get out of His Chruch! If in a position to do so, this witness would surely refuse to serve you the Communion Elements at The Lord's Supper. John Calvin said the one who eats and drinks unprepared "swallows the wrath of God!" The Apostle Paul tells us there are some who should be *"turned over to Satan that the Spirit might be saved in the day of the Lord Jesus."*

If we find out -- and we will -- but maybe too late, that a whipping post and gallows faithfully used will soon cut crime to a minimum, doubtless, we will fill the bill of those of whom The Prophet Daniel speaks: *"Many of them that sleep in the dust of the earth shall awake -- some to shame and everlasting contempt"* (Daniel 12:2).

We may give our children everything that money can buy, position, popularity, influence, ease, education, pleasure, travel. But if we have not helped them where they would rather die than be false, where they prefer poverty to duty dishonored, where they would rather go hungry than tell a lie, starve than steal, wear rags than be arrayed at the price of duty and duplicity; we are only a cheap counterfeit of parenthood!

If your parents do not bring you to the place where you would rather die than be false, where you prefer poverty to duty dishonored, where you would rather go hungry than tell a lie, starve than steal, wear rags than be arrayed at the price of duty and duplicity, The Lord Jesus Christ will surely do so if you hear Him call and answer:

"Come unto me, all ye that labor and are heavy laden, and I will give you rest; take my yoke upon you, and learn of me: for I am meek and lowly in heart, and ye shall find rest unto your souls, for my yoke is easy, and my burden is light!" (Matthew 11:27-30).

"Blessed are they which do hunger and thirst after righteousness, for they shall be filled. . . Blessed are the pure in heart, for they shall see God" (Matthew 5:6, 8).

"Be ready when He comes again; He is coming again so soon!"

May 27, 1972

† † †

Recently received a letter that said: "A friend says your column is of the Rosicrucians. Is he correct? Don't know, don't know what that word means, and up until the present, lacked interest and ambition to look it up. Maybe your friend "thinks of me more highly than he ought to think."

Am much concerned and interested in many words I do know the meaning of. For example: "steal" and *"Thou shalt not steal."* About an hour ago, I read in a newspaper about a man in high position and office in a great city who stole, knocked down and dragged out hundreds of thousands of dollars that belonged to others. And about two weeks ago I read in a newspaper -- one that runs this column at present -- and saw the picture of a former Governor of one of our great States who was indicted and got in the "hoosegow" for "cheating, swindling and stealing!" Alas! Alas! Where are we going?

77

About a month ago, the writer stopped at a country store for gas and oil. Said the Store Man: "While I service your car, please go in my store and watch those boys. They might steal all I got!"

"God knoweth your hearts -- that which is highly esteemed among men is abomination in the sight of God" (Luke 16:15). And then follows immediately the words of Christ warning of adultery, divorce, and His drawing back the curtain and giving the vision of the rich man in hell! It appears that not only some things highly esteemed among men are an abomination in the sight of God. **But some folks, too!**

Reckon we got a lot of preachers today who preach about things and use words that many of us do not know the meaning of! "If you would promote faith, defeat the devil and save souls, preach hell! The facts of life cry out of hell. Walk around the wards of the hospitals and note the many diseases which wrack man's frame. Go to the shores of the Dead Sea and look down into its mysterious bitter waters. Observe the wandering Jew, scattered over the face of the world. Then preach with conviction that God most surely hates evil and punishes sin!

The conscience of man cries out of hell. Go to the bedside of some dying child of the world and fear not to talk to him of God's judgment upon sin and wrath upon the sinner. Preach of a Saviour that went into the yawning jaws of hell that forgiveness might be purchased at great price -- His own shed blood -- and offer him mercy but only by faith in that blood, and watch his gnawing anxiety about the future turn to calmness and marvel as he departs in peace!

"The interests of holiness and morality cry out of hell! Tell men it matters how they conduct themselves, that there is an eternal difference between Abraham and the Sodomites, between Paul and Nero, between the drunkard who dies unrepentant and a Baxter, a Wilberforce, or a M'Cheyene. Preach hell as the final end of men who will not have the Christ in whom they may say, "Live soberly, righteously, and Godly!"

78

"The Bible speaks of hell from the beginning to end. Hundreds of texts in God's Word reminds us of the wages of sin, the end of the flesh and the reward of ungodliness. Jesus cried that the gate to hell is wide, the road broad and well traveled. When you stand before the people, preach hell!"

-Bishop J.C. Ryle

August 21, 1971

† † †

"And thou shalt remember all the way the Lord thy God hath led thee these forty years" (Deuteronomy 8:2). For your consideration: The same Lord God has led our nation these 150 odd years, 1777-1930. Generally speaking, it was in the 1930s our nation and her government began to turn away from honoring and following after the God of our fathers. The God of the Bible, His Ways, His Laws, and His Commandments. However, we kept on writing on our money "In God We Trust," and still do, in spite of the fact that we have *"Cast away the law of the Lord of Hosts . . ."* in many respects; concerning idolatry, profaneness, Sabbath desecration, dishonoring of father and mother, murder, adultery, stealing, false witnessing, and coveteousness -- *"Coveteousness is idolatry,"* Christ said of Himself, *"The Son of Man is Lord of the Sabbath Day."* Have we not taken away His Lordship of the sacred day and turned it over to the King of Sport, the world, the flesh, and the devil? Also, do we not almost boast that we have nearly done away with the Death Penalty commanded by The Almighty, and are saving the lives of murderers, rapists, whoremongers, homosexuals, and others whom God commanded His people to put to death and send their spirits back to Him who gave them? We will not take time to speak of our heavy and growing crop of crime, thieves, liars, coveteous, etc.!

"Be not deceived; God is not mocked; for whatsoever a man soweth, that shall he also reap. For he that soweth to his flesh shall of the flesh reap corruption; but he that soweth to the spirit shall of the spirit reap life everlasting" (Galatians 6:7, 8).

79

Since this column began, about 325 times it has presented God's question to man in the Second Psalm: *"Why do the heathen rage?"* together with His statement as to who are the heathen: *"People who imagine a vain thing, their kings and rulers,"* and that their rage is against God Himself, and His Anointed," and for the purpose of getting rid of His Law and Commandments: *"Let us break their bands asunder, and cast away their cords from us."* In this Psalm, God also reveals to us the fruit and harvest of this anarchy will bring the "contempt of the Almighty: *"He that sitteth in the heavens shall laugh: The Lord shall have them in derision. Then shall He speak to them in His wrath, and vex them in His sore displeasure."*

During the past thirty years or more, have we not been very successful and made a good job of "breaking God's and Christ's bands asunder, and casting away their cords from us?" Is not the rise of crime, rape, riots, pillage and burning of our cities good evidence that God meant what He said about *"holding in derision and vexing with all adversity"* those who reject His Laws and Commandments?

"And God is angry with the wicked every day. . . the wicked shall be turned into hell, and all the nations that forget God!. . ." (Psalm 7:11 and Psalm 9:17).

"I have not sent these prophets, yet they ran: I have not spoken to them, yet they prophesied. But if they had stood in My counsel, and had caused My people to hear My words, then they should have turned them from their evil way, and from the evil of their doings" (Jeremiah 23:21, 22).

"Of making many books there is no end . . . Let us hear the conclusion of the whole matter [of life and death]; Fear God and keep His Commandments; for this is the whole duty of man. For God shall bring every work into judgment, with every secret thing, whether it be good, or whether it be evil" (Ecclesiastes 12:12-14).

"Now, therefore, fear the Lord, and serve Him in sincerity and truth . . . And if it seem evil unto you to serve the Lord,

*choose ye this day whom ye will serve . . . but as for me and my
house, we will serve the Lord"* (Joshua 24:14, 15).

January 30, 1970

† † †

Consider God's message in Deuteronomy 17:18-20: **Get a
Bible. Keep it with you. Read therein all the days of your life.
Learn to fear the Lord your God. Keep all God's Commandments and do them.** Obey and follow these instructions to keep
your heart from being lifted up above your brethren, and from
turning aside from The Commandment to the right hand, or to
the left: to the end you and your children might live a long and
blessed life in your land. This is the sixth time this message has
been presented in the year 1970.

The following is a reprint of the article that first appeared in
this column on February 2, 1963.

Back in the days when execution of criminals was by public
hanging, it is said that they were very popular attractions. One
writer says that often twelve or fifteen thousand attended. On
one occasion, when the weather was stormy and threatening,
he reported that only eight thousand came to see the sight.
Another story tells of a wife and children attending the hanging
of the husband and father. The man was brought to the gallows,
sitting on his coffin, which was in a one-horse wagon, and there
right in front of the mob near the gibbet stood his wife with a
baby in her arms and several children holding to her skirt. "Go
home, Mary," he said, "This is no place for you and the
children." "Yeah," she replied, "That is the way you have
always been, never willing for me and the kids to have a little
pleasure!"

In the 21st chapter of II Samuel, there is the account of a
multiple hanging, seven men at one time. The Jewish Law
required that the bodies should be taken down before sun
down, but these seven men, though Jews, were hung by the
Gibeonites, non Jews, and their bodies were left hanging

indefinitely. All these men were cousins, descendants of King Saul. The mother of two of them camped near the horrible scene and kept the birds off their bodies by day, and beasts by night. After she had kept this up for quite a while, King David heard about it, and sent and had them taken down and buried.

This, and other terrible judgments found in the Bible, God Almighty's Book revealing Himself to man, if traced back to their source, will reveal the cause of the calamity. They are written for our instruction and example that we may avoid the curse of God falling on us for similar sin, or sins! In this case, we will have to go back about 500 years to the time of Joshua. In the 9th chapter of the Book of Joshua is the record of how Joshua and the princes of Israel were tricked and deceived by the pagan Gibeonites whom God had ordered should be destroyed. They accepted and acted on lying speech, circumstances, and appearances, instead of asking and waiting upon God who had already told them what to do, and swore to let them live, making the oath "In the Name of the Lord."

We might well ask ourselves if our nation and its leaders have been tricked and deceived in the past two decades by people who are the open and avowed enemies of the God we profess. Under such circumstances, most men probably would consider wuch a vow void. However, the Almighty did not consider it void since it was made "In His Name," and when it was violated about 500 years later, judgment fell! The vow was made by the proper government authorities of the nation, and was broken many centuries later by the supreme governing authority, King Saul. He killed some of the Gibeonites, a people who were their servants according to the ancient treaty, and which protected them, and a people whom so far as we know, had lived up to their part of the treaty and therefore, were in no position to defend themselves. We are told that Saul's purpose was the fame and exaltation of his own reputation and name among his people.

The real important thing for us to note in this account, as well as in all Biblical records, is to "watch God work," and observe

His ways, actions, and attitudes in order that we might learn of Him whom to know is Eternal Life. He is the Judge of all the earth," and we are on our way to appear before His judgment seat! God's judgment for this "breach of promise" did not fall in the days of King Saul, but later, when David was King. The judgment was a famine of three years duration. How many starved and perished we are not told. *"And David inquired of the Lord and the Lord answered, It is for Saul and his bloody house, because he slew the Gibeonites."* David consulted with the Gibeonites that were left, and an agreement was made that seven of Saul's sons were to be turned over to them to be hung to make atonement. This accounts for the hangings recorded in II Samuel, 21st chapter: *"And after that, God was intreated for the land"* (verse 14). And the famine came to an end.

God's terrible judgments we find in the Old Testament of the Bible might well be likened to "child's play" in comparison with those declared in the New Testament: *". . . outer darkness, everlasting fire prepared for the devil and his angels; the worm dieth not and the fire is not quenched; weeping and wailing and gnashing of teeth, and no rest day and night forever and ever; and other such statements, practically all of which were spoken by Christ Himself and the beloved Apostle John"* (Revelation). It appears that probably the judgments in the Old Testament, or most of them, might be temporal only, and the sufferings and agony relieved by death. In the punishment foretold in the New Testament, death flees from some who long for it.

The reaction of the present day "top brass" in the ecclesiastical world regarding the judgments foretold in the New Testament is one of dismissal with a "sneer," and a "smear" upon those who warn men that this is the Word of God, and urge them to *". . .flee the wrath to come . . ."* The reaction of this same class towards those in the Old Testament is usually to attack the character of the Holy Lord God Almighty; one who is *". . . highly esteemed among men. . ."* and in the church world has called Him a "dirty bully," and another has said He is Hitler-like, and another has said, "He is my devil," and one so-called Christian minister remarked he would not walk across the street to speak to the God of the Old Testament! These men could be borne with a little better if they were outside of the Protestant Christian Church, but probably all of them at their ordination, took solemn vows accepting the Authority of the Scriptures of the Old and New Testaments as the Infallible Word of God, the only rule of faith and practice.

But for the time being, "Let them alone" -- that is what Christ told His disciples regarding the Church leaders when He was upon earth in the flesh. *"Look to yourselves!"* In Psalm 138:2, the Psalmist says of God: *"For Thou hast magnified Thy word above all Thy Name."* How have we magnified our word, our vows made in His name, maybe in His house, maybe with one hand raised towards heaven and the other placed on His Book, the Bible? How have you magnified your word, church member, preacher, citizen, lawyer, policeman, sheriff, judge, legislators, senators, governors, presidents, all men! Has lapse of time, change of customs, change in your beliefs, justified a "breach of promise," or voiding a vow made to God, or man! To know God is Eternal Life. Visit this public hanging scene recorded in His Word, and meditate on the cause of it in connection with your own vows to God and man. *"Be sure your sin will find you out,"* was spoken to those who made a vow in case they failed to fulfill it. Here we have the record in God's Book of a vow made, and after 500 years had rolled by, it was broken, and judgment fell! Don't think I would like to attend a public hanging, but think it is very profitable to me that I have stopped and looked a while at the multiple hanging in the 21st chapter of II Samuel. Thank God that we can get forgiveness for broken vows, even if it means some judgment in this life. But if we ask and accept that forgiveness, let us beware of further neglect and carelessness concerning them!

May 27, 1970

† † †

84

A week ago in this column, a letter was quoted from a visitor to Georgia from the state of Ohio: "In your article answering the woman in *The Atlanta Journal,* November 30th, you struck a new note and one much needed. God." This statement in the letter we considered quite a compliment; however, this is not a new note for this column. There have been over 400 articles published. Anyone somewhat familiar with *"Every word that proceedeth out of the mouth of God"* from Genesis 1:1 through Revelation 22:21, we believe, will find God's Note and God's Trumpet sounded in accordance with the last two verses of the book of Ecclesiastes: *"Let us hear the conclusion of the whole matter: Fear God and keep His Commandments, for this is the whole duty of man. For God shall bring every work into judgment, with every secret thing, whether it be good, or whether it be evil."*

In the following, we are seeking "Blow the Trumpet of the Lord" and sound His Note concerning something we have heard much about of late in these parts: **"The Speckled Bird!"** The writer thinks and is of the opinion that it is none other than God Almighty Himself who introduced "the Speckled Bird" to mankind and into their languages and literature. It was the Holy Spirit of God speaking through His servant Jeremiah. Are you familiar with the occasion and the circumstances? You ought to be if you have in sincerity taken upon yourself Christian vows and Church membership! In the very first article in this column, we quoted II Chronicles 35:21: *"Forbear thee with meddling with God . . . that He destroy thee not!"* One of the best Kings that Judah ever had lost his life on account of not taking heed to this warning!

Doubtless, one of the greatest causes of the "curse and confusion" upon us and the world today is due to those who call themselves Christian, but have utterly failed in making a reasonable effort to get familiar with -- not, we did not say "understand every word" -- the entire Bible. *"Man shall not live by bread alone, but by every word that proceedeth out of the mouth of God"* -- Matthew and Luke 4:4. May we suggest that the young, middle age, and old even if you are "seventy-eleven" and more, begin at Genesis 1:1 and read some every day, praying and looking to God to shine His Light into your heart with His Inspired Word; and aim at seeing how much of "Every Word of God" you can get familiar with before Mr. Undertaker "calls for your carcass"! There is no telling how much sincere action like this may affect your Eternity and that of others. Christ said: *"To him that hath shall be given, but to him that hath not shall be taken away that which he seemth to have!"* Lack of use in the long run results in lack of possession.

"Hear the Word of the Lord" as found in Jeremiah 12:7-11: *"I have forsaken Mine House, I have left Mine heritage; I have given the dearly beloved of My Soul into the hand of her enemies. Mine heritage is unto Me as a lion in the forest; it crieth out against Me; therefore have I hated it.*

"Mine heritage is unto me as a 'speckled bird', the birds round about are against her, come ye, assemble all the beast of the field. Come to devour.

"Many pastors have destroyed My vineyard, they have trodden My portion under foot, they have made My pleasant portion a desolate wilderness. They have made it desolate, and being desolate, it mourneth unto Me; the whole land is made desolate, because no man layeth it to heart."

The writer has several dictionaries. The one just used was put out in the 1930s. One definition it gives of heritage is "The people of God," maybe modern man knows better. Anyhow, in the Word of God quoted above, God says His Heritage is His people: the kings, the princes, the judges, the soldiers, the common people, etc. He likens them to a lion in the forest, roaring, tearing with his claws and paws and devouring with his teeth. He also likens His Heritage to a Speckled Bird -- the margin of my King James Version says speckled might be translated "taloned." Here is then the picture The Almighty gives of His Heritage, His People: the roaring lion, the speckled or taloned Big Bad Bird tearing and clawing and exercising his terrible beak. The Lion's enemy is His Creator. The Bird's enemy is its Creator.

If you have had such an experience: Remember the time you stood up in the House of God, in the presence of God's people, making promises to God and man. How has your conduct been since that day? How is your conduct today? Was the Almighty talking about you, about me, in telling all generations, all mankind about "a lion roaring in the forest, and about a 'speckled bird'?" Forget all other "speckled birds" until you have made a sincere examination of self. *"For if we would judge ourselves, we should not be judged"* (I Chronicles 11:31).

Read the book of Lamentations: And behold God's terrible judgment upon 'speckled birds'!

Read Luke 13:1-5 where the Lord Jesus Christ says: *"Repent or perish!"*

December 14, 1968

† † †

On Saturday, January 25th, there appeared in *The Atlanta Journal* on the editorial page an article under the heading: "Who are candidates for Hell?" Next day, Sunday, this writer was asked if he saw it. The reply was no, but later, he looked it up and read it. To appraise it in just a word or two, our opinion and judgment is that it mocked and scorned the most fearful and terrible Truths our great Creator has made known to us; and then ridiculed by name one servant of God who in faithfulness to God and his own vows proclaimed God's Word to mankind. The First Psalm declares: *"Blessed is the man that walketh not in the counsel of the ungodly, nor standeth in the way of sinners, nor sitteth in the seat of the scornful. . . The ungodly are not so but are like the chaff which the wind driveth away. Therefore the ungodly shall not stand in the judgment. . . . the ungodly shall perish. . .* '' Immediately following is the 2nd Psalm, the opening words of which head this column and tell us such folks are the enemies of God raging against His Laws, His King, His Son, and His Government.

Here follows a quote from this "profane" article: 'Although there are a few references to damnation attributed to Jesus, they are not only microscopic in comparison to the numerous passages such as *"I if I be lifted up will draw all men unto myself"* (John 12:31). With this introduction, we are presenting a reprint of the article in this column on November 21, 1964. As noted, in it all these Scripture references to future and/or eternal punishment are found in just one Book of the Bible, first of The New Testament -- Matthew! Judge if they are "few and microscopic."

Concerning Eternal Punishment! In the following, it is our purpose to acquaint you with references and revelations concerning "Future and/or Eternal Punishment," found in just one book of the Bible -- the First Book of the New Testament, St. Matthew. Some of them we point out quote, and seek to give the setting and circumstances in which they occur. Hebrews 9:27 says: *"It is appointed unto men once to die, but after this the judgment.* '' No doubt all will agree that we are going to die -- and the time mighty close by for a lot of us -- but many will disagree or are indifferent about the judgment to follow. But there is surely a lot about the judgment in this one Book of the sixty-six books that make up God's Revelation of Himself to man, the Bible. All is spoken by the Lord Jesus Christ with the exception of the first paragraph following.

John the Baptist, forerunner of Christ, called the Pharisees and Sadducees *"A generation of vipers,* '' and asked *"Who had warned them to flee the wrath to come?"* He told them that the axe was not laid at the root of the tree and if there was not good fruit it would be cut down and *"Cast into the fire!"* Also, there was One at hand who would *"Burn the chaff with unquenchable fire!"* (Matthew 3:7, 10, 12).

Matthew 5:22 -- Christ says the man angry with his brother "without a cause" is in danger of the judgment -- *"But whosoever shall say, thou fool, shall be in danger of hell fire!"* Again, in verses 29 and 30, Christ tells us it is better to pluck out your eye, cut off a hand and cause one member of the body to perish, rather than *"That thy whole body shall be cast into hell."* Here He was warning about adultery and "looking at a woman with lust"! (If we believed this, would we permit women to dress or rather undress as they do? Would we permit the flood of lewd literature and pictures on every hand? Are we not by our customs mocking Christ's Words *". . . sitting in the seat of the scornful . . ."* and inviting hell fire?

In Matthew 8:12, Jesus, in contrasting the faith of a Gentile Roman Army Captain with the unbelief of His own people, the Jews, said: *"But the children of the kingdom shall be cast out into outer darkness; there shall be weeping and gnashing of teeth!"* In the same chapter, verse 29, devils cried out and testified of torment to come, begging that it might not come ahead of time!

Matthew 10:15 and 11:21-24 -- Fire and brimstone were rained from heaven and destroyed Sodom and Gomorroh. Christ mentioned the names of several cities in which He preached and ministered, saying Sodom and Gomorrah would have a better chance in the day of "eternal fire" than they: *"And thou, Capernaum, which are exalted unto heaven, shall be brought down to hell . . ."*

In Matthew 12:32, Christ speaks of the "unpardonable sin" that shall not be forgiven in this world, nor in the world to come. We better be careful how we low-rate orthodox fundamentalists, less perhaps it turn out the Spirit of God is upon him or them and we call it the spirit of the devil.

The following quotations are words of Christ from the 13th chapter of Matthew: *"In the time of the harvest, I will say to the reapers gather ye together first the tares, and bind them in bundles to burn them"* (verse 30). "The field is the world; the good seed are the children of the kingdom; but the tares are the children of the wicked one; the enemy that sowed them is the devil; the harvest is the end of the world; and the reapers are the angels. As therefore, the tares are gathered and burned in the fire, so shall it be in the end of the world. The Son of Man shall send forth His angels, and they shall gather out of His Kingdom all things that offend, and them which do iniquity; and they shall cast them into a furnace of fire; there shall be weeping and gnashing of teeth" [*verses 38-42*]. [*One cast into an earthly furance of fire does not remain conscious -- thank God -- long enough to wail and gnash his teeth!*]

Matthew 18:8, 9: Here Christ repeats again the message in the Sermon on the Mount to the end it is better to cut off hands, feet, pluck out the eye rather than having the whole body cast into everlasting fire -- be cast into hell fire. In the Sermon on the Mount, He issued the warning while speaking of adultery and looking at a woman with lust. In the latter passage, His warning is concerning "offending little children." It appears to us that in view of our disregard of proper sex relations and the sort of examples being set before little children, we are daring the Almighty to bring on His "Hell Fire!" The last two verses of this 18th chapter has this message: *"My heavenly father will deliver you to the tormentors.* You whom He has forgiven that turn about and refuse to forgive those who have done you wrong!

In Matthew 22:13, we read: *"Then said the King to the servants, bind him hand and foot, and take him away, and cast him into outer darkness; there shall be weeping and gnashing of teeth!"* Who was or who is this man? He is the self-righteous man. The man whose pride and presumption has sold him on the idea of his own importance and "the dignity of the individual"! He is the man who does not need to prepare for eternity and to meet his God. Does not need to be washed in the atoning blood of Christ; and does not need the "robe of righteousness" obtained by "Grace through Faith, the gift of God." He is very talkative in this world, and quite a scribe in writing essays and books. But when the King came in and looked him over, He said, *"Friend, how camest thou in hither not having a wedding garment? And he was speechless!"* This is the man who the kin ordered His servants: *"Take him away, cast him into outer darkness; there shall be weeping and gnashing of teeth!"*

Matthew 23:14: *"Therefore, ye shall receive the greater damnation!"* This was said to Church leaders guilty of "pretense in prayer"! Here, Christ reveals there are grades of damnation, even as God did through Moses in Deuteronomy 32:22: *"For a fire is kindled in Mine anger, and shall burn into the lowest hell, and shall consume the earth with her increase and set on fire the foundations of the mountains . . ."*

Matthew 23:33: *"Ye serpents, ye generation of vipers, how can ye escape the damnation of hell?"* These terrible words were spoken by Christ to Church leaders and authorities who forsook the message of God by the mouth of Jeremiah to *"Stand in the ways, and see, and ask for the old paths, where is the good way, and walk therein."*

Matthew 24:51: *"Cut him asumder, and appoint him his portion with the hypocrites; there shall be weeping and gnashing of teeth!"* This message was to the unfaithful servant who neglected his duty. To another unprofitable servant, it was said in Matthew 25:28-30: *"Take vherefore the talent from him . . . and cast ye the unprofitable servant into outer darkness; there shall be weeping and gnashing of teeth!*

In Matthew 25:41, 46, Christ speaks to those whom He appraised as "leftists": *"Then shall the king say unto them on the left hand, depart ye cursed into everlasting fire, prepared for the devil and his angels . . . and these shall go away into everlasting punishment; but the righteous into life eternal!"*

Matthew 24:26: *"Woe unto that man by whom the Son of Man is betrayed; it had been good for that man if he had not been born."* This was spoken concerning Judas, the man who put self-interest and money above the Christ of God.

"For the wages of sin is death, but the gift of God is eternal life through Jesus Christ our Lord" (Romans 6:23). *"Flee the wrath to come -- and be thou faithful unto death to our Lord Jesus Christ."*

February 15, 1969

† † †

"Say to the righteous, that it shall be well with them . . . woe unto the wicked! It shall be ill with him for the reward of his hands shall be given him" (Isaiah 3:10).

The Voice of Retribution: *"For I, the Lord thy God am a jealous God, visiting the iniquity of the fathers upon the children unto the third and fourth generation of them that hate me; and showing mercy unto thousands of them that love me, and keep my commandments"* (Part of the Second Commandment, exodus 20:5-6).

History makes some singular developments in respect to the retributive justice of God. Nations, communities, families, individuals, furnish fearful illustrations that *". . . the wicked is snared in the work of his own hand,"* and that *". . . the way of the transgressor is hard."* Wrong doing, oppression, crime, are by no means reserved only for a future retribution. They draw after them an almost certain retribution in this world. *"There is no peace to the wicked saith my God!"* He may seem to prosper -- riches may increase -- he may revel in pleasures, and shine in honors, and seem to have all that heart can wish; yet there is a canker-worm somewhere gnawing at the very vitals of happiness -- a blight somewhere upon all that he possesses. History bears at least an incidental, yet decisive testimony on this point.

Perilous it is indeed to a man's well being in this life -- to his peace, his reputation, his best interest -- to do wrong. Possibly the wrong doer may not suffer himself, yet most certainly, his children, and his children's children will pay the penalty of his misdeeds. Man is undoubtedly so constituted, whether regard he had to his physical, social, intellectual, and moral nature, as to make him a happy being. The right, the unperverted use of all his powers and susceptibilities would not fail to secure to him a high and continual state of earthly happiness and prosperity. And not only is the human machine itself so fitted up as to accomplish such an end, but the whole external world, the theatre in which man has to live, act, and enjoy, is fitted up in beautiful harmony with the same benevolent end. Every jar of human happiness, every arrest or curtailment or extinction of it, is the fruit of the transgression or perversion. The violation of a natural law is as sure to be followed by retribution, as the violation of a Divine Law. The history of individuals, families, communities, nations, is full of such retributions.

"Be sure your sin will find you out" (Numbers 32:23).

"It shall not be well with the wicked" (Ecclesiastes 8:13).

"As I have done, so God hath requited me" (Judges 1:7).

"Oh, that they would consider their latter end" (Deuteronomy 32:29).

The domestic peace and prosperity of the good old patriarch Jacob was sadly marred. He is compelled to become at an early age an exile from his father's house -- to flee before the aroused wrath of his brother -- to suffer a long oppression and wrong in the family of Laban, his kinsman; and no sooner is he relieved from these domestic afflictions than suddenly he is bereaved of his favorite wife -- Joseph is violently torn from his embrace of his own sons -- and at length Benjamin, the only object on which the affections of the aged father seemed to repose, must be yielded up to an uncertain destiny, and his cry is heard: *"All these things are against me."*

Pharaoh defied the God of heaven and raised his hand to oppress the chosen people, and he perished miserably amid the ruins of his own kingdom. Egypt never recovered from the shock of Pharaoh's sin, but since has been the basest of kingdoms.

David was a good man, yet he sinned a great sin. And his sin was of a domestic character. And how grievously was he afterward afflicted in his domestic relations, his subsequent history remains the sad memorial. The Voice of God announced: *"The sword shall never depart from your house!"* His son, Amnon raped his half-sister Tamar. Absalom, her brother, killed Amnon. Later on, Absalom usurped his father's throne and drove him out, etc., etc. Yet David was a ". . . *man after God's heart* . . ." a man after God's heart in the way he repented and accepted the severe judgment of God, reminding one of the words of Job: *"Yea, though he slay me, yet will I trust Him!"*

Adonibesek, who had conquered 70 kings, and having cut off their thumbs and big toes, made them eat under his table, is at length conquered by the invading Israelites, who in turn cut off his thumbs and big toes. He acknowledged the retributive justice of the act when he said: *"As I have done, so God hath requited me."*

Examples crowd upon us from every quarter; every neighborhood furnishes them. Haman was hung on the gallows he built for Mordecai. Dogs ate the carcass of Queen Jezebel, and licked up the blood of her husband, King Ahab. The Herods furnish fearful examples. But consider Pontius Pilate: Many of us quote his name every Sunday in public worship: "Suffered under Pontius Pilate!"

Pilate, vacillating between the monitions of conscience and a miserable time serving policy, delivered up Jesus to be crucified. He believed him to be innocent; yet that his own loyalty to Caesar might not be suspected, he did violence to his conscience and condemned the innocent. He must secure his friendship of Caesar, though it be at the expense of the most appalling crime. But how miserably he failed; and there was in the retribution which followed a striking fitness of the punishment to the crime. He hesitated at nothing to please his imperial master at Rome. Yet but two years afterward he was banished by his same emperior into a distant province, where, in disgrace and abandonment, and with a burden on his conscience which was as the burning steel, he put an end to an existence which was too wretched to be borne! *Be sure your sin will find you out!" "He that confesseth and forsaketh his sin shall find mercy.*"

"Say ye to the righteous, that it shall be well with him; for they shall eat the fruit of their doings. Woe unto the wicked! It shall be ill with him for the reward of his hands shall be given him."

August 11, 1973

† † †

Lawlessness

Division Five

Concerning Bombing and Burning Churches: From meditation on the Scriptures of the Old and New Testaments, it appears that The Almighty Himself has been doing a lot of such things ever since He bombed Eden, figuratively speaking, the Church home of Adam and Eve, and drove them out: *"Therefore, the Lord God sent him forth from the Garden of Eden, to till the ground from whence he was taken. So He drove out the man; and He placed at the east of the Garden of Eden, Cherubims, and a flaming sword which turned every way, to keep the way of the tree of life"* (Genesis 3:23, 24).

Some Bible scholars have estimated, and with good logic, there might have been several hundred times as many people on the earth in the days of Noah as at present. Considering how religious man is by nature, and how "too superstitious" he is, surely there must have been a lot of magnificent temples and churches on the earth when the flood came. They were all "washed up" and destroyed, except the floating "Boat church" built by Noah, according to the detailed specifications given him by God: *"Thus did Noah; according to all that God commanded him, so did he"* (Genesis 6:22).

After the completion of the conquest of Canaan, The Tabernacle, or Church, was set up at a place called Shiloh. God blasted and destroyed this Church, overturned the High Priest's high seat -- his neck was broken in the fall -- his two sons were killed in battle along with thirty-four thousand others; and The Ark, the symbol of God's Presence that contained within it the tables of stone on which the Ten

Commandments were written "with the finger of God," this Ark was captured by the pagan Phillistines and put in the temple of their idol god, Dagon! However, even there, God did not have too much trouble in looking after His own business without any human hands to help -- He did use some beasts! In Jeremiah 7:12, God, in threatening the destruction of the Temple built by Solomon, said: *"But go ye now unto my place which was in Shiloh, where I set My name at the first, and see what I did to it for the wickedness of my people Israel"* (Samuel, chapters 1-6).

The fame and glory and magnificence of Solomon's Temple spread far and wide over the earth. The Queen of Sheba, who doubtless herself was accustomed to magnificence, came to see and hear. The wonder and glory of it all just about "knocked her out," for we are told: *"When the Queen of Sheba had seen . . . his ascent by which he went up to the house of the Lord; there was no more spirit in her . . . "* (I Kings 10:5). But God got displeased with it, or rather, with the way it was being used and misused, and brought the King of Babylon over to sabotage and burn it -- it is an old and ancient custom to burn churches: *"Now in the fifth month . . . came Nebuzaradan, captain of the guard, which served the King of Babylon, into Jerusalem, and he burned The House of the Lord, and the King's house and all the houses of the great men, burned he with fire"* (Jeremiah 5:12, 13).

The great Temple in Jerusalem standing when Jesus was on the earth was forty-six years in being built. *"And as He went out of the Temple, one of His disciples saith unto Him, Master, see what manner of stones, and what buildings are here! And Jesus answering, saith unto him, Seest thou these great buildings? There shall not be left one stone upon another, that shall not be thrown down."* About forty years later the Roman General Titus did that job, also destroying the city and a million inhabitants, more or less!

If knowledge was available, time and space is not to tell of many instances in history where great temples, cathedrals, and churches built to honor God, were later on rejected by Him and blasted because of their abuse, misuse, neglect, and the hypocrisy of those who had taken solemn vows to serve and obey Him! Think of how many have been bombed and blasted in the two great wars of our day and generation! Imagine what may be in store for those stillstanding and being built in view of the present day engines of destruction! Great numbers of them have new and fine educational buildings, and yet many of us have not learned enough to put on enough clothes to cover our nakedness!

There is much concern, talk, and effort these days to stop "war on churches," and rightly so. The following is a quote from a morning paper in reference to the arrest of certain men for burning a church: "An FBI spokesman said the four confessed they were drinking beer, and just decided to burn the church before dawn Monday." Could this be an indictment of the makers, the sellers, and the advertisers of beer? Maybe in God's sight they have some responsibility for the burning of the church! If so, be sure you will not escape His judgment: *"Woe unto him that giveth his neighbor drink, that putteth thy bottle to him"* (Hab. 2:15). Maybe these men were "driven to drink" by the thoughts and prospects of losing their God-given "white race birthright," and becoming with their children and posterity a mingled people, amalgamated, and mongrelized, which is surely coming to pass in time if we continue forcing together little white and colored children in schools, churches, social life, etc. We might as well put fire and straw together and expect the straw not to burn! Another aspect of the situation that may have depressed these men and "driven them to drink" is that the great power of this nation with many of its so-called great and wise men in the political, educational, and even ecclesiastical world strongly backing up this devilish design -- we say it is devilish because it strikes at acts and providences of Almighty God Himself! Race pride is a God-given quality. Of course, it can be abused and is by weak and sinful human nature, but it was ordained for our good, our profit, and our purity. Even in wold animals God has placed a "natural affection" that keeps them segregated. It appears that the devil has destroyed such a natural affection out of many today, especially among those in high and lofty places among men: *That which is highly esteemed among men, is abomination in the sight of God*" (Luke 16:15). Read the rest of the chapter. "I admire gorillas above most animals," says Dr. Schweitzer: "They are completely amiable until their families are threatened. Then they become noble in their strength and purpose." And another familiar with these animals says: "Gorillas defend their families unto death." With our families being threatened with amalgamation and mongrelization by the highest powers of our nation forcing little children of white and colored races together, some of us need the spirit of the gorillas to become noble in strength and purpose to defend our families unto the death. In the first few verses of the Book of Isaiah, God says the ox and the ass have more sense than his people. Yet those through sincere conviction and faith seek to maintain race purity as a God-ordained providence are called "race haters," bigoted, and prejudiced. However, if we don't turn back to God and His ways and paths, we might end up mongrelized, and it could be that we have already so "sold out to the devil" that the Almighty will send it upon us as a curse: *For, behold, I will shake Mine hand upon them, and they shall be a spoil to their servants*" (Zech. 2:9).

In driving men out of the Temple with a lash of cords, Jesus told them they were using His Father's House for the wrong purpose. Did it ever occur to you that God may be displeased and angry with the use of a house dedicated to His honor and worship for politics? Jesus told Pilate: ". . . *My kingdom is not of this world.*" The proper use is for men to go there and worship and learn of God and His Word, to become partakers of His righteousness and receive strength to go out into the affairs of the world of government, politics, business, society, and by their example and conduct, sow the seeds of righteousness, character, integrity, chastity, and all the other virtues. In the two passages -- Isaiah 2 and Micah 4 -- where God tells of the conditions that will prevail when there is peace among the nations and they learn war no more, God's House is set above all else in the earth and nations flow up to it to learn His ways and walk in His paths. Does it promote peace and safety to the House of God, as well as all mankind's homes and houses, to use a house built and dedicated to the honor of God for politics and mobocracy that stirs up anarchy against the "powers that be," ordained of God and charged with the responsibility of keeping law and order? To stop bombing and burning of churches, it looks like we are going to have to "change our ways" to the "ways of God," or else get out an injunction against The Almighty -- The Russians are trying to do that. Please take note, Mr. President, Congress, The Supreme Court and Judges, Attorney Generals, Lawyers, FBI, GBI, and all law enforcement agencies charged with the duty of stopping church burnings!

"Let us hear the conclusion of the whole matter; Fear God and keep His Commandments; for this is the whole duty of man. For God shall bring every work into judgment, with every secret thing, whether it be good, or whether it be evil."

(Ecclesiastes 12:13, 14)

May 23, 1968

† † †

Surely there is a lot of raging, rioting, rape, crime, lawlessness and anarchy all over tqe world, in your community and mine, here, there, yonder and all around. We need to think! The heathen are those ". . . *Who do not believe in the God of the Bible.*" In the Second Psalm God names them as ". . . *people who imagine a vain thing, kings and rulers striving to break the bands and cast away the cords . . .*" of His Moral Law, His Ten Commandments!

The first of these ten is: *"Thou shalt have no other gods before me"* (Exodus 20:3).

The "Me" is the Almighty and Everlasting God, Creator of the Heavens and Earth, He Who hath ". . . *measured the* waters in the hollow of His hand, and meted out the earth with the span and comprehended the dust of the earth in a measure, and weighted the mountains in scales, and the hills in a balance . . . Behold, the nations are as a drop of a bucket, and are counted as the small dust of the balance . . ." The great "I AM" with whom Jesus Christ identified Himself in the 8th chapter of John: "Verily, verily, I say unto you, before Abraham was I Am." Would any dare rage against Him? Consider the matter: "Thou shalt have no other gods before Me."

Other gods! There are other gods the creation of men and devils: made by the hands, minds and imaginations of men inspired by the devil! Consider two of them. Call them "other god no. 1" and "other god no. 2".

No. 1 created man in the image of some very low form of life, maybe jelly-fish or tadpole, and placed him in a "garden of Eden" of the slime, scum, mud, muck, and mire of a swamp! There, he grew, developed, and evolved up, up, and up. (One is reminded of the old saying that you "can't keep a squirrel on the ground in timbered land" -- surely, there were trees in that Eden.) Up and up came no. 1's creature, got to be a frog, and later a monkey, baboon, etc., on and on. (There is one school of thought which thinks this creature when it got to be an "ass" its development was arrested and stopped, and it stayed put. They may have something there in view of Jeremiah 2:24 and Hosea 8:9.

Other god no. 2 is probably best understood and seen by pronouncements of his seers and prophets. No. 2 seeks to dethrone "The God of the Bible" by attacking His character! Because of His terrible judgments -- and indeed, they are terrible, the Apostle Paul said: "Knowing the terror of the Lord, we persuade men . . ." -- upon wicked and vile individuals, cities, nations, and the world in the days of Noah, one of no. 2 god's prophets said He is Hitler-like; another of his seers classed Him as a "dirty bully", and still another of these prophets told us people who believe in and trust the God of the

Bible: "Your God is my devil!" By the way, all three of these prophets have held very high positions in Protestant Denominations and within the past decade all have visited our community and spoken in some of our greatest institutions -- institutions which were founded, supported, and preserved for many years by God fearing men and women, who with all their heart trusted in the God of the Bible.

"O God, the heathen are come into thine inheritance, Thy holy temple have they defiled." This Scripture in Psalm 79:1 is again being fulfilled!

"If the foundations be destroyed, what can the righteous do?" Psalm 11:3. They can do their duty: *"Trust in the Lord with all thine heart, and lean not unto thine own understanding."*

"Cursed be the man that trusteth in man, and maketh flesh his arm, and whose heart departeth from the Lord" (Jeremiah 17:5). We can search the Scriptures and earnestly strive to be a faithful witness, seeking the help and grace of God to the end we might *". . . magnify the Law and make it honorable . . ."* by obedience, *"seeking first the kingdom of God and His righteousness."* Doubtless, much blame lies at our door for all this "raging" and it may be the judgment of God because we have so miserably failed to give God the first place in our ambitions and actions, and only lip service when we pray, *"Thy will be done on earth as it is in Heaven."* We should not forget that it is only the mercy and grace of God that has kept us back from "sitting in the seat of the scornful" as these men are doing. We should pray for them, that God would *"Open their eyes, turn them from darkness to light, from the power of Satan unto God, that they may receive forgiveness of sins and inheritance among them which are sanctified by the faith that is in Christ Jesus."*

Also, it may be our duty to pray that God would either **save or strike**. *"It is better that one man perish than the whole nation."*

"Did not Achan, the son of Zerah, commit a trespass in the

103

*accursed thing, and wrath fall on all the congregation of Israel?
And that man perished not alone in his iniquity"* (Joshua
22:20).

January 10, 1976

† † †

"The fundamentals of **Vice** are **sensuality, pride** and
ambition, and **avarice."** Sensuality is "the doctrine that
gratification of the senses is the highest good, indulgence of
bodily appetites, carnal gratification." Are we not in this great
and blessed country now building on these foundations, and
have rejected "The firm foundation laid for the saints of the
Lord in His excellent Word?" If so, we had better look out for
the lightning to strike!

"The dread foes of man are not belligerent circumstances,
but the riotious passions . . . the leopard of incontinence, the
lion of violence, and the wolf of avarice -- after food she is
hungrier than before!"

The Leopard of Incontinence: The dictionary says incontinence means "Lack of restraint, especially undue indulgence of
sexual passions, licentiousness, etc." How many great nations
and empires of history have for this cause rotted from within,
fallen in decay, perished! Is that not largely true of our great
land today! "Chastity is driven away as an enemy by all men,
like a snake!

The Lion of Violence: Riot, rebellion, rape, murder and
violence of all sorts and description stalk the globe in our days!
Some of the most miserable and hypocritical Violence of the
present and recent times has dressed itself up in the garb of
"Non-Violence," and even taken the Name of God in vain and
calls itself "Christian"! And many, if not the majority, of the
great men of our government, our educational and ecclesiastical institutions, are lending their support and power and
influence. *"That which is highly esteemed among men is*

104

abomination in the sight of God,'' so said Jesus Christ, God, just before telling of the dead rich man's trip to hell and his reception there! We *''. . . do err, not knowing the Scriptures, nor the power of God!''* Do we even know the ABCs of Christianity? Here they are, consider them:

"A" . . . Abandon Self. "B" . . . Bear the Cross. "C" . . . Come after Me, Jesus Christ, God! "A" . . . Abandon Self: The first thing the would be follower of Christ is called up to do is to "deny self". *"Foxes have holes, and the birds of the air have nests, but the Son of Man hath not where to lay His head . . .''* and with these words, Jesus turned back one follower. Another said: *"Lord, I will follow Thee, but first let me go home and bury my father.''* The answer he got was: *"Let the dead buryt the dead, but go thou and preach the Kingdom of God.''* And to still another who said he wanted to follow, after he had attended to some other affairs: *"He that putteth his hand to the plow and looketh back is not fit for the Kingdom of Heaven.''* Someone has written and expressed himself as believing that most of our present day "revivals" are a farce! There are grounds for such attitude; we call folks to join the Church, accept Christ, without teaching and impressing upon them the ABCs of the Faith. *"Break up your fallow ground; sow not among thorns; sow to yourselves in righteousness, reap in mercy!''*

"B" -- Bear the Cross: Crossbearing does not mean just patiently enduring the aches and pains and disappointments and losses more or less common to all men in the flesh, but rather, the Cross of Christ means the rejection and suffering at the hands of an evil world, men, and devils because of their hatred and rage against the righteousness and holiness of God, His Word, Moral, Law, Ten Commandments. The Band, the Cords of Restraint He has placed to hold us back from His wrath and the pit of hell! In John 7:7, Jesus said: *"The world hates Me because I testify of it, that the works thereof are evil. . .''* Have we forgotten, or did we never know it, that when Jesus began His ministry and went back to His home town of Nazareth what He said made the folks so mad that they took Him out of town to throw Him off a precipice? But they did not know Who they were fooling with, and He just walked off and left them! Do we know who we are dealing with in our churchianity? We think we believe in Christ! Test it out with the question He asked in John 5:44: *"How can ye believe, which receive honor of one another, and seek not the honor that cometh from God only?"*

"C" -- Come After Me: If we have not learned the Cs in the ABCs of Christianity, it is because we failed to learn the As. . . abandon, deny self. In the Sermon on the Mount, Jesus said: *"Not every one that said unto Me, Lord, Lord, shall enter the Kingdom of Heaven, but he that doeth the will of My Father which is in Heaven. Many will say unto Me in that day, Lord, Lord, have we not prophesied in Thy Name? and in Thy Name cast out devils? and in Thy Name done many wonderful works? And then will I profess unto them, I never knew you; depart from me, ye that work iniquity."* How many of us church members are definitely and deliberately making effort day by day to learn of and to know Him, whom to know is life eternal? If one does "the will of the Heavenly Father" and neglects the Bible, the Word of God, the Day of God, the House of God, the Prayer Life, he does even more than Jesus Himself did! In view of the fact that our land, our cities, and our lives are filled with sin, rebellion, and rage against The Almighty, and in view of the fact that the nuclear bombs hang heavy, heavy, heavy over our heads, would it not be wise to take up and learn or brush up on the ABCs of Christianity?

Daniel interpreted King Nebuchadnezzar's dream recorded in the second chapter of the Book of Daniel. He told him that he and his kingdom were the "head of gold" of the great image he saw in his dream. Probably, that put the notion in the king's noodle to make the great image of gold we are told about in the third chapter, and to gather all the great ones of his empire to its dedication, and demand that they all fall down and worship it when "the band began to play." There were three men present, friends of Daniel: Shadrach, Meshach, and Abednego, who refused to disobey their God and bow down to the king's idol, although warned if they did not, they would be thrown into a furnace of fire! But let them speak as "*. . . they said to the king, O Nebuchadnezzar, we are not careful to answer thee in this matter. If it be so, our God is able to deliver us from the burning fiery furnace, and He will deliver us out of thine hand, O king. But if not, be it known unto thee, O king, we will not serve thy gods, nor worship the golden image which thou hast set up. Then was Nebuchadnezzar full of fury -- he commanded the most mighty men that were in his army to bind S., M., and A., and cast them into the midst of the burning fiery furnace -- and these three men -- fell down bound into the midst of the burning fiery furnace. Then Nebuchadnezzar the king was astonished, and rose up in haste, and said unto his counsellors, Did not we cast three men bound into the midst of the fire? They answered and said unto the king, True, O king. He answered and said, Lo, I see four men loose, walking in the midst of the fire, and they have no hurt; and the form of the fourth is like the Son of God! Then Nebuchadnezzar came near to the mouth of the burning fiery furnace, and spake, and said: Shadrach, Meshach, and Abednigo, ye servants of the most high God, come forth and come hither. Then S., M., and A. came forth of the midst of the fire. And the princes, governors, and captains, and the King's counsellors, being gathered together, saw these men upon whose bodies the fire had no power, nor was a hair of their head singed, neither were their coats changed, nor the smell of fire had passed on them!*" That was a pretty good crowd of witnesses to a mighty good bomb and fallout shelter; is it not so?

"*Let us hear the conclusion of the whole matter: Fear God and keep His Commandments; for this is the whole duty of man. For God shall bring every work into judgment, with every secret thing, whether it be good, or whether it be evil!*" (Ecclesiastes 12:13-14).

July 13, 1974

† † †

Why do we have riots? Who is responsible? Read Isaiah 3:10-11: *"Say ye to the righteous, that it shall be well with them . . . Woe unto the wicked! It shall be ill with him for the reward of his hands shall be given him."* In the following we quote from the article in this column on October 30, 1965.

The voice of retribution: *"For I the Lord thy God am a jealous God, visiting the iniquity of the fathers upon the children unto the third and fourth generation of them that hate me; and showing mercy unto thousands of them that love me, and keep my commandments"* (Part of the Second Commandment, Exodus 20:5-6). (If you are one of those who belong to a Protestant Christian Church, and yet rail at God here revealed, may we suggest that you make haste and delay not to have your name rubbed off the rolls -- if it may be a lengthening of your tranquility!

History makes some singular development in respect to the retributive justice of God. Nations, communities, families, individuals, furnish fearful illustrations that "the wicked is snared in the work of his own hand," and that "the way of the transgressor is hard!" Wrong doing, oppression, crime, are, by no means reserved only for a future retribution. They draw after them an almost certain retribution in this world. *"There is no peace to the wicked, saith my God!"* He may seem to prosper -- riches may increase -- he may revel in pleasures, and shine in honors, and seem to have all that heart can wish; yet there is a canker-worm somewhere gnawing at the very vitals of happiness -- a blight somewhere upon all that he possesses. History bears at least an incidental yet decisive testimony on this point.

Perilous it is indeed to a man's well being in this life -- to his peace, his reputation, his best interest -- to do wrong. Possibly the wrong doer may not suffer himself, yet most certainly, his children and his children's children will pay the penalty of his misdeeds. Man is undoubtedly so constituted, whether regard be had to his physical, social, intellectual, and moral nature, as to make him a happy being. The right, the unperverted use all

108

of his powers and susceptibilities would not fail to secure to him a high and continual state of earthly happiness and prosperity. And not only is the human machine itself so fitted up as to accomplish such an end, but the whole external world, the theatre in which man has to live, act, and enjoy, is fitted up in beautiful harmony with the same benevolent end. Every jar of human happiness, every arrest or curtailment or extinction of it, is the fruit of transgression or perversion. The violation of a natural law is as sure to be followed by retribution as the violation of a Divine law. The history of individuals, families, communities, nations, is full of such retributions!

"Be sure your sin will find you out" (Numbers 32:23).

"It shall not be well with the wicked" (Ecclesiastes 8:13).

"As I have done, so God hath requited me" (Judges 1:7).

"Oh, that they would consider their latter end!" (Deuteronomy 32:29).

The domestic peace and prosperity of the good old patriarch Jacob was sadly marred. He is compelled to become at an early age an exile from his father's house -- to flee before the aroused wrath of his brother -- to suffer a long oppression and wrong in the family of Laban, his kinsman; and no sooner is he relieved from these domestic afflictions, than suddenly he is bereaved of his favorite wife -- Joseph is violently torn from his embrace by his own sons -- and at length, Benjamin, the only object on which the affections of the aged father seemed to repose, must be yielded up to an uncertain destiny, and his cry is heard: *"All these things are against me!"*

Pharoah defied the God of heaven and raised his hand to oppress the chosen people, and he perished miserably amid the ruins of his own kingdom. Egypt never recovered from the shock of Pharoah's sin, but since has been the basest of kingdoms!

David was a good man, yet he sinned a great sin. And his sin was of a domestic character. And how grievously was he afterward afflicted in his domestic relations, his subsequent history remains the sad memorial. The Voice of God announced, *"The sword shall never depart from your house!"* His son Amnon raped his half-sister Tamar. Absalom, her brother, killed Amnon! Later on, Absalom usurped his father's throne and drove him out, etc., etc. Yet David was a "man after God's heart" -- a man after God's heart in the way he repented and accepted the severe judgment of God, reminding one of the words of Job: *"Yea, though he slay me, yet will I trust Him!"*

Adonibesek, who had conquered 70 kings, and having cut off their thumbs and big toes, made them eat under his table, is at length conquered by the invading Israelites, who in turn, cut off his thumbs and big toes. He acknowledged the retributive justice of the act when he said: *"As I have done, so God hath requited me."*

Examples crowd upon us from every quarter; every neighborhood furnishes them! Haman was hung on the gallows he built for Mordecai. Dogs ate the carcass of Queen Jezebel, and licked up the blood for her husband, King Ahab. The Herods furnish fearful examples. But consider Pontius Pilate: Many of us quote his name every Sunday in public worship: *"Suffered under Pontius Pilate!"*

Pilate, vacillating between the monitions of conscience and a miserable time serving policy, delivered up Jesus to be crucified. He believed him to be innocent; yet that his own loyalty to Caesar might not be suspected, he did violence to his conscience and condemned the innocent. He must secure his friendship of Caesar, though it be at the expense of the most appalling crime. But how miserably he failed; and there was in the retribution which followed a striking fitness of the punishment to the crime. He hesitated at nothing to please his imperial master of Rome. Yet but two years afterward he was banished by this same emperor into a distant province, where, in disgrace and abandonment, and with a burden on his conscience which was as the burning steel, he put an end to an existence which was too wretched to be borne! *"Be sure your sin will find you out!"* *"He that confesseth and forsaketh his sin shall find mercy."*

110

"Say ye to the righteous, that it shall be well with him, for they shall eat the fruit of their doings. Woe unto the wicked! It shall be ill with him for the reward of his hands shall be given him."

March 24, 1973

✝ ✝ ✝

Faith

Division Six

"*Thus saith the Lord: Cursed be the man that trusteth in man, and whose heart departeth from the Lord. For he shall be like the heat in the desert, and shall not see when good cometh; but shall inherit the parched places in the wilderness in a salt land and not inhabited.*

"*Blessed is the man that trusteth in the Lord, and whose hope the Lord is. For he shall be as a tree planted by the waters, and that spreadeth out her roots by the river, and shall not see when heat cometh, but her leaf shall be green; and shall not be careful in the year of drought, neither shall cease from yielding fruit.*

"*The heart is deceitful above all things, and desperately wicked: who can know it? I the Lord search the heart, I try the reins, even to give every man according to his ways, and according to the fruit of his doings. As the partridge sitteth on eggs, and hatcheth them not; so he that getteth riches, and not by right, shall leave them in the midst of his days, and at his end shall be a fool*" (Jeremiah 17:5-11).

On August 11, 1962, the following appeared in this column. In the above we are told of the horrible wilderness and salt land of the "man who trusteth in man!" But below we are told of the blessings and happiness of those who "come out of the wilderness" -- the souls that truly "*trusteth in the Lord, and whose hope the Lord is.*"

One Sunday morning over 40 years ago, the gates of a jail in Atlanta, The Old Tower, opened up and the writer walked in -- believe it or not, he went in voluntarily, oh, yes, he did! He went in with others to conduct a religious service for the guests, large numbers of whom registered the Saturday night just passed. Heard of a Doctor who was mending and sewing up some Colored patients who had been broken and cut up in a Saturday night party. He remonstrated with them about their violent and savage conduct, and got this reply: "Doctor, if you could be a 'nigger' just one Saturday night you would not want to be 'white folks' no more." Were much surprised to see how well dressed and refined looking were many of the white guests, especially women and girls -- Were you there?

Out of respect for the Creator's Acts and Providences, one part of this "hotel" was reserved for White guests, and another part for Colored. One service was held for the White, and another for the Black. If this appraisal is correct, there was a much better spirit of worship in the Colored service than there was in the White. We figured this was accounted for by such Scriptures as *"God resisteth the proud, but giveth grace to the humble,"* and *"He that humbleth himself shall be exalted, and he that exalteth himself shall be abased."* Just as the speaker finished his message to the Colored people, voluntarily and spontaneously, someone in the audience "raised the song": *Didn't You Feel Happy When You Come Out of the Wilderness Leaning on The Lord Who Died on Calvary.* As we recall, some of the words in this song were:

"Didn't you feel happy when you come out of the wilderness, come out of the wilderness leaning on the Lord. I'm leaning on the Lord, I'm leaning on the Lord, who died on Calvary. My hands looked new, when I come out of the wilderness, my feets looked new, when I come out of the wilderness a leaning on the Lord. I'm leaning on the Lord, I'm leaning on the Lord, didn't you feel happy when you come out of the wilderness leaning on the Lord who died on Calvary."

One of the party said that hearing those several hundred humble people sing that song was one of the most inspiring experiences of his life. Some might call it all emotion, but we judged it to be motion stirred up by the Spirit of God fulfilling

114

His promise to give grace to the humble, as they seemed to be moved by that spirit of the Publican who would not so much as lift up his eyes to heaven, but smote upon his breast saying: "God be merciful unto me a sinner." No telling how many of those souls are now among "The Cloud of Witnesses" accompanying about those who in faith and humility are waiting on the Lord for their "Advancement," and "fighting the good fight of faith," those who "got good religion and can truthfully sing "I'm a going to trust in the Lord till I die."

It may be that song was born during slavery time in the heart and experience of some poor slave -- but he got to be rich -- who had a cruel master that "sold him down the river." In his bonds he heard the Gospel, the Good News of the Lord Jesus Christ who said:

"Come unto me, all ye that labour and are heavy laden, and I will give you rest. Take my yoke upon you, and learn of me; for I am meek and lowly in heart; and ye shall find rest unto your souls, for my yoke is easy and my burden is light."

As he heard and listened, "The Trumpet of the Lord sounded in his soul," and he said to himself: "I ain't got long to stay here, so steal away, steal away to Jesus." He did "steal away to Jesus," quit stealing from his master and others and kept on "stealing away to Jesus" until he came forth singing "Didn't you feel happy when you come out of the wilderness a leaning on the Lord who died on Calvary." Doubtless, he did not know his own background enough to realize just what a "wilderness" the Lord has used his temporary slavery to bring him out of: the "wilderness" of his former condition in the jungles of Africa with its frightful nightmare of darkness, ignorance, superstition, oppression, cruelty, and witch-doctor led devil worship! His relatively short period of physical suffering and slavery, even if he had a cruel master, was mighty small pay to be delivered from all that natural and spiritual darkness into the happiness of sins forgiven and some knowledge of God and His Son, the Saviour Jesus Christ, and the good hope of everlasting life where *"Eye hath not seen, ear hath not heard, neither have entered into the heart of man the good things God hath prepared for them that wait for Him.''*

God marvelously and miraculously delivered His people out of the slavery and oppression of the Egyptians, yet afterwards, he permitted them to suffer hunger and thirst and many privations to test and discipline them, and to teach them that ''man cannot live by bread alone, but by every word that proceedeth out of the mouth of God.'' When they continued to murmur and complain, He became angry, and all that generation died ''in the wilderness'' and failed to get in the ''promised land'' except two -- Joshua and Caleb. Murmurings and complainings at the Providences of God are great sins, especially for those who claim to be trusting Him and say:

''God is our refuge and strength, a very present help in time of trouble.'' However, if your hope for advancement is in man, man made governments and laws and organizations, etc., you might as well go ahead complaining when things don't go to suit you, grumble, and growl, and bite the hand God has provided for near a hundred years to feed you in providing work and a means of making a living. Get all the help you can and advance yourself as much as you can. God permitted the rich man destined for hell to be ''. . . *clothed in purple and fine linen and to fare sumptuously every day.*''

This closing word is one I have heard from the Colored people: ''You better mind, you better mind, God is going to set your sins before you some of these days.'' You better mind and leave it to The Almighty to correct and handle those whom you think do you wrong!

April 18, 1969

† † †

Virtue alone could procure true happiness. This column has appeared over 700 times in the past 13½ years. In about the 400th column, the above quotation appeared: *Virtue alone could procure true happiness.*

The following is the entire article as it appeared about 6 years ago:

"**Chastity is driven away by all men, like a snake!**" Think this quote was spoken of the generation of Dante's times. There is cause to fear that it is fearfully true and applicable to our day and generation. Sitting on the "high seat" and "handling the reins" in this "drive", it appears there are some highly esteemed Clergymen and Educators! According to the statement of the Lord Jesus Christ, such should have "a millstone tied about their neck and drowned in the depth of the sea!" -- And I would comment there ought to be apologies made to all maritime life in the sea for so polluting their water. The following appeared in this column February 19, 1966.

The past few articles in this column have dealt with how Abraham, Friend of God, was the means of delivering some of his kinsfolk out of Sodom just before the judgment of God fell -- fire and brimstone falling from heaven consuming the city and the inhabitants. Sins of sex obsession was one of the causes of the terrible judgment. The account of these things are written for our admonition and warning. And how we need to take heed of this warning! Being plagued with sex obsession sins and in danger of the curse of God falling upon our nation.

"Chastity is driven away by all men, like a snake!" The following is the historical testimony of a beautiful Christian young woman whose "chastity" all men failed to drive away: "Her chastity was impregnable" and she testified by life, suffering, and death "Virtue alone could procure true happiness."

In the year 249 A.D., Decius was the Roman Emperor. He became angered and enraged because of the amazing increase of Christianity which caused the heathen temples to be forsaken and the Christian Churches thronged. For these reasons, he attempted the very exterpitation of the name Christian. In general, his subjects, raging heathen, were ambitious to enforce the imperial decrees, and looked upon the murder of Christians as a merit to themselves. At that time, under such conditions, there lived in Sicily a lady by the name of Agatha. She was remarkable for personal and acquired endowments, but most of all, for Christian consecration and piety. On account of her great beauty, the governor of Sicily, Quintian, fell in love with her, and made many attempts upon her chastity without success. In order to gratify his passion with greater convenience, he put the virtuous lady in the hands of Aphrodica, a very infamous and licentious woman. This wretch tried every artifice she could to win her to the desired prostitution; but found there was "nothing doing," for her chastity was impregnable, and she well knew that virtue alone could procure true happiness. Aphrodica reported to the Governor the failure of all her efforts, who, enraged at being foiled in his design changed his lust into resentment. When Agatha confessed she was a Christian, the Governor, being encouraged and supported by the Emperor's effort to wipe Christianity, determined to gratify his revenge as he could not his passion. Agatha was scourged, burnt with red hot irons, and torn with sharp hooks. She bore these torments with admirable fortitude. Next, she was laid naked upon live coals, intermingled with glass, and then being carried back to her prison, she died there on February 5, 251 A.D. She lost her life, but not her virtue: "Her chastity was impregnable!"

October 4, 1975

✝ ✝ ✝

Recently, we advised a friend who wrote to have "A dialogue with God Almighty" (If dialogue is a strange word to you: it means "two talking together.") Anyone can do that, we read a number of times in God's Book, the Bible, where even the Devil talked with God. Hope and trust, you are not a member of the Devil's family: If so, have a dialogue with the Almighty about cutting your bonds and setting you free! If you love "the world, the flesh, and devil so much you do not want to be set free, then consider your latter end and eternal curse, and ask God to change your appetite and desires and put "The fear of the

118

Lord" in your heart to the place where you will "delay not," but make haste to "flee the wrath to come!"

Faith is essential and necessary to have a dialogue with God -- *"The devils believe, fear, and tremble!"* Hebrews 11:6 tells us: *"For he that cometh to God must believe that He is, and that He is a rewarder of them that diligently seeketh Him."* And Romans 10:17 tells us: *"So faith cometh by hearing, and hearing by the Word of God,"* and that is the reason this column urges that everyone read all of God's Word and get familiar with what it says as much as possible, asking God and His Holy Spirit to be your teacher.

"Unbelief" will prevent or cut off a dialogue with God. Several examples: In both the 4th chapters of Matthew and Luke, we have the account of Christ's Temptation by the Devil. The Devil quoted Scripture, misapplying it in order to tempt Christ. Christ quickly cut off that part of the dialogue saying, *"Get thee hence, Satan: For it is written, thou shalt worship the Lord thy God, and Him only shalt thou serve."* And in Luke: *"Get thee behind me, Satan: For it is written --"* and note how Christ fought the Devil with what the Bible said, *"It is written; It is written!"* We submit that God's attitude towards His own people if they try to dialogue with Him in unbelief is the same as His attitude towards the Devil! Did He not say to Peter about the same thing in Matthew 16:23 and Mark 8:23: *"Get thee behind me, Satan, thou art an offense unto me: for thou savorest not the things that be of God, but those that be of men?"* What did Peter do or say that caused Christ so abruptly cut him off and refuse to dialogue? It was because Peter did not believe and rejected God's message of "The Death Penalty for Sin!" Are we not as individuals, states, and the nation doing the same thing when we refuse to visit the "death penalty" as God's Word commands, to put a stop to murder and other horrible crimes? Without faith, you cannot have a dialogue with God. However, the Devil will not only talk with you, but also put a hook in your nose and lead you where he wants you to go!

Permit me to tell you of a dialogue I had with God, or an

119

attempted one. It was about ten or twelve years ago. I have never since thought that God was displeased with the effort, but on the contrary, felt and believed He was pleased. It was concerning the subject of pornography. Often think of it when I see news items telling of the unsuccessful efforts of those authorities whose duty it is to stop it -- and doubtless, the desire of many of them -- yet their efforts are so thwarted by evil, lustful, devilish men and woman, legal manipulation with judges, and courts, etc. that these authorities appear at times about ready to "throw in the towel," not knowing what else to do!

About ten or twelve years ago, some authority here in DeKalb County took a strong stand against the evil and warned all places that sold books and literature of severe penalties for the guilty. Shortly after this, I was in one of these side-of-the-road places that stay open about 16 hours per day and looked at the books for sale. Some of them "stunk terribly" from the standpoint of modesty, chastity, morality, decency, etc. What impressed me as being far worse than the filth was the disregard and scorn of the recent Law announcement. The thought came, and I fear time has proved it to be about correct, the Devil will win out over The Law.

It was shortly after this experience that the effort was made to "have a dialogue with God Almighty." I recalled what God said through Christ: That when Christ returned in power, He would give some whom He found faithful "authority over some cities." I then told the Lord how I would handle this store owner who had just defied the legal authorities by continuing to sell dirty books: He would be given one hour to clean up his place. If it was not clean at the end of the hour, orders would be to set the place afire and oil fed to the fire until everything was consumed, good and bad; and in case he belly-ached unduly about this action, orders would be to throw him into the fire when it was the hottest! (And do not believe The Devil, though a great Imitator of the Son of Man, could imitate the Son of Man's action as when He went into the fiery furnace and walked with the Three Hebrew Children and brought them out

120

without the smell of smoke on them!) While terrible indeed, this action might save the man, his wife and little children from spending Eternity in the Lake of Fire, as well as multitudes of other men, women, and children thus warned of "The Wrath to come."

If the foregoing offends any "fine folk" who have learned to "swallow anything", then take comfort by remembering this was said to God in dialogue, and if the Almighty and you are in one accord in this matter, never would I be given authority over a city.

The above is a reprint. What brought its message to the writer's mind was that magnificent God-inspired letter on sex corruption recently received from a sixteen-year-old young lady from over in Alabama.

December 26, 1970

† † †

We trust it will be an encouragement to all the true and sincere people of God to be reminded of several long periods of time in the earth when men dwelt without fear for their families, loved ones, and property, due to kings, rulers, and families, loved ones, and property, due to kings, rulers and governing authorities who would not countenance or put up with lawlessness. May I ask any of the "birds," or "beasts," or "humans," or in whatever category you may belong who claim to believe that the "death penalty" does not prevent crime: Did you ever see a dead man commit murder? Did you ever see a dead man rape a woman or girl? Do you reckon there was any rape, adultery, homosexuality, or other crimes in Sodom on that morning shortly after Lot went out of the City and God rained fire and brimstone from heaven upon it?

The following statement is made not for the purpose of offending any many, but rather for the purpose of the writer not offending God Almighty: From my knowledge of the Bible if I

121

take the position the "death penalty" does not restrain and prevent, I make God out to be a liar many times in His Word, and in fact reject the entire economy of The Almighty revealed in John 3:16: *"For God so loved the world that He gave His only begotten Son, that whosoever believeth in Him should not perish, but have everlasting life."* Maybe we need to meditate on these words of The Lord Jesus Christ: *"Ye do err not knowing The Scriptures, nor the Power of God!"* Meditate on them, and repent!

Regardless of what others do, or profess, you continue to *"Fear God and keep His Commandments: For this is the whole duty of man." "Be not weary in well-doing, for in due season we will reap, if we faint not."* Continue to pray as Christ taught us: *"Thy Kingdom come, Thy Will be done, in earth, as it is in Heaven. Deliver us from evil."* Remember that a number of times God has told us in His Word: *"The earth shall be full of the knowledge of the glory of the Lord, as the waters cover the sea."* For nothing should the people of God more devoutly pray than that "their great men might be good and God-fearing men!

Democratic institutions exist by reason of their virtue. If ever they perish, it will be when you have forgotten the past, become indifferent to the present, and utterly reckless as to the future. (From the Monument of Thos. E. Watson on the Capitol Grounds in Atlanta.) Our Democratic institutions are now perishing as they are being "integrated" with socialist and communist ones. This is a great day for "integrations" of many kinds! *When you have forgotten the past!* The following is a reminder of a few incidents of the past:

"1358 years ago in the year 617 A.D., Edwin was crowned King of Northumbria, one of the seven divisions of England in the period of the Heptarchy. It was from this King that Edinburgh got her name. He was the most powerful of the several kings, and they were more or less subject to him. It was said first of him that in his days "a woman with her babe might walk scatheless from sea to sea." The people tilled their fields and gathered their harvests in quiet and safety. Men no longer feared the thief and robber; stakes were driven by the roadside spring, where the traveler found a brass cup hanging for his use, and no thief durst carry it off . . . "Thus the church as the great civilizer, had already begun its work in Teutonic Britain."

What is the trouble? The answer is as plain as the nose on your face: We have forsaken the Commandments of our God! There is almost no end to the numbers of our churches, but righteousness is about as scarce as hen's teeth. There is no end to our schools and educational institutions, church and secular, but it looks as if we are "fools for want of sense!" I will accept my part of the responsibility, but I don't want to unload! God help us!

March 1, 1967

† † †

"And let us not be weary in well doing; for in due season we shall reap, if we faint not" (Galatians 6:9). The writer is thinking of quite a number of correspondents who have written telling of evil and corruption they know of in high and low places, of things all decent and God fearing men and women should be ashamed. In the 9th chapter of the Book of Ezekiel, God orders a mark put upon all those crying and troubled concerning society's corruptions and abominations. This mark was to protect them from the man with the "slaughter weapon" sent forth by The Almighty for judgment and vengeance. *"Woe unto them that call evil good."*

Many consider fine and o.k. the things the Bible calls abominations in the sight of God. Said Jesus Christ in Luke 16:15: *"For that which is highly esteemed in the sight of men is abomination in the sight of God."* Are you familiar with the context of the Scripture in which the statement was made? It was followed with Christ's "record of a certain rich man" in the fires of hell, who, in his effort to get his brethren warned, was told: *"They have Moses and the prophets; let them hear them .*

123

. . if they hear not Moses and the prophets, neither will they be persuaded, though one rose from the dead. " The testimony of this column, whether any hear or forbear to hear, is to beware of all those who set the New Testament against the Old Testament. One of the early Christian martyrs, Polycarp, said such were the "first born of the devil." The first recorded words of Christ after His baptism were approval of ". . . *every word that proceedeth out of the mouth of God,* " which means all Scripture (read Matthew and Luke 4:4). And later, Christ said: *"Ye do err, not knowing the Scriptures, and the power of God!"* So we say at the close of this paragraph, as at the beginning: *"And let us not be weary in well doing; for in due season, we will reap, if we faint not!"* We do well to worry and warn of evil and disobedience to God's Commandments! In fact, we do unwell and are in danger if we fail to give God's warning!

To those sincere in their witness against the evils all about, and know Judgment and Wrath is ahead unless we repent and turn away from evil, would suggest you read and meditate upon the 9th chapter of Nehemiah, and again the 9th chapter of Daniel. In these chapters, the Congregation of Israel, and later Daniel, appear to repent and apologize to God for the great sin of the people as well as their own, and seek pardon and forgiveness, though undeserved.

Several letters recently received tell of a man, or men, who operate an ince-cream truck, but sell many other things. Some months back a man wrote telling that he used to be a night clerk in a hotel, and how at the request of one of our honorable (?) Legislators he acted as a "procurer" to obtain a partner for this man in his adultery and fornication -- a self-admitted family man who claimed to love his family! (I trust this former night-clerk has sincerely repented of his part, of the wickedness, and debasement of the girl, and is sincerely seeking to bring about righteousness. *"Righteousness exalteth a nation, but sin is a reproach to any people"* (Proverbs 14:34). I wish our honorable Legislature, or some of them, had gone on record regarding their attitude towards such a "state father," if perchance there should be such a one among them. They went on record concerning one elected member, and I agree with them, whom they believed guilty of acts treasonable to the nation in its war effort.

During the summer of 1964, the writer received an article concerning the "Washington Scene." It told of the horrible sex evils and influence in our national Capitol. In our Article submitted to the Atlanta papers for September 5, 1964, we quoted largely from this article. It was rejected, and never published. We expect to get this article published in the *DeKalb Tribune* to appear July 5th, the day after the 4th, the nation's birthday. We suggest it would be well for such as "believe in the God of the Bible and have the fear of the Lord in their hearts" to get this article and read it, and make this July 4th a season of repentance, humiliation and apology to The Almighty for the great wickedness in our "high places" as well as the "low places". Let us take heed to II Chronicles 7:14: *"If my people, which are called by my name, shall humble themselves, and pray, and seek my face, and turn from their wicked ways; then will I hear from heaven, and will forgive their sins, and will heal their land."* The writer recalls a 4th of July during World War One set aside nationally as a day of fasting and prayer. The nation was troubled, and many really observed the day. Shortly afterward, there came the news of a great victory for American, English and French forces.

June 22, 1967

† † †

"There is no place, saith my God, to the wicked, cry aloud, spare not, lift up thy voice like a trumpet, and shew my people their transgression, and the house of Jacob their sins" (Isaiah 57:21).

No peace to the wicked! There are two places in the Bible that tell of peace among the nations when they shall beat their swords into plow-shares, and their spears into pruning hooks --

Isaiah, second chapter, and Micah, 4th chapter. Both messages are practically the same. The following quote is from Isaiah!

"And it shall come to pass in the last days, that the mountain of the Lord's House shall be established in the top of the mountains, and shall be exalted above the hills; and all the nations shall flow unto it, and many people shall go and say, come ye, and let us go up into the House of the Lord, to the House of the God of Jacob; and He will teach us of His ways, and we will walk in His paths; for out of Zion shall go forth the Law, and the Word of the Law from Jerusalem, and He shall judge among the nations, and shall rebuke many people; and they shall beat their swords into plow-shares, and their spears into pruning hooks; nation shall not lift up sword against nation, neither shall they learn war anymore. O House of Jacob, come ye, and let us walk in the Light of the Lord."

This shall come to pass in the last days, when the House of God is exalted above all else in the earth; on the highest hill of a mountain in the top of the mountains. All nations shall flow unto that High Place to be taught God's ways in order to walk in His paths. It is then that The Lord will judge among the nations and bring peace. As you and I who claim to be Christian and heaven-bound flowing up to that High Place, or, are we flowing downward seeking another level? It is our duty and business to seek and proclaim peace for ourselves and as many others as we can. Jesus Christ took a whip of cords and lashed out at the hypocrites and profane wretches in the Temple, and later, His disciples remembered that it was written of Him: *"The zeal of Thine House hath eaten me up."* What is "eating on us?" The story is told of a goat being shipped by express: the agent sent his porter to find out where it was to go, who returned and reported: "Dat goat done 'et up' where it gwine." It is to be feared that many of us so-called Christians have "eaten up" our heaven-bound tag, if we ever had one. Our zeal for the world, the flesh, and the devil has consumed us, and our love for money, pleasure, sport, etc. has caused us to lower and degrade the House of God, His Day, His teachings, and His paths. How then can we expect peace!

Charles the First, of England, in opposition to the Puritans' strict obedience to The Law of God promulgated the "Declaration of Sports" which made it lawful for the people to spend The Sabbath Day otherwise than in worship and reverence. Cromwell tried to run away from it all and come to America and was on the boat to sail, but Charles' boys took him off and would not let him leave, or it may be more correct to say that God took him off as He had a job for him in England -- to lead the movement that was eventually to "chop off the king's head." Think he was the only King of England legally executed. The story of Cromwell being kept in England to upset the "apple cart" of Charles and his Cavaliers reminds one of Haman in the Book of Esther, who thought he was building a gallows on which to hang Mordecai, when in reality, he was building it for himself and his ten sons!

Last year, we think it was, the newspapers reported that The Georgia Legislature had made it "no sin" to fish on Sunday -- the one day in seven set aside by most Christians to be observed in obedience to God's Fourth Commandment: *"Remember the Sabbath Day to keep it holy."* It might be well for you Sunday fishermen to get a copy of that Law and give instructions that it be put in the pocket of your funeral suit, or shroud, so as to have it to take along to the other world. *"If it seems evil unto you to serve the Lord,"* don't do it. That is Scripture. *"Choose ye this day whom you will serve,"* is also Scripture. Speaking of the shroud, the late Sam Jones was often criticized for lack of dignity. He said: "Dignity is the starch in a shroud. When I am in my coffin, I will have as much dignity as any of you." We hear a lot today about the "dignity of the individual," regardless of his character, or lack of it. If we would seek to impress upon the individual the importance and necessity of "humility and the fear of the Lord" the dignity part would take care of itself. Today we seem to think that that "expression" should come ahead of "impression." Don't forget to "climb the mountains" for peace!

August 25, 1962

† † †

Last week's article closed with this sentence: "Hope to comment more on all the above later." The "above" contained the witness of three people: 1) A man who worked at one of the South's great universities, testified "things were awful" regarding some conduct, character, righteousness, etc.; 2) The testimony of a worried parent who sent a college newspaper containing what she called "disgusting filth" and saying the State paid for its publication. This voice cried aloud and lifted itself up like a trumpet saying "What shall we do to stop this? What would you do?"; 3) A letter from a lady saying the Bible did not permit her to speak out in the Church. She quoted three different passages from the Bible saying she believed they meant just what they said: *"The Scripture cannot be broken"* even as Jesus said. The passages she quoted were as follows: I Corinthians, chapter 11:14: *"Doth not nature itself teach you, that, if a man have long hair it is a shame unto him?"* (Deuteronomy 22:5). Woman shall not dress as a man and a man shall not dress as a woman for it is an abomination unto the Lord. Also, I Corinthians, Chapter 14, Verses 34 and 35: *"Let the woman keep silence in the church; for it is not permitted unto them to speak; but they are commanded to be under obedience, and, if they will learn anything, let them ask their husbands at home, for it is a shame for women to speak in the church."*

In commenting on the above, we undertake to cover numbers one and two together, inasmuch as both refer to evil conduct, character, literature, etc. One of our articles last year testified about as follows concerning pornography and a store keeper who defied and resisted legal action. Undertook to have a dialogue with God Almighty, recalling God said through Christ on His return He would give some of the faithful power over cities, we told the Lord how we would handle this revolting and rebellious wretch: Give him five minutes to make his store decent and clean, and if he defied and failed, orders would be to set the store on fire and consume all his stuff good and bad, and in case he belly-ached unduly, throw him in the fire when hottest. (However, hope I would have enough of the Spirit of Christ in me to be willing to take the evil man's place if it would mean his salvation and conversion. If I was "Safe in the Arms of Jesus", He would come and walk with me in the fire and lead me out, or if it was best for me to be consumed, He would gather up my ashes and built out of them a body that could never perish! "I said not to the house of Jacob, seek ye me in vain!"

Sometimes back the writer made the statement in one of his articles that it was as easy as "falling off a log" to keep law and order anywhere anytime provided there was "Genuine faith in the God of the Bible" who said to the first man created: *"Obey or die!"* However, instructing man in the work of redemption, God said whip an evil man, not more than forty stripes, and if punishment would not correct him, then put him to death, stoning, hanging, sword or spear and sometimes by fire." *"It is a fearful thing to fall into the hands of the Living God"* (Hebrews 10:31). *"And so terrible was the sight that Moses said, I exceedingly fear and quake"* (Hebrews 12:21). *"For our God is a consuming fire!"* (Hebrews 12:29). And the Book of Revelation tells of kings and great men and rich men and chief captains and mighty men and others: *". . . hid themselves in the dens and the rocks of the mountains; and said to the mountains and rocks, fall on us, and hide us from the face of him that sitteth on the throne, and from the wrath of the lamb!"* "From the Wrath of the Lamb!"

Yes, the more I read the Bible, the more I am persuaded it is as easy as "falling off a log" to keep law and order where there is genuine faith in God: *"Let us hear the conclusion of the whole matter: Fear God and keep His Commandments for this is the whole duty of man!"* *"Forbear thee from meddling with God!"* (II Chronicles 35:21).

Concerning comment on number three in first paragraph:

129

Beware of mocking by word or act God's Word that tells us nature teaches it is a shame for a man to have long hair -- some great man of the past has said: "Nature never tells a lie." Certainly, it is true that often, maybe mostly, long hair on man is an indication of dedication and holiness unto God. Certainly, the Bible says an "hairy scalp" is offensive to God if the feet walk in evil and disobedience to God -- Psalm 68:21. Beware of mocking by word or act God's Word concerning a woman wearing man's clothes and a man woman's clothes in view of these firm foundations found written in God's Book: *"For Adam was first formed, then Eve. And Adam was not deceived, but the woman being deceived was in the transgression"* (I Timothy 2:13, 14). Consider that other great fundamental stating man is created in the image of God, the woman in the image of the man.

April 17, 1971

† † †

Many years ago there was a man by the name of Mr. Hall who owned, operated, and edited the DeKalb New Era weekly newspaper. It had a column called "Random Remarks" -- am borrowing the name today. The writer lived across the street from Mr. Hall and every day, morning and evening, he could be seen walking to or from his office -- on the Lord's Day or Christian Sabbath, his walking trips were to the Baptist Church. Think he was a Democrat, but do not believe he went along with Tom Jefferson, and some present day folks, in their testimony they would rather live in a town that had newspapers and no government than in a place that had a government but no newspapers. Our opinion is that Mr. Hall was too good a Baptist to go along with Tom Jefferson and his present day buddies along that line, because that attitude rejects God Almighty's Word as recorded in Romans, chapter 13: *"Let*

130

every soul be subject unto the higher power, for there is no power but to God." The powers that be are ordained of God. Whosoever therefore resisteth the power, "*. . . resisteth the ordinance of God; and they that resist shall receive to themselves damnation!*" Reckon Tom Jefferson's unbelief and appreciation of Tom Paine could be partly responsible for the recent report that crime increased 148 percent during the 1960s. *"The curse shall not causeless come"* (Proverbs 26:2).

Joshua was a mighty man of faith who worked miracles; one time he called on the Sun to stand still in the heavens, and it did so for about a day; and another time he commanded the River Jordan to open up so the people could go over on dry ground, it obeyed. However, Joshua and his officers made one bad mistake that caused the curse to fall on Israel and David about 500 years later -- and many perished. We are living only about 200 years the other side of Tom Jefferson; let us give thanks for his great wisdom and abilities, but refuse to go along with him in his unbelief and rejection of God's Word.

The writer purposed in January of this year to call attention every month, the Lord willing, to his appraisal of what God says to His people in Deuteronomy 17:18-20, as follows: *"Get yourself a Bible, Keep it with you. Read in it all the days of your life that you may learn to fear the Lord your God, and to keep pride out of your heart causing you to think you are better than your brethren. Also to keep you from turning to the right or left from God's Commandments and Statues, to the end you and your children might live a long and blessed life in the land God gives you"* -- "Thinking you are better than your brethren!" These days as I read what the political candidates say about themselves and their opponents, wonder if there could be some folks in our days whom pride has caused to think are "better than their brethren!"

Another class of folks that appear to think they are "better than their brethren" are those who band together to tell folks who own their own business and property how to operate, how much to pay, etc., etc. It brings to mind the passage in Matthew 20:1-16 which was spoken by Him ". . . *who created all things, and for Whom all things were created*" - the Lord Jesus Christ. "*Is it not lawful for me to do what I will with mine own*" -- given me by God.

Numbers 15:30-31: "*But the soul that doeth aught presumptuously -- the same reproacheth the Lord, and that soul shall be cut off from among his people, because he hath despised the word of the Lord, and hath broken his commandments, that soul shall be utterly cut off: His iniquity shall be upon him!*" In the following chapter: Numbers 16, there is quite a record of God's judgment upon certain men who "acted presumptuously." Quotes are from that chapter: "*Now Korah --Dathan and Abiram -- and On, took men; and they rose up before Moses, with certain of the children of Israel, two hundred and fifty princes of the Assembly, famous in the congregation, men of renown; and they gathered themselves together against Moses and against Aaron, and said unto them, ye take too much upon you, seeing all the congregation are holy every one of them, and the Lord is among them; wherefore then lift ye up yourselves above the congregation of the Lord? And when Moses heard it, he fell upon his face; and he spake unto Korah, and all his company, saying, even tomorrow the Lord will show who are His and who is holy; and will cause him to come nigh unto Him; even him who He hath chosen . . . and Moses sent to call Dathan and Abiram . . . which said, we will not come up . . . And Korah gathered all the congregation against them unto the door of the congregation; and the glory of the Lord appeared unto all the congregation. And the Lord spake unto Moses and Aaron, saying, Separate yourselves from among this congregation that I may consume them in a moment, and they fell upon their faces, and said, O God, the God of the spirits of all flesh, shall one man sin, and wilt Thou be wroth with all the congregation? . . . And Moses said, hereby ye shall know that the Lord hath sent me to do all these works; for I have not done them of mine own mind. If these men die the common death of all men . . . then the Lord hath not sent me. But if the Lord make a new thing, and the earth open her mouth, and swallow them up, with all that appertain unto them, and they go down quick into the pit; then ye shall understand that these men have provoked the Lord, and it came to pass as he had made an end of speaking these words, that the ground clave that was under them; and the earth opened her mouth, and swallowed them up, and their houses, and all the men that appertained unto Korah, and all their goods, they, and all that appertained unto them went down alive into the pit, and the earth closed upon them; and they perished from among the congregation. And all israel that were round about them fled at the cry of them; for they said, lest the earth swallow us up also, and there came a fire from the Lord, and consumed the two hundred and fifty men." "But on the morrow all the congregation murmured against Moses and Aaron, saying, ye have killed the people of the Lord."* The result of this attributing God's judgment by presumption to Moses and Aaron was the appearance of the glory of God, the breaking out of a plague destroying the people, and 14,700 dying before Moses could make atonement.

Random Remark Number One: Beware of putting newspaper messages above God Almighty's Word.

Random Remark Number Two: Beware of pride causing you to think you are better than your brethren.

The remedy is the fear of the Lord that comes from reading and believing God's Word.

Random Remark Number Three: Thou shalt not covet anything that is thy neighbor's, his position, or anything God has given him.

September 12, 1973

† † †

133